GEORGE TUCKER

MORAL PHILOSOPHER AND MAN OF LETTERS

GEORGE TUCKER

MORAL PHILOSOPHER AND MAN OF LETTERS

By

ROBERT COLIN McLEAN

Chapel Hill

THE UNIVERSITY OF NORTH CAROLINA PRESS

PRINTED BY THE SEEMAN PRINTERY, DURHAM, N. C.

To my wife

KATHLEEN

PREFACE

Clearly enough, to understand the literature of the Old South, we must have studies of the lives and thought of the men whose writings make up that literature. One notable ante-bellum Southern author was George Tucker (1775-1861), novelist, critic, and philosopher. Although almost all literary historians concerned with the development of American letters in the first half of the nineteenth century recognize Tucker's prominence among the writers of his age, there has been no full-length study of his life and works. This deficiency is regrettable not only because Tucker himself was an interesting person, but also because his intellectual curiosity was such that he was connected with many of the most important intellectual trends in a particularly interesting and significant period in America's past.

In this study, it has been my first aim to provide an accurate, unvarnished account of Tucker's life. Past accounts of his career are unsatisfactory for several reasons. Most surveys—all those in standard reference works—are very brief, and some contain serious errors of fact, as does the otherwise valuable commentary in the *Dictionary of American Biography*. The usefulness of longer and more detailed sketches has been impaired chiefly by too uncritical a tone. George Sherley, whose essay in a University of Virginia magazine in 1880 has done much to determine scholars' conception of Tucker, gathered information for his study from Tucker's two surviving children, in whose presence he heard a reading of selections from Tucker's unpublished autobiography. Sherley portrayed Tucker as an aristocratic planter and lawyer who, having for a time served Virginia and the nation as a statesman, abandoned public life for the calm of Charlottesville, where he lived in academic seclusion as a dispassionate scholar searching for elusive truths. Tucker's life, concluded Sherley, was "one exquisite poem, unruffled by . . . jarring discords."[1] This interpretation, which seems to owe a good deal to preconceptions as to what the life of a Virginia gentleman ought to be like, has never been seriously questioned. In recent years, Leonard C. Helderman,[2] Malcolm Lester,[3] and Jay B. Hubbell[4] have related some new information about Tucker, but they have not essentially modified the image established by Sherley.

The principal source for a biography of Tucker—Part I in this study—is Tucker's unpublished autobiography. But this document must be read judiciously, with its limitations in mind. Writing at the age of eighty-two for the moral edification of three generations of descendants, Tucker carefully restricted the depth of his narrative, refusing to "rend the veil" which concealed the motivations for his acts, lest he follow the example of Rousseau's *Confessions,* in which "the bold avowal of flagrant vice and lawlessness and the fake glosses . . . are calculated to do more harm than good."[5] Moreover, the autobiography lacks perspective and balance, failing to give proper weight to the struggles and disappointments which characterized Tucker's early life. I have therefore supplemented this primary source of information with other materials, especially with Tucker's published works, his letters, and the correspondence of some of his contemporaries.

The Tucker which emerges from such a study is a much more interesting and believable figure than past interpretations would allow. He took an unusually active part in the affairs of his age, and, in the years preceding his appointment at Jefferson's University of Virginia, he enjoyed anything but a placid existence. Only after the age of fifty, after thirty long and largely unsuccessful years following his emigration to America, did Tucker attain the success and serenity usually attributed to him.

1. "Our University, II: George Tucker, Professor of Moral Philosophy in the University of Virginia, 1825-1845," *Virginia University Magazine,* XIX (1880), 539-540.

2. "A Social Scientist of the Old South," *Journal of Southern History,* II (1936), 148-174.

3. "George Tucker: His Early Life and Public Service, 1775-1825" (University of Virginia M.A. thesis, 1946).

4. *The South in American Literature, 1607-1900* (Durham, N. C., 1954), pp. 243-255.

5. "Autobiography," manuscript copy, Tucker-Harrison-Smith Papers, University of Virginia Library, opposite p. 21. The autobiography is written on right-hand pages numbered in two sequences—from 1 to 35 and from 1 to 18. I have renumbered the pages to run in one sequence from 1 to 53. Tucker's occasional writings on left-hand pages I have designated "opposite page."

Since an important part of the story of Tucker has to do with his frustrated desires to become a professional writer and with his achievements as a chronicler and critic of Southern life, I have devoted Part II to a description and evaluation of his imaginative writings. Here I have discussed his works in the order of their composition and have tried to explain how his development as a writer of imaginative literature was influenced by various social and economic pressures. Tucker could not afford to be a professional writer. In this respect, he was representative of the writers of his age and culture, and his unsuccess throws some light on the old but interesting question of why the South's literary accomplishments were inferior to those of the North in the first half of the nineteenth century. At the same time, it is important to note that Tucker's fictional works, crude as they sometimes are, have an intrinsic interest for the literary and social historian for their interpretation of Southern life and society in the light of a deeply-rooted doctrine of human progress. Tucker's economic interpretation of the advancement of civilization and his concern with broad economic and social problems mark him as an unusual figure in the Southern literature of his time, one who deserves closer and more accurate attention than has been given him.

In Part III, which deals with Tucker's thought, I have devoted a chapter to each of four subjects which were of paramount interest to him. Except in the chapter dealing with philosophy, which is arranged topically, I have treated Tucker's works in chronological sequence within each chapter, in order to illustrate how his opinions developed or changed. Studies of Tucker as an economist are both comprehensive and sound, and I have therefore not systematically discussed his contributions in this field. Although I have tried to exercise independent judgment, I have leaned heavily upon the work of professional economists whose analyses illuminate those writings of Tucker's in which I have been most interested.

From a study of Tucker as Southern thinker, there have emerged several important, largely revisionary, conclusions about the man and his age. First of all, the nature of Tucker's thought has been seriously misconstrued. He did not follow or advocate the policies of Virginia's eighteenth-century patrician liberals, nor was he at war with the institution of slavery. In reality Tucker was a radically conservative thinker who devoted much of his ability to defending slavery. An admirer of the Old South's hierarchical caste system who viewed changes in Virginia's social order with a sense of loss, Tucker was, on the other hand, a prophet of the "New South," looking forward to and preaching the necessity of the industrialization of his region. A second significant result of this study, stemming from an investigation of the sources for Tucker's ideas, is documentation for the great influence in the Old South of the Scottish "common sense" philosophers and aestheticians, in whose writings Tucker found the materials for his most important discussions of literature, philosophy, and economics.

Materials for the examination of Tucker as a writer and thinker are chiefly his published works, but unpublished pieces are also valuable. Tucker's manuscript novel is especially helpful for understanding his literary career; and the manuscript notes for his lectures on rhetoric and belles lettres at the University of Virginia provide information about his literary criticism which is nowhere else available. Notes taken by Tucker's students in mental philosophy expand and clarify points which Tucker made in printed pieces, and they help in identifying some of his pseudonymously published writings. Wherever doubt exists about Tucker's authorship of unsigned or pseudonymous publications, I have tried to explain in the text my reasons for assigning each work to Tucker. In the bibliography of this study I have listed all the compositions which I believe to be his.

I have received the help of many institutions and individuals. I owe a special debt of gratitude to Mrs. Edward G. Gamble, who gave me permission to read and quote from the Tucker-Harrison-Smith Papers on deposit at the University of Virginia Library; to the directors of the Institute of Early American History and Culture, who made available to me the manuscripts of the Tucker-Coleman Collection on deposit at Colonial Williamsburg; and to Mr. W. B. McDaniel, 2nd, Curator of the Historical Collections at the Library of the College of Physicians of Philadelphia, who allowed me to read and microfilm portions of Dr. Robley Dunglison's autobiography. Dr. George E. Davie of the Queen's University of Belfast made helpful suggestions about the Scottish writers discussed in this book. The staffs of the following institutions made it possible for me to read otherwise unavailable printed and manuscript materials by and about Tucker which enhanced my understanding of him and his works: The American Philosophical Society, the Virginia State Library, the Historical Society of Pennsylvania, the New York Public Library, and the Library of Congress. I am grateful for the aid which has been given me by the whole staff of the University of Virginia Library, and particularly by Francis Berkeley, William H. Runge, and Robert E. Stocking, of the manuscript and rare book division, who have been extremely generous in providing advice and information whenever sought. I would also like to acknowledge a generous grant by the Ford Foundation under its program for assisting American university presses in the publication of works in the humanities and the social sciences.

I wish to thank the Washington University faculty committee for reading this work during its preparation as a dissertation. Especially, I wish to express my debt and thanks to Professor Guy A. Cardwell, who suggested this study, for his criticism and many helpful suggestions. My wife has given me invaluable help in every stage of this work.

Robert Colin McLean

Rochester, New York
November, 1960

CONTENTS

PART III

TUCKER AS SOUTHERN THINKER

PART I

GEORGE TUCKER, HIS LIFE

CHAPTER I

EARLY YEARS AND
EDUCATION

GEORGE TUCKER was born on St. George's Island in Bermuda on August 20, 1775, the second child and first son of Daniel and Elizabeth Tucker. Both of his parents, distant cousins, were descendants of a family that at the time of Tucker's birth had lived in the British colony for over one hundred and fifty years.[1] Most of the islands' white settlers—a little over half of the population—earned precarious livings chiefly by building ships or carrying merchandise for the North American Colonies and the British West Indies. Competition for business among the merchants was keen, especially during the years of the American Revolution and the French War. One Henry Tucker of Somerset, who amassed a considerable profit by dealing indiscriminately with the British and the Americans during the Revolutionary War, provided jobs for many of his less fortunate relatives, among them his brother and George Tucker's father, Daniel.[2] After the war, when a degree of peace and prosperity returned to Bermuda, Daniel Tucker became an independent merchant and, as his son was to be, something of a financial speculator. Daniel and his three brothers joined with four other ambitious islanders to found a "mercantile partnership." They set up a number of stores on Bermuda and hired Yankee seamen to man a fleet of seven vessels, which carried cargo to the United States, Newfoundland, and the West Indies. When the firm finally

---

1. The best account of the early Tucker family is Thomas Addis Emmet, *An Account of the Tucker Family of Bermuda from a History of the Emmet Family* (New York, 1898). See also Lewis Leary, *The Literary Career of Nathaniel Tucker, 1750-1807* (Durham, N.C., 1951), pp. 3-4, 97-101.

2. See Wilfred Brenton Kerr, *Bermuda and the American Revolution: 1760-1783* (Princeton, 1936), pp. 1-4, 17, 60-61, 72. Kerr (p. 17) says that Daniel Tucker was one of the islands' "petty Tuckers."

failed because of mismanagement, Daniel helped to found the "projected metropolis" of Hamilton to compete as a shipping center with the wealthier eastern portion of Bermuda, and he served as its first mayor.[3]

George Tucker's formal education in Bermuda lasted only six years, but it was probably equal in quality to that of contemporary students on the American continent. At eleven he began study in a "Latin school" under a tutor engaged from Great Britain by his father and other Bermudians.[4] To satisfy his "ruling propensity for reading," Tucker read John Newberry's books for boys, the *Arabian Nights*—"by stealth"—and such standard eighteenth-century novels as *Tom Jones, Roderick Random, Gil Blas,* and *The Vicar of Wakefield.* By fifteen he had helped to form a literary club, the Calliopean Society, and had read some history and a standard work in belles lettres, Hugh Blair's *Lectures*—"the first book which awakened in me the habit of serious reflecting."[5] In Hamilton he continued his classical training under "another Scotch teacher," a Mr. Dalziel, before traveling ten miles to St. George's to receive instruction in natural philosophy from the lawyer Josiah Meigs, later professor of natural philosophy at Yale College and president and founder of the University of Georgia. Meigs successfully petitioned Governor Henry Hamilton to open his library to Tucker, who, it seems, applied himself diligently to his work, closeting himself throughout the day and presenting himself to Meigs in the evenings for examination. After a year of such directed study, in 1792, Tucker began to prepare himself for a profession by reading law in the office of George Bascomb, a prosperous lawyer.[6]

When Bascomb died in 1795, Tucker was faced with an important decision. He was asked by several of Bascomb's clients—British privateers who brought captured French and American ships into Bermuda's ports—to represent them in the admiralty courts. Tucker was sorely tempted to accept the job, which promised security and wealth to one who could prove himself a competent trial lawyer. But he reluctantly refused, partly because he recognized that he was un-

---

3. "Autobiography," manuscript copy, Tucker-Harrison-Smith Papers, University of Virginia Library, pp. 1, opposite p. 5, 5, 7. According to Tucker, the business failed because the company had no one central head and because each of the partners was allowed to draw supplies for his family without reimbursing the firm.

4. *Ibid.,* p. 4.

5. *Ibid.,* p. 8.

6. *Ibid.,* pp. 6-8. The George Bascomb whom Tucker mentions perhaps is the George Bascome whom Kerr discusses in *Bermuda and the American Revolution, passim.*

qualified to handle the complicated cases, but especially because he had political ambitions too great for the small islands.[7]

He determined to seek his career in America. His wish to leave what he considered the imprisoning confines of Bermuda for the greater opportunities in the new nation was not unusual. For years numerous Bermudians, among whom were many members of the Tucker family, had been emigrating there, and two of his relatives had achieved eminence. One, St. George Tucker, after successive marriages to wealthy Virginia widows—Mrs. Frances (Bland) Randolph in 1778 and, after her death, Mrs. Lelia Carter in 1791—had become a great landowner and in 1795 was a judge and professor of law at William and Mary College; another, Thomas Tudor Tucker, had practiced medicine in Charleston and had been elected to Congress from South Carolina. George Tucker probably never had met St. George, but he knew of his success and of his heroism in the Revolutionary War. The influence of Thomas Tudor was more direct, especially in forming Tucker's pro-American, anti-Tory politics, which, in 1795, bordered on French Jacobinism. Although Tucker already sympathized with the French Revolution, partly because of his association with his republican tutor, Josiah Meigs, it was the visit of the American Congressman to Bermuda in the 1790's which caused Tucker to overrate greatly the merit of his "republican predilections."[8]

In July, 1795, shortly after the death of his mother, Tucker sailed for Philadelphia, intending to continue the study of the law, either in America or preferably in London, if he could be sure that English training would not prejudice his chances for "political advancement" in America. With three other Bermudians who planned to proceed to London on an American ship to avoid the risk of French capture, Tucker enjoyed an exhilarating, free-spending good time in the capital city. Then, almost out of funds, he traveled to Williamsburg to ask St. George Tucker's advice and to borrow money—two favors which he was to continue to solicit for a long time in life. At Williamsburg Tucker found that St. George, then a judge of the Virginia General Court system, was visiting the courts under his jurisdiction. Too

7. "Autobiography," pp. 8-9.

8. *Ibid.*, pp. 7-8, 9-10. For an account of the life of St. George Tucker, see Mary Haldane Coleman, *St. George Tucker, Citizen of No Mean City* (Richmond, Va., 1938), and Jay B. Hubbell, *The South in American Literature, 1607-1900* (Durham, N.C., 1954), pp. 150-152. Leary's *The Literary Career of Nathaniel Tucker* contains biographical information on both St. George and Thomas Tudor Tucker. For Meigs, see William M. Meigs, *Life of Josiah Meigs* (Philadelphia, 1887), and Ellis Merton Coulter, *College Life in the Old South,* rev. ed. (Athens, Ga., 1951), pp. 14-20.

impatient to await his return, Tucker set out to seek him on horse-back. He was "handsomely dressed in a black coat & waistcoat, in white casimire breeches and silk stockings with shoes," a mode of dress very different from that of the Virginians he met, and Tucker feared he might be arrested as a "runaway clerk from Richmond." Saddlesore and bitten by bedbugs, by the time he located St. George in western Fluvanna County, Tucker was beginning to wish himself back among the comforts of a clean Philadelphia hotel, making plans to travel to London. His spirits revived, however, when St. George lent him suitable traveling clothes and money. Advised to study law in Virginia, Tucker returned to Williamsburg to enroll at William and Mary.[9]

The Williamsburg in which Tucker spent his first years in America had but twelve hundred inhabitants and was declining from the flourishing position it had held in the years preceding the Revolution as the colonial capital. One contemporary traveler described it thus: "The town consists of one principal street, and two others which run parallel to it. At one end of the main street stands the college, and at the other end the old capitol or state house, a capacious building of brick, now crumbling to pieces from negligence. The houses around it are mostly uninhabited, and present a melancholy picture."[10] In a similar vein, Tucker at first thought the village to have "such an air of decay & dullness as to produce great disappointment."

But that first appearance was deceiving, and Tucker soon found that Williamsburg had "a very refined and intelligent society" and was a place of "really luxurious living."[11] There dwelt a limited circle of well-to-do physicians, judges, and retired planters, as well as enough attractive women to cause Judge John Coalter, St. George's son-in-law, to remember the village as "the land of lovely dames."[12] Men and women, pleased to show their wit and conviviality, composed verses to memorialize weddings, picnics, courtships, flirtations, and other diversions. St. George, for example, wrote about a musical evening in which relatives and friends met at his home to play violin, violincello,

9. "Autobiography," pp. 10-12.

10. Isaac Weld, Jr., *Travels Through the States of North America and the Provinces of Upper and Lower Canada, during the Years 1795, 1796, and 1797* (London, 1799), II, 95.

11. "Autobiography," pp. 10, 12.

12. John Gardiner Tyler, *The Old Colonial Capital* (Richmond, Va., 1907), p. 174. A good description of the Williamsburg of the period can be found in Tucker's *The Valley of Shenandoah; or, Memoirs of the Graysons* (New York, 1824), II, 48-55.

harpsichord, flute, and timbrels.[13] Selected college students and visitors, whose stays sometimes lengthened into months, joined in the sociality, helping to put on dances and amateur musicals.

That Tucker was warmly welcomed by the Tidewater aristocracy was due in part to his sponsorship by the esteemed St. George; but as great a cause for his success was his prepossessing appearance and his manners and accomplishments, which well fitted him for life in the small but genteel community. By his own description, Tucker was, at twenty, five feet ten inches in height, with a slender though "well proportioned" figure and a handsome face, which was "somewhat of a feminine cast." He enjoyed conversing on literature, architecture, and drawing, could play the violin with some skill, "excelled in dancing," and, perhaps most important, had an extreme "fondness for female society and a lively sensibility to the charm" of feminine "beauty and conversation."[14] Shortly after settling in Williamsburg, he "had entrée into the best houses" and was the frequent guest of some "12 or 15 families, in easy circumstances," who gave balls and entertained friends with dinner and evening parties during which they played charades and composed poetical "effusions."[15]

Tucker found polished and enlightened friends among the students, as well as in Williamsburg society. Two of his "special friends" at the college were James P. Preston, who became governor of Virginia, and Benjamin Howard, later a congressman and governor of the Missouri Territory.[16] Also enrolled in William and Mary at this time and probably acquainted with Tucker were Joseph C. Cabell, John H. Cocke, and David Watson, all of whom were to help Jefferson organize the University of Virginia; and John Tayloe Lomax, who was appointed Professor of Law at the University in 1827.[17]

Tucker's studying seems in no way to have interfered with his social life, and he confessed that during his stay in Williamsburg he attended few classes and studied only in bed before breakfast.[18] Such laxity was possible partly, perhaps, because William and Mary, as one foreign visitor described it at about the time of Tucker's enrollment, was more "a grammar school than a college," including in its

13. See William Stevens Prince, "St. George Tucker As a Poet of the Early Republic" (Yale University diss., 1954, pp. 30-31).

14. "Autobiography," pp. 4-5.

15. *Ibid.*, opposite p. 12, p. 12.

16. *Ibid.*, p. 12.

17. Malcolm Lester, "George Tucker: His Early Life and Public Service, 1775-1825" (University of Virginia M.A. thesis, 1946), p. 27.

18. "Autobiography," p. 12.

student body about thirty young boys learning the rudiments of classical languages.[19]   Although both St. George Tucker and Bishop James
Madison, the college president, were outstanding teachers, the faculty
was generally undistinguished.[20]   Tucker may have felt, in addition,
that his training in Bermuda allowed him to relax his efforts at
William and Mary, and the college would seem to have acquiesced.
After spending one year as a general student in lieu of the two years
prescribed, and another learning the law, Tucker was graduated in
1797 *ex speciali gratia.*[21]

In the summer of 1796, recuperation from a series of intermittent
fevers provided Tucker with a reason for visiting New York City and
for seeing more of his adopted country.   With letters of introduction
from relatives and friends, Tucker met the governor and the ex-
governor of New York, John Jay and George Clinton.   On his return
home in November he stopped in Philadelphia to observe the election
then in progress.   There was, he said, "as much laudatory as
calumnious falsehood," for he heard one voter successfully sway
another, a holder of fifteen electoral votes, to Jefferson on the ground
that his "negroes sit down with him at the meal table every day."[22]
Tucker was still a strong republican, but already he had begun to
doubt the desirability of a classless society.   He found his trip up the
Chesapeake unpleasant, with "a dirty set of French Canaille for the
crew and passengers."[23]   More to his taste was a brief and hard-
worked-for meeting with General Washington, who, dressed in black
velvet, solemnly received guests in his oval room on Market Street in
Philadelphia.[24]

In spite of his visits with the "best society" in Philadelphia and
New York, Tucker was anxious to return to Williamsburg, in com-

19. Weld, *Travels Through North America,* II, 95.   See Duc de La Rochefoucauld-
Liancourt, *Travels Through the United States of North America, the Country of the
Iroquois, and Upper Canada, in the Years 1795, 1796, and 1797; With an Authentic
Account of Lower Canada* (London, 1799), II, 23-28.   According to Percy Winfield
Turrentine, "Life and Letters of Nathaniel Beverley Tucker" (Harvard diss., 1952),
p. 183, Weld's description is inaccurate, because he failed to distinguish young gram-
mar school students from regular college students.

20. Lester, "George Tucker," pp. 26-27; "Autobiography," p. 26; La Rochefoucauld-
Liancourt, *Travels,* II, 23-70.

21. "Autobiography," p. 12.

22. *Ibid.,* p. 14.

23. Tucker to St. George Tucker, Sept. 23, 1796, Tucker-Coleman Collection,
Colonial Williamsburg.

24. "Autobiography," p. 13.

parison with which he found all else "insipid and uninteresting."[25] He was courting Mary Byrd Farley, the wealthy great-granddaughter of William Byrd II, who was living in Williamsburg with her widowed mother. The girl, whose charm and fortune, Tucker said, attracted a host of suitors, was seriously ill, probably with consumption. Tucker proposed to her and was accepted. Although he had intended to postpone his marriage until he had a license to practice law, he changed his mind and, borrowing money for his wedding expenses from his uncle William Hall, married her in October, 1797, in order to take her to Bermuda to improve her health.[26]

Tucker's visit to his old home in 1797 only served to convince him of the wisdom of his emigration. He wrote that, though the island trade was growing, he was not so simple-minded as to believe that new trade regulations would "make this rock a paradise, convert Turks Island salt . . . into gold."[27] Tucker's plans now were all laid in Virginia, the home of his rich and beautiful wife. After ordering a set of expensive furniture from London, he returned to the United States in May, 1798, and set up a temporary residence in Williamsburg, intending to read for the bar examinations. But except for a few trips to North Carolina to collect rents from his wife's tenants, Tucker, who found many reasons for not reading dull and difficult legal writings, enjoyed a year-long vacation. He attended the races in Fredericksburg, made the circuit of Virginia's fashionable watering places, and visited his wife's friends and relatives. As a guest at the Albemarle estate of his wife's sister and brother-in-law, the Champe Carters, he met Jefferson for the first time and found him a man of "easy politeness and familiar conversation."[28] Tucker, who had come to America with only his wits and his family connections as assets, seemed well on his way to social eminence in Virginia.

The death of his wife on May 25, 1799, however, checked the easy flow of Tucker's life. When he tried to settle her affairs, he ran into difficulty. Mary Tucker left to her husband a large part of a profitable sugar plantation in Antigua, a share in thirteen thousand acres of land in North Carolina on the Dan River (Saura Town), some smaller tracts in Virginia, and a share in the Dismal Swamp Company. But, as Tucker's sisters-in-law were quick to point out, some of Mary

25. Tucker to St. George Tucker, Sept. 23, 1796, Tucker-Coleman Collection, Colonial Williamsburg.

26. "Autobiography," opposite p. 12, p. 13.

27. Tucker to St. George Tucker, Jan. 20, 1798, Tucker-Coleman Collection, Colonial Williamsburg.

28. "Autobiography," opposite p. 14.

Tucker's conveyances were defective, because both North Carolina and West Indies law prescribed that deeds be signed, as hers were not, in the presence of the governor or his representative. Disgusted with that "delicacy" and fastidiousness which on his honeymoon had prevented him from selling his wife's properties, as a lawyer from Antigua had counseled him to do, Tucker worked hard to protect his interests, bringing forth in court proof that Mary Tucker's sisters had voluntarily signed their sister's will, and citing the testimony of an attending physician, Dr. Philip Bauraud, that his wife's last wish was that Tucker should be her sole heir.[29]   But the dispute continued for twenty years, and in the end Tucker salvaged only part of Mary's estate.

About three months after his wife's death, Tucker left Virginia to collect the rents from the still unrelinquished Antigua plantation. After several months in Antigua, Martinique, and St. Vincent's in the West Indies, and a long stay in Bermuda, he traveled to Baltimore and Norfolk, accompanied by his younger brother, James Tucker, for whom he found a job in a Norfolk counting house. By the time he returned to Williamsburg, Tucker had made up his mind what to do with himself. In the summer of 1800 he moved to Richmond, intending to set up a law practice and to make himself an important political figure.

29. *Ibid.*, pp. 13-14.

CHAPTER II

LIFE IN RICHMOND

THE RICHMOND OF 1800 was an appropriate residence for a man like Tucker who enjoyed the bustle of society, was interested in commerce and banking, and harbored hopes for political office. Situated at the head of navigation on the James River, the town with a population of a little over five thousand—half of whom were Negroes—was the state capital and the center of social, commercial, and political life for all Virginia. Aristocratic planters rode blooded horses down the main street, and nationally famous statesmen could be seen on many a corner. Here John Marshall and George Wickham gave their famous "lawyers' parties," where the Virginia elders—Judge Pendleton, Chancellor Wythe, and Patrick Henry—gathered with such promising new members of the bar as William Wirt and George Hay. From December to March, when the General Assembly was in session, politicians from all over the state convened, debating during the day and drinking, dining, and gambling at night. Enterprising merchants such as John Allan, Poe's foster father, worked long hours buying and selling produce and dry goods, and sanguine bankers and land speculators gave an air of prosperity to the town. Richmond newspapers, perhaps the best in the South at the time, published belletristic essays and poetry as well as partisan political polemics and statewide and national news. The town's varied entertainments—museums, theaters, a library society, and many evening parties—provided diversions well suited to Tucker's tastes.

A letter of recommendation sent by the ever-helpful St. George to his friend Governor James Monroe throws light on Tucker's character at this time and helps explain his future career in Richmond. "To the best qualities of the heart," wrote St. George, "he unites an excellent understanding, which has been well cultivated, and a very comprehensive knowledge of the world; Nature has blest him with a most exuberant flow of spirits, which sometimes betray him into acts of levity. . . ."[1]

When Tucker first moved to the capital, he was apprehensive of what his social standing might be. The talents which had stood him in good stead in Williamsburg, however, were also appreciated in Richmond, and he promptly reported his social success to St. George. He entertained guests in his expensively furnished home near the Governor's and was, he wrote in a letter, "creeping into notice . . . rather faster than my first reception promised"—by August 4, 1800, he had been invited out to dinner three times![2] As a result of careful cultivation, within a year Tucker could number among his acquaintances Judge Pendleton, George Hay, George Wythe, and, of course, Monroe, that "dull slow man," who introduced him to the town.[3]

In February, 1802, Tucker married Maria Ball Carter, the seventeen-year-old daughter of Charles Carter, a member of the "Blenheim" branch of the Carter family. She was the niece of Mrs. Champe Carter, the sister of Tucker's first wife, who introduced the couple in the summer of 1799, shortly after Mary Tucker's death. Tucker's first impression of Maria was not favorable, but a year later, when he paid court to her at the Fredericksburg races, he found her, he said, "much improved, and very interesting." During Maria's visit to Richmond in the spring of 1801, Tucker proposed to her, having come to the conclusion that, though she was not "a decided beauty she had a face distinguished for sweetness and intelligence, conversed sensibly & sung sweetly" and was, in short, worthy to be his bride.[4]

Though her wealth and beauty could not match those of Tucker's first wife, Maria certainly proved to be a social asset to her husband. Because of her, Tucker said, he gained access to "much of the best society." For example, John Marshall, whom Tucker greatly admired, was especially kind to the young lion-hunter from Bermuda because he knew that Maria Tucker was the great-niece of George Washington, and, for the same reason, George Wickham, the town's leading Federalist lawyer, welcomed the Tuckers to his whist and loo parties.[5]

1. St. George Tucker to James Monroe, July 19, 1800, Monroe Papers II, Library of Congress.

2. Tucker to St. George Tucker, Aug. 4, 1800, Tucker-Coleman Collection, Colonial Williamsburg.

3. "Autobiography," manuscript copy, Tucker-Harrison-Smith Papers, University of Virginia Library, pp. 22-23.

4. *Ibid.*, pp. 15-16.

5. *Ibid.*, p. 23.

Interest in literature and the arts led Tucker to seek the friendship of the chief littérateurs of Richmond. During his first year in the capital, he published an essay suggesting a remedy for the slavery problem. This was favorably received and brought him recognition as a "man of letters," worthy to join such established writers as William Wirt and James Ogilvie in writing a number of essays which were published in the leading Richmond papers. Under various pseudonyms Tucker also wrote verses published in the local press and achieved fame as a satirist of the follies which he himself enjoyed.[6]

As a lawyer, however, Tucker was an utter failure. He was licensed to practice law in 1801, but, cursed with an awkward and faltering manner of public speaking and with insufficient knowledge of common law and court procedure, he made a poor showing in court.[7] St. George once drew up an argument on a matter-of-fact case and asked Tucker to represent his client. Tucker became so confused in court that, as he said, he hardly knew whether he was on his head or his feet.[8] He tried practicing law in the courts of chancery—again through the offices of St. George—but before any case was brought to an end he was always replaced or aided by other counsel.[9] Of all the legal positions offered him through family or political friendships, Tucker found only one he could handle. For a year he served successfully as commissioner of bankruptcy, a lucrative job, because there were numerous cases "always prompted by the bankrupts, by way of sponging off their debts."[10]

In politics Tucker was a Jeffersonian Republican, pleased at the split in the Federalist party between Adams and Hamilton,[11] and lavish in his praise of proud Virginians who resented Federalist attempts to use a caucus to "appoint a president."[12] But Tucker was no longer a near-Jacobin; he had become a conservative, pro-bank Republican. His early letters reveal that his political allegiance was strongly influenced by a belief that the Jefferson administration would sensibly support the policies of the banking institutions. Like many

6. For an account of Tucker's writings during this period, see below, Pt. II, pp. 51-59.

7. "Autobiography," pp. 4, 10.

8. *Ibid.*, p. 16.

9. *Ibid.*, p. 18.

10. *Ibid.*, p. 17.

11. Tucker to St. George Tucker, Oct. 2, 1800, Tucker-Coleman Collection, Colonial Williamsburg.

12. Tucker to St. George Tucker, Jan. 18, 1800, Tucker-Coleman Collection, Colonial Williamsburg.

people in Richmond, he told St. George, he was happy about Jefferson's 1801 election, for "now that the pilot is chosen, the federal bank will glide on smoothly," unless, he added without elaboration, "the waves of democracy arise."[13]

Of immediate concern to Tucker were the efforts of the Republican state legislature to regulate the Bank of Virginia. He published a series of essays defending the state bank as a private institution and was rewarded for his propaganda efforts by being taken onto the bank's board of directors.[14] Yet, though he expressed a belief that government regulation of business was harmful to the state's welfare and apparently feared for his own heavy investments in bank stocks, he could assure St. George that the alarms resulting from legislative "meddling" provided "for men of prudence and foresight" a wonderful opportunity for profitable speculation.[15]

It was, seemingly, Tucker's antipathy to the economic policies of Jefferson's followers and his intimacy with prominent Federalist politicians which caused one of his party's members to insult him and accuse him of being a Federalist in Republican disguise. At one of the party's caucuses, in which Tucker participated despite a professed dislike for party politics, "some of the more zealous republicans," according to Tucker, "carried their bitterness & violence so far that all of their party could not join them." Tucker made a speech on behalf of certain Federalists who were candidates in the coming election. When Lewis Harvey challenged his party faith and "gave him the lie," Tucker, who seems always to have had an extremely hot temper, struck at him, only to have his arm caught by John Brockenbrough, Harvey's brother-in-law and Tucker's friend. "I had always determined to preserve my honor untarnished, according to the prevailing code," Tucker wrote, "and had several times demanded and received satisfaction, though I had never fought a duel."[16] Tucker admitted that he could have regarded himself as the provoker of the quarrel and thus honorably have avoided challenging Harvey, but he preferred as a gentleman not to resort to "these subterfuges." Be-

---

13. Tucker to St. George Tucker, Feb. 24, 1801, Tucker-Coleman Collection, Colonial Williamsburg. Joseph Dorfman, *The Economic Mind in American Civilization, 1606-1865* (New York, 1946), II, 540, states that in early life Tucker was a "Jeffersonian Republican, but he belonged to the conservative wing which never ceased to deprecate the errors of extreme 'democracy.'"

14. "Autobiography," p. 19.

15. Tucker to St. George Tucker, Jan. 19, 1806, Tucker-Coleman Collection, Colonial Williamsburg.

16. "Autobiography," p. 21.

cause both men were "bound to the peace in a heavy penalty," Tucker waited to issue his challenge until the period of recognizance was over, meanwhile trying to prepare his affairs. From what we know of his financial and family circumstances—his wife was carrying their second child—Tucker must have been secretly appalled at his predicament. But he challenged Harvey, drew up his will, and, since he was a poor marksman, arranged to exchange shots from a distance, to reduce the disparity in his and his opponent's abilities. Mutual friends, fortunately, interfered and stopped the duel on the day before it was to take place.[17]

During these years, 1800 to 1806, in Richmond, Tucker's financial situation became extremely complicated. When he moved to Richmond shortly after his first wife's death, he was a moderately wealthy man. His right to part of his first wife's estate was being contested in the courts, but Tucker held free title to Mary Tucker's Virginia lands, and he seems to have felt that he could make a favorable settlement on the balance if he waited long enough. Expenses increased, of course, with his second marriage and with the addition of two children to the family—Daniel George born on November 23, 1802, and Eleanor Rosalie on May 4, 1804. Tucker made little or no money from his law practice and was fast using up the capital of his inherited estate; yet he failed to lower his scale of living or to change his habits. When he wasn't entertaining in his own home, he played cards elsewhere late into the night—sometimes losing as much as three hundred dollars in one game—and during the day he loafed away his time with "lawyers & jesters."[18] He speculated heavily in bank stocks and tied up most of his cash in buying, selling, and trading a great deal of real estate. Among other investments he purchased a lot for fifteen hundred dollars and erected on it an office building, "modelled after a Grecian temple," and derisively called by some "the little capitol." With his father-in-law and others he bought a share in an estate which eventually was to profit him ten thousand dollars but which brought in no needed cash at the time. To finance such transactions, he sold his Norfolk estate and his claim in the Dismal Swamp Company, and, finally, tried to negotiate a compromise with the co-heirs to his first wife's estate whereby, for relinquishing any future claim to the

17. *Idem.*
18. *Ibid.*, pp. 16-17, 22-23. The extent of his losses at cards is seen in his losing in a single evening all of the money he had with him and $276 he borrowed from a friend.

rich Antiguan sugar plantation, he was to receive free title to the Saura Town lands.[19]

Tucker's tangled financial affairs and his lack of responsibility are perhaps best represented by his involvement in a financial scandal which threatened to blight his social and professional reputations and to destroy whatever hopes he may have still held for elective political office in Richmond. The details of the shady transaction are vague, but the general outlines are clear enough. In 1803, along with such distinguished citizens as George Wythe, John Marshall, Edmund Randolph, John Page, George Hay, and John Brockenbrough, Tucker was appointed a trustee of the Richmond Academy. He organized a lottery to raise money for the institution and sold chances for various cash prizes, the largest of which was worth five thousand dollars. He also bought a sizable number of chances for himself which he sold to other people, sometimes at very large profits, for each became more valuable as the lottery progressed and the number of undrawn chances diminished. Finally Tucker held one of the remaining four or five chances, one of which was sure to win the grand prize. The holders of these chances decided to divide the prize, but, to satisfy their curiosity, to draw from a large turning container the last ticket to see who among them held the matching ticket and would have won the five thousand dollars. Embarrassingly enough for Tucker, the winning ticket was his, "found stuck in the joints between two parts of the wheel." If this stroke of miraculous good luck on the part of the lottery manager disturbed the other ticket-holders, they gave no sign of disapproval. Indeed, Tucker seems to have persuaded a few prize winners to allow him to hold their winnings for them, and he "prevailed upon the other trustees" to make him custodian of the profits of the lottery, some five thousand dollars. He promptly blended all this money with his own and spent it in high living and land buying.[20] Three years later, when he made plans to leave Richmond and was finally asked for settlement by the unpaid prize winners and the Academy, he was unable to pay them. The other trustees paid the discontented prize winners from their private funds and allowed Tucker to pledge his property as security for his debt to the Academy.

19. *Ibid.*, p. 19. Tucker's early attempts to settle with his co-heirs were unsuccessful because one refused to compromise, claiming that possession was nine-tenths of the law. (See Tucker to St. George Tucker, Sept. 30, 1803, Tucker-Coleman Collection, Colonial Williamsburg.) As late as 1815, his title to the Saura Town lands was still not clear. (See "Autobiography," p. 30.)

20. "Autobiography," p. 19.

In about a year, Tucker reimbursed both the trustees and the Academy. Nevertheless, a committee investigated his trusteeship and demanded more money for the Academy. Tucker appealed the decision, and a board of arbitrators reduced the amount of his payment and even, said Tucker, awarded him a commission for selling tickets. This charge of mishandling funds was revived in 1819, the year in which Tucker was nominated to the office of president of the Bank of Lynchburg and ran for Congress. Forced to appear in person at the Virginia General Assembly to defend himself, he did obtain official clearance. But the whole matter besmirched his reputation and symbolized the irresponsibility of his life during the years in which he lived in Richmond.[21]

21. *Ibid.*, pp. 23, 28-29.

CHAPTER III

RUSTICATION

AFTER SIX YEARS in Richmond, Tucker came to the realization that he needed to start life afresh. He was totally unsuccessful as a lawyer, and he stood little chance of election to political office in Richmond, where he was not thought to be a completely loyal party member and where the local citizens knew him as a gambler and man about town. Most of the fortune left to him by Mary Farley Tucker had been spent in gambling and entertaining or was pledged as security to creditors who were pressing him. He determined to escape Richmond and to put his affairs in order.[1]

In the fall of 1806 Tucker moved to the home of his wife's parents, the Charles Carters, in Frederick County in the Shenandoah Valley. His connections with Richmond were not completely severed, however, for business affairs brought him back to the capital frequently.[2] On one such visit in 1807, a loan company to which he owed six thousand dollars had him arrested and filed a complaint in court against him. Tucker hired an attorney to defend him and was released without bail. After instituting a counter-action for false arrest to help clear his name, he used the endorsements of Thomas Tudor and St. George Tucker to borrow from a Richmond bank the sum to repay his debt. The arrest was one of the most embarrassing events in his life, but it served the useful purpose of reminding him that only by hard work could he free himself from debt and rebuild his reputation.[3]

1. [Tucker], *Recollections of the Life of Eleanor Rosalie Tucker* (Lynchburg, Va., 1818), p. 18.
2. Malcolm Lester, "George Tucker: His Early Life and Public Service, 1775-1825" (University of Virginia M.A. thesis, 1946), p. 60.
3. "Autobiography," manuscript copy, Tucker-Harrison-Smith Papers, University of Virginia Library, p. 29.

For almost two years, Tucker economized by living in rural Virginia with the Carters and friends. During this time he purchased an estate in Virginia just across the Dan River from his Saura Town lands in North Carolina. He did not wish to leave Virginia, probably because he still entertained hopes of political advancement in the southern part of the state, once he remade his life. Although he had little ready money, he had control of or rights in much property, and by satisfying new creditors of his ability and willingness to pay his debts, he was able to finance the purchase of slaves and the remodeling of his new eight-room house.[4]

In May, 1808, Tucker at last settled his family at "Woodbridge," his home in Pittsylvania County. Mrs. Tucker recognized that the retreat to the backwoods of Virginia was necessary if her husband was to retrench financially and build his professional reputation. Yet she loathed the change. Having borne Maria in 1806 and Eliza in December, 1808, seven months after settling at "Woodbridge," she was faced with the necessity of raising four children with fewer servants and more primitive facilities than she was accustomed to. Consequently, she found it difficult to forgive those "sordid relatives" of Tucker's first wife who, in her mind, by disregarding the death-bed wish of their "amiable sister," deprived Tucker of the wealth which would have allowed him to remain in Richmond.[5]

To Tucker, who missed the "gaieties and dissipations" of Richmond, the greatest privation of frontier life lay in mingling only with the uneducated and boorish. Although Pittsylvania County had rich farm land, it was one of the last Virginia areas to develop the plantation system, and there were, as he recognized, few prominent politicians or polished planters for the fashionable Tuckers to associate with. The chief entertainment was to be found in the sessions of the county courts, during which tobacco-chewing lawyers and small farmers discussed politics and economics.[6] All of his neighbors, Tucker said, were "friendly & civil, but extremely plain & unpolished in their manners & style of living."[7] Life certainly would be more pleasant, he told St. George, if he and his wife could find "but one or

4. *Ibid.*, p. 23.
5. Maria B. Tucker, "Commonplace Book," typed copy, University of Virginia Library.
6. William Cabell Bruce, *John Randolph of Roanoke* (New York, 1939), II, 169 ff., as cited by Lester, "George Tucker," p. 56.
7. "Autobiography," p. 24. Lester, "George Tucker," pp. 53-54, 56, 60, describes briefly the inhabitants and customs of the Pittsylvania-Lynchburg area.

two neighbors of cultivation and refinement."[8]   Yet, when Tucker, who had begun the practice of conscientiously tallying his income and expenses, compared his present financial situation with that during his life in Richmond, he was more than willing to forgo Richmond society for the security of a balanced budget.   His greatest wish was that he had moved sooner, for, as he said, he "should have been so much more advanced in . . . profession, so many thousands richer in purse, and so many years younger in health and ambition."[9]

Gradually Tucker achieved some success in the courts, not that the competition was less keen than it had been in Richmond, but simply because he worked harder and longer.   In his first appearance in the Pittsylvania County Court, he was forced to decline an opportunity to address a grand jury because he was ignorant of criminal law, but he studied it, prepared a charge, and was appointed attorney for the Commonwealth, though admittedly through the influence of friends and the chance of the office-holder's quitting without notice.[10]   In addition to having to learn the law with which he should have been familiar after seven years of practice, Tucker had also to moderate his distaste and disdain for the facile rhetoric which characterized the speeches of lawyers in general and of rural lawyers in particular.[11] His recognition as a competent lawyer was slow in coming, but, although he seems never to have achieved the self-confidence needed to speak easily in court, he increased the number of his clients and practiced law in three, then four counties, traveling an average of three hundred and forty miles a month.[12]

Tucker also became active in politics.   With Isaac W. Coles and Peachy Gilmer, he successfully urged the state legislatures of North Carolina and Virginia to take steps to clear the Roanoke, Dan, and Staunton rivers for navigation, so that planters could transport their produce cheaply to Norfolk, avoiding expensive land trips to Petersburg and Richmond.   In support of his proposal, in 1811 he published *A Letter to a Member of the General Assembly . . . on the Navigation of the Roanoke. . . .*   His agitation for this improvement led him to

8. Tucker to St. George Tucker, July 31, 1808, Tucker-Coleman Collection, Colonial Williamsburg.

9. Tucker to St. George Tucker, Oct. 9, 1808, Tucker-Coleman Collection, Colonial Williamsburg.

10. Tucker to St. George Tucker, April 14, 1809, Tucker-Coleman Collection, Colonial Williamsburg.

11. "Autobiography," pp. 25-26; Tucker to St. George Tucker, April 14, 1809, Tucker-Coleman Collection, Colonial Williamsburg.

12. "Autobiography," p. 26.

bid in 1813 and 1814 for a seat in the state legislature, but he was twice defeated. In 1816 Tucker once more "offered himself" at the urging of friends and was elected. During his tenure as a state representative he never excelled in debating, but he drafted a respected report on the revision of the Virginia Constitution and later proposed and drafted a valedictory address on Madison which was accepted by both houses on February 22, 1817.[13]

Although Tucker did not produce much writing while practicing law in rural Virginia, yet he then did some of his best literary work. In 1814 and 1815, under the title "Thoughts of a Hermit," the Philadelphia *Port Folio* published his series of essays written in 1813 as part of a disciplinary program which he had laid out for himself. During moments salvaged from "more pressing business," he told St. George, "I . . . prepare . . . once a month an essay on some serious subject . . . which I have previously written upon by way of exercise— and I am compelled to perform this engagement on the road—at Courthouses—& after everyone else is asleep."[14]

Good fortune seemed to come all at once for Tucker. Success in selling his contributions to the *Port Folio* for two dollars a page increased his confidence in his intellectual pursuits, and he found that, with the peace of 1815, his property rose rapidly in value. He promptly unloaded some land at considerable profit, settled all his debts, and —with Walter Coles, who bought a quarter of the land—paid $26,800 for a three-quarters share of an estate along the Staunton River, which he planned to break up and sell in small lots. By the time he had sold his "Woodbridge" home for $7,200 and moved to Lynchburg, in March, 1818, Tucker could estimate his property holdings to be worth $80,000. Success followed success, and Tucker found that a man with considerable wealth stood in a good way to gain even more: as his reputation as a shrewd financier increased he received many jobs as a debt collector. In the same period he became a trustee of the Lynchburg Female Academy and a vestryman in St. Paul's Episcopal Church, and in 1819 he was elected to Congress from Lynchburg.[15]

But Tucker's financial success was short-lived, and after his election to Congress he found himself again in debt. His recent purchase

13. "Valedictory Address on the Retirement of President James Madison," *Acts of the General Assembly of Virginia* (1816-17), pp. 201-202. See Lester, "George Tucker," pp. 69-76, for a discussion of Tucker's work in the General Assembly.

14. Tucker to St. George Tucker, Feb. 3, 1814, Tucker-Coleman Collection, Colonial Williamsburg.

15. "Autobiography," pp. 30-31.

on the Staunton River had only eighty-five hundred acres instead of its estimated thirteen thousand, and he was pressed into paying off a claim, later proved to be fraudulent, of seven thousand dollars. Part of his loss he recouped by selling one quarter of a four hundred dollar purchase in Danville lots for twenty-five hundred dollars, but "from a repugnance to be regarded as a land speculator" he left the rest untouched.[16] From 1811 to 1821 his father-in-law, Charles Carter, had been plagued with financial woes and was continually calling upon Tucker for help. After selling his Shenandoah Valley plantation at a loss, Carter bought in Culpeper County an estate much too expensive for him to manage. He was in debt for six thousand dollars, and his creditor, bitter because Carter had proved him a forger in court, refused to grant him any mercy. While Carter was traveling through Virginia in an unsuccessful attempt to borrow money from friends, Tucker joined with Lawrence Lewis, Carter's brother-in-law, to salvage what goods and slaves they could from Carter's estate and to prevent the family from moving to Kentucky. During the auction Lewis contrived to buy twelve of Carter's field hands, whom he conveyed in trust to Tucker for Carter. Tucker mingled the slaves with those he had on his "Deerwood" estate and made arrangements to settle the Carters there for life, with his father-in-law running the plantation for their joint profit.[17]

Difficulties with his and his father-in-law's property were but two sources for Tucker's worry during his three terms in Congress. A return to his old habits of stylish living, indolence, and gambling made his stay in Washington expensive and relatively unproductive. He spent, he said, more time playing chess and cards than he did working, and on one occasion lost a thousand dollars to a professional cardsharp, introduced to him by a representative from Pennsylvania. Moreover, troubles within his immediate family required much of his attention. In the years preceding the purchase of a home in Lynchburg, Mrs. Tucker had given birth to her fifth and sixth children, Lelia in October, 1810, and Harriett in May, 1813. The death of Harriett in 1816 was painful to her, but her anguish was almost uncontrollable when Rosalie, the oldest girl and the family favorite, died unexpectedly in 1818, at the age of fourteen. Combined with Mrs. Tucker's grief was continuing ill-health. Though warned by physicians not

16. *Ibid.,* pp. 31-32.

17. *Ibid.,* pp. 20, 32-33; Betty Lewis Carter to Maria Tucker, Jan. 20, 1814, and Maria Tucker to Betty Lewis Carter, Nov. 23, 1819, Tucker-Harrison-Smith Papers, University of Virginia Library.

to have more children after the birth of Harriett in 1813, she again conceived and died during pregnancy in February, 1823. In the carriage on his way back to Washington after Maria's funeral in Lynchburg, Tucker muffled his face with a handkerchief to hide his tears, feigning a toothache to explain his conduct to overly-curious fellow passengers. Reviewing his years with Maria, he called up all his errors and failures, irrationally but understandably seeing himself as the cause for her suffering and privation. The property they had worked long and hard to retain was still encumbered with debts and might well be lost. And at about the same time that he thought the past was wasted, he was worried about his only son, who in his indolence and unbalanced behavior was manifesting symptoms of a mental disorder which was to lead, years later, to his hospitalization and death in a Philadelphia institution.[18]

With such troubles, it is understandable that Tucker made no original or important contributions to legislation while in Congress. In general, he supported the standard Virginia positions. "He opposed the admission of Missouri with a slavery restriction, the bankruptcy bill, the protective tariff, and internal improvements at Federal expense." He was, in short, during his tenure, a Jeffersonian Republican—at least in voting.[19] Yet, as one student has pointed out, his expressed beliefs are different not only from those held later as a rampant nationalist and anti-Jacksonian, but also from the earlier opinions expressed in the essays published in the *Port Folio* in 1814 and 1815—so different that one has to conclude that, had the voters known of his authorship, they would not have sent him, as they did, to Congress to oppose nationalism.[20] The reasons for the disparity of the opinions expressed in his voting record and in his anonymous writings are hard to find. On May 12, 1824, he wrote privately to Peachy Gilmer that the problem of the tariff was "greatly overrated" by friends and foes.[21] But less than a month later in the Lynchburg *Virginian* he said in a "Letter to the Freeholders" that he was strongly opposed to the tariff because farmers suffered dearly from it.[22] It may be that political theory allowed him, as he held in the essay

18. "Autobiography," pp. 34-36. See Tucker to St. George Tucker, Oct. 4, 1820, and Jan. 28, 1823, Tucker-Coleman Collection, Colonial Williamsburg.

19. Leonard C. Helderman, "A Social Scientist of the Old South," *Journal of Southern History*, II (1936), pp. 150-151.

20. Lester, "George Tucker," p. 88.

21. Cited by Lester, "George Tucker," pp. 99-101.

22. "To the Freeholders of the Counties of Campbell, Pittsylvania, and Halifax," Lynchburg *Virginian*, June 11, 1824.

"On Instructions to Representatives," to think one way, yet vote as he knew his constituents would wish.[23]

In 1824, the year before his third term in Congress ended, Tucker received an offer from Jefferson, sanctioned by Joseph C. Cabell and James Madison, both members of the Board of Visitors, to go to the University of Virginia as Professor of Moral Philosophy. The commission which had met at Rockfish Gap in 1818 to discuss plans for the University decided that moral and political training was to be given through three professorships of law, government, and ideology. But in 1824 a shortage of money led the Board of Visitors to reduce the positions to law and moral philosophy.[24] Both posts, according to the board's minutes, were to go to Americans, and both, probably, to non-Federalists.[25] It is impossible to know whom else the board considered for the professorship of moral philosophy, but it seems likely that Tucker's name was mentioned early. Personal recommendations may have come from either St. George or Thomas Tudor Tucker, the latter of whom was still serving as Treasurer of the United States, to which position he was appointed in 1801 by Jefferson. Tucker's friendship with Cabell, begun when they were students at William and Mary and strengthened by Cabell's marriage to St. George's step-daughter, was undoubtedly influential.[26] Also Tucker's 1817 valedictory address on Madison in the General Assembly caught both Madison's and Jefferson's notice, and his voting record in Congress from 1819 to 1824 was looked upon with favor by the Republicans.

23. *Essays on Various Subjects of Taste, Morals, and National Policy* (Georgetown, D.C., 1822), pp. 273-288.

24. Herbert B. Adams, *Thomas Jefferson and the University of Virginia*, U.S. Bureau of Education Circular of Information No. 1, 1888, in *Contributions to American Educational History*, No. 2 (Washington, D.C., 1888), pp. 95, 119, 135; Philip Alexander Bruce, *History of the University of Virginia* (New York, 1920), II, 19.

25. "Minutes of the Board of Visitors of the University of Virginia," April 7, 1824, typed copy, University of Virginia Library, p. 62. Joseph Dorfman (*The Economic Mind in American Civilization, 1606-1865* [New York, 1946], II, 547) claims that Jefferson and Madison tried to make sure that "no Federalist in letter or spirit" should be appointed to the professorships of law or moral philosophy.

26. Lester, "George Tucker," p. 109. In 1824, before Cabell tendered Jefferson's offer to Tucker, he had requested Tucker's help in Congress on behalf of the Corrotoman estate in settling claims against the British, who had kidnapped slaves in the War of 1812 (Joseph C. Cabell to Tucker, Feb. 2, 1824, Cabell Deposit, University of Virginia Library). In January and February, 1825, Cabell also was in close correspondence with St. George on the appointment of Henry St. George Tucker to fill the law professorship in place of Francis Walker Gilmer, whose sickness and unpopularity would make it prudent "*to let him off*, on the ground of ill health," or Thomas Cooper, who was odious to the clergy (Joseph C. Cabell to St. George Tucker, Jan. 9, Feb. 7, Feb. 11, 1825, Cabell Deposit, University of Virginia Library).

But most instrumental, perhaps, in enhancing Tucker's chances for the appointment was his volume *Essays on Various Subjects of Taste, Morals, and National Policy* (Georgetown, 1822), composed of papers originally published in the *Port Folio* in 1814 and 1815. Tucker sent Madison a copy in the year it was published, and Madison, who found the essays "among the best answers to the charges of our national . . . backwardness,"[27] recommended it to Jefferson. The nationalism evident, for example, in the *Port Folio* essay "On the Future Destiny of the United States" was toned down when that essay was reprinted. In a footnote to a sentence predicting the control by federal government of the construction of "canals, roads, and public institutions," Tucker added that at first writing he did not fully consider "the constitutional question" and "was not aware that strong arguments may be urged against the existence of this power under the Constitution, and against the policy of granting it by amending that instrument."[28] The whole volume, moreover, shows an interest in civil society and aesthetics which must have pleased Jefferson, biased as he was toward the philosophical program of the Scottish Enlightenment.[29]

Lastly, Tucker may have been selected partly because of his acceptability to those who were constant enemies to Jefferson's plan. Generally speaking, Jefferson's University was opposed by the Episcopalians, who wanted to strengthen William and Mary, by the western Presbyterians, who wished the school to be located west of the Blue Ridge, and by the Federalists. Tucker was an Episcopalian educated at William and Mary, had represented rural Virginia in the General Assembly and in Congress, and had, in addition, many Federalist friends and associates.[30]

On December 29, 1824, Cabell wrote to Tucker that Jefferson and Madison both "thought with predilection of yourself for the Professorship of Ethics" and offered Tucker the position.[31] The proposal

27. James Madison to Tucker, July 15, 1822, Madison Papers, Library of Congress.

28. *Essays* (1822), p. 16.

29. Adrienne Koch, *Jefferson and Madison: The Great Collaboration* (New York, 1950), p. 274.

30. William Minor Dabney, "Jefferson's Albemarle: History of Albemarle County, Virginia, 1728-1819" (University of Virginia diss., 1951), pp. 116-117, has background information on the founding of the University.

31. Joseph C. Cabell to Tucker, Dec. 29, 1824, Cabell Deposit, University of Virginia Library. Cabell was following closely the terms set forth in Jefferson's letter of Dec. 22, 1824, to him: "We want a professor of Ethics. Mr. Madison and myself think with predilection, of George Tucker, our member of Congress. You know him, however, better than we do. Can we get a better? Will he serve? You know the

was a tempting one for several reasons. Tucker's duties as congressman and lawyer kept him away from his children for most of the year. Although his widowed sister, Eliza Jane Tucker, had come from Bermuda after Maria Tucker's death to help run his household, he believed that a job which allowed him to live at home would benefit his family. His children and his sister's daughter, Mary Byrd Farley Tucker, he reasoned, would profit by living in a university environment, and he himself would enjoy the cultured conversation of his colleagues.[32] Another and more pressing argument for taking the post at Charlottesville stemmed from doubt about his future in politics. Tucker's participation in the closed Republican caucus to select William Crawford as the party's presidential candidate greatly reduced his chances for re-election to Congress, because many of his constituents were ardent supporters of Andrew Jackson, Crawford's rival.[33] At the very time when Tucker was threatened with the likelihood of losing his seat in Congress, he again found himself deeply in debt. Some two months before he received Cabell's offer of a professorship, Tucker wrote to St. George that attempts to buttress his finances through a loan from New York had failed because he could not get needed letters of recommendation from Richmond bankers. If he could not borrow a comparable amount from other sources, he would, he said, "sell my property for whatever it will bring, for the purpose of extricating myself from debt, the painful consciousness of which I find insupportable."[34] The professorship clearly offered a solution for his financial difficulties. It guaranteed him lifetime tenure, it paid him a fixed amount of fifteen hundred dollars a year and allowed him to collect an extra twenty dollars from each student who enrolled in the School of Moral Philosophy, and it provided him with attractive rent-free quarters on the University Lawn.

Despite the apparent advantages of taking the post, Tucker was at first reluctant to accept it. His autobiography of 1858 relates some details of the appointment. He wrote to Jefferson asking for post-

---

emoluments, and that the tenure is in fact for life, the lodgings comfortable, the society select, &c." Nathaniel Francis Cabell, *Early History of the University of Virginia, as Contained in the Letters of Thomas Jefferson and Joseph C. Cabell* (Richmond, Va., 1856), p. 324.

32. "Autobiography," p. 36.

33. Dorfman, *Economic Mind*, II, 547.

34. Tucker to St. George Tucker, Nov. 11, 1824, Tucker-Coleman Collection, Colonial Williamsburg.

ponement of his decision until the close of Congress, at which time he would visit Monticello. The delay, Tucker wrote, was occasioned by a desire to evaluate the advantages of remaining in politics and, especially, to estimate his chances for selection as an ambassador.[35] This, of course, is partly true, for Tucker had nursed hopes for political advancement since 1800, and Henry Clay had promised him a foreign post if he were elected to the presidency.[36]

But Tucker, writing his autobiography in 1858, did not relate what obviously was uppermost in his mind in 1825. He would have it that he surrendered his ambitions in politics and government in the belief that the professorship might enable him "to cultivate letters, to which I was then strongly inclined."[37] From Tucker's letter to Cabell on January 1, 1825, however, the case appears to have been almost the reverse. He explained to Cabell that he had a dread of taking a job which he could never quit should it become distasteful. But more important than this "fantastic prejudice" was the objection that teaching "would almost put a stop to my efforts as an author, or would confine them in a channel in which I have already found that little reputation is to be acquired and no money." Admitting hopes of becoming a professional novelist and pointing out that Cooper "made about $5000 by each of his novels—and the Valley of Shenandoah, my new work, was written in two months," Tucker asked for time before deciding about the professorship in order to see how successful *The Valley* might be.[38]

Sometime between January 1 and February 21 Tucker realized that *The Valley* was a financial failure and that he could not turn down the professorship in the hope of freeing himself from debt by writing. On February 21 he wrote to Cabell that, though he would prefer to remain in public life, yet "on mature consideration, I have come to the conclusion, to accept the situation tendered me."[39] Two days later he wrote to Jefferson substantially the same acceptance, now attributing his hesitation to a "distrust of my qualifications as well as of my

35. "Autobiography," p. 36.
36. George Sherley, "Our University, II: George Tucker, Professor of Moral Philosophy in the University of Virginia, 1825-1845," *Virginia University Magazine,* XIX (June, 1880), 562.
37. "Autobiography," p. 36.
38. Tucker to Joseph C. Cabell, Jan. 1, 1824 [1825], Cabell Deposit, University of Virginia Library.
39. Tucker to Joseph C. Cabell, Feb. 21, 1825, Cabell Deposit, University of Virginia Library.

industry & steadiness"[40]—objections which, in his autobiography of 1858, he said Jefferson persuaded him to dismiss.[41]

Tucker had committed himself to a career as a professor of philosophy more from necessity than from desire. On April 25, after his acceptance of the professorship, he wrote to St. George, telling his old friend of his hopes for the future:

I promise myself to be for some time a close student; and if the spirit moves me, to essay the public favor again as an author—tho' I have not met with but sorry encouragement hitherto—I know not whether you have chanced to meet with a hasty ill-printed production called "The Valley of Shenandoah"—It was the employment of an idle & melancholy hour— and was written in two months in which short time I ought to have known that nothing could please generally or very much could be produced. It however seemed to take very well in Washington—but so far as I can learn has been received in New York with frigid indifference, so much so as not even to have provoked comment.[42]

As Tucker himself made clear, however, the stillbirth of *The Valley* merely dampened—and did not extinguish—his hope of succeeding as an author. Meanwhile, until he won recognition as a writer, he would be able to keep his real estate holdings and still support his family in comfort.

40. Tucker to Thomas Jefferson, Feb. 23, 1825, Henry E. Huntington Library.
41. "Autobiography," p. 36.
42. Tucker to St. George Tucker, April 25, 1825, Tucker-Coleman Collection, Colonial Williamsburg.

CHAPTER IV

THE ACADEMIC YEARS

IN THE SPRING of 1825, Tucker moved with his family into Pavilion No. 9, his quarters on the University of Virginia Lawn, beginning an association with the school which was to last twenty years. His six colleagues, chosen for Jefferson by Francis Walker Gilmer, included George Long, Professor of Ancient Languages, Thomas H. Key, Professor of Mathematics, Charles Bonnycastle, Professor of Natural Philosophy, and Dr. Robley Dunglison, Professor of Anatomy and Medicine, all English born and educated; George Blaetterman, Professor of Modern Languages, a German trained in England; and John P. Emmet, Professor of Chemistry, Irish born though educated in America.[1] All, wrote Tucker, "were agreeable, well-informed men; they had all travelled quite extensively in foreign countries. We were very sociable, often dining and passing the evening together, and the life which we then led, though seemingly monotonous and devoid of interest, has no doubt appeared to all, on a retrospect, as one of the happiest portions of our lives."[2]

Family life in Charlottesville contributed to Tucker's general contentment. After Maria's death Tucker "found solitude unbearable," and in 1827 he began a serious search for a third wife. His proposals were turned down by several ladies, but Louisa A. Thompson, a widow living in Baltimore, accepted his suit, and in December, 1828, Tucker married her. In the thirty years in which they lived together Tucker found, he said, "the same warmth & devoted affection" with which he "had been previously blest."[3]

1. Philip Alexander Bruce, *History of the University of Virginia* (New York, 1920), I, 356-376; II, 1-36 and *passim*.
2. "Autobiography," manuscript copy, Tucker-Harrison-Smith Papers, University of Virginia Library, p. 36.
3. *Ibid.*, p. 39.

In the year following Tucker's marriage, his only son, Daniel George, was judged to be hopelessly insane and was committed to a Philadelphia institution, where he died in 1838. Except for remarking in his autobiography that visits to his son were inordinately painful,[4] Tucker said little about what must have been one of the most tragic facts of his life. He wrote more fully of the careers of his daughters, two of whom made advantageous marriages which allowed them to remain in or near Charlottesville. In 1830 Eliza married Gessner Harrison, a University of Virginia graduate who succeeded George Long as Professor of Ancient Languages in 1829,[5] and Maria, Tucker's second daughter, in 1840 became the wife of George Rives, a prosperous planter and businessman living in Albemarle County.[6] Tucker's niece, Mary Byrd Farley Tucker, in 1827 married John P. Emmet, Tucker's friend and colleague, and also remained in Charlottesville.[7]

As Professor of Moral Philosophy, Tucker was expected to lecture on what Jefferson described as "mental sciences generally, including Ideology, general grammar, logic and Ethics."[8] Although he had long been interested in philosophy, Tucker had little formal training in the field and was compelled at first to work hard to prepare himself. "Convinced," he said, ". . . of my insufficient acquaintance with the subjects on which I was required to lecture, I very assiduously applied myself to their study, and read & wrote to a late hour in the night, so as sometimes to apprehend from the grotesque images that floated before my fancy when I returned to rest, that my brain might be seriously affected."[9]

In a year or two Tucker felt confident enough of his grasp of philosophy to increase considerably the number of subjects he taught.

4. *Idem.*

5. Walter A. Montgomery in *DAB*, s.v. "Gessner Harrison."

6. For information on George Rives, see Edward Younger, *John A. Kasson: Politics and Diplomacy from Lincoln to McKinley* (Iowa City, 1955), p. 417 n.

7. Tucker, *Memoir of the Life and Character of John P. Emmet, M.D., Professor of Chemistry and Materia Medica in the University of Virginia* (Philadelphia, 1845), p. 12; and Tucker to St. George Tucker, June 21, 1827, Tucker-Coleman Collection, Colonial Williamsburg.

8. Thomas Jefferson to Tucker, March 9, 1825, Jefferson Papers, University of Virginia Library. "Ideology," or the general theory of ideas, was a term which Jefferson borrowed from the French philosopher, Destutt de Tracy, and used to include "philosophical inquiry into the operations of the mind (psychology) and into the knowledge and kinds of proof obtainable thereby (logic and epistemology)." See Adrienne Koch, *The Philosophy of Thomas Jefferson* (New York, 1943), p. 55. For a good discussion of the importance of ideology in Jefferson's thought, see Koch, pp. 54-82.

9. "Autobiography," p. 36.

Upon petition to the Board of Visitors, he was allowed to advertise Political Economy, originally assigned to the Professor of Law, as being included in the School of Moral Philosophy. Shortly afterwards, when he discovered that the Professor of Ancient Languages, George Long, wished to rid himself of the chore of teaching Belles Lettres and Rhetoric, Tucker adopted these subjects. Political economy and belles lettres and rhetoric had always been of interest to him, and, being drastically in need of money, he felt that the fees received from students attracted to his school because of the additional courses would more than compensate for the time he would expend in preparing his lectures.[10]

An unexpected duty fell upon Tucker when he was elected by his colleagues to serve as chairman of the faculty for the first session. In view of the duties accompanying the administrative position, Tucker's selection was a natural one. The chairman was expected to represent the faculty on all occasions, to supervise the actions and conduct of employees and students, and, in general, to see that the University ran efficiently and quietly.[11] At fifty Tucker was the oldest member of a young faculty, and, with the exception of the twenty-eight-year-old Emmet, he was the only teacher who had been educated in America. As Robley Dunglison pointed out, it was presumed that Tucker, who had lived for thirty years in Virginia, would be "acquainted with the manners, customs, and feelings of the young men . . . and would be more acceptable to them and their parents" than foreign born and educated men, against whom there had been considerable distrust and dislike expressed in American newspapers.[12]

In the first year of his chairmanship (he served again in 1831-32), Tucker was placed in an impossible position. Although he was responsible for student conduct, neither he nor the faculty in general was given authority to compel obedience to school regulations. Under Jefferson's plan of organization, which called for faculty-appointed students to report offenders, students enjoyed a large degree of self-government, the erroneous assumption being that Southern gentlemen would conduct themselves in an exemplary fashion.[13] According to Tucker, all the professors were eager to avoid administrative work

10. *Ibid.*, p. 39.

11. Bruce, *History of the University of Virginia*, II, 46-52.

12. Robley Dunglison, "Autobiographical Ana," manuscript copy, Library of the College of Physicians of Philadelphia, I, 240; Bruce, *History of the University of Virginia*, II, 1-2.

13. "Autobiography," p. 37; Bruce, *History of the University of Virginia*, II, 258-266.

and at the first of the academic year acquiesced in Jefferson's scheme; and one English professor, with whom Tucker disagreed, expressed the view that students should be allowed to drink, gamble, and carouse as much as they pleased, so long as they prepared their class work.[14] By the fall of 1825, all recognized the impracticability of Jefferson's lenient policy. Students refused to attend classes or take examinations, drank and gambled in defiance of school rules, fought on and off school grounds, and intimidated and insulted local citizens and faculty at will.[15]

Hooliganism culminated in October in a demonstration in which masked students paraded on the University lawn, chanting slogans against European teachers and destroying school property. One student hurled a bottle filled with urine through the sitting room window of Professor Long, who was serving tea to three pious, mannerly students, the brothers Tiffin and Gessner Harrison, and Henry Tutwiler.[16] Twenty-four hours later the rioters again assembled, daring Professors Long and Key to show themselves. Professor Emmet was stoned as he tried to disperse the crowd, and Tucker, who rushed to his rescue, was threatened with a beating.[17]

Shortly afterwards, when the Visitors assembled at nearby Monticello, the faculty presented their grievances, and, on the following day, three ex-presidents of the United States, Jefferson, Madison, and Monroe, rode to the campus to address and quiet the students, more than half of whom confessed to having participated in the riot. Long and Key, who had sent letters of resignation, were persuaded to remain at the University, but, according to Dunglison, the later resignations of both resulted from the October, 1825, riots.[18]

Although disorders continued throughout Tucker's years at the University, he seems to have avoided the worst of the students' resentment and even to have been treated with a degree of deference. His popularity as a teacher and his charm have been mentioned by almost all who have written about him. In his official history of the University, Bruce states that Tucker was the most beloved of all the professors and describes him as one "the fountain of whose geniality

14. "Autobiography," p. 37.

15. *Idem;* Bruce, *History of the University of Virginia,* II, 266-317.

16. Gessner Harrison to Peachy Harrison, Nov. 28, 1825, Tucker-Harrison-Smith Papers, University of Virginia Library.

17. "Autobiography," p. 37. Bruce, *History of the University of Virginia,* II, 299, asserts that Tucker *was* caned; but Tucker says that he faced the student rioters down.

18. "Autobiographical Ana," I, 289.

never ran dry, and who never failed to delight with his keen sense of humor, his inexhaustible fund of anecdotes, and his racy information on every subject that arose in conversation."[19]   Harriet Martineau, who visited the campus in 1837, characterized as "lively, sensible, and earnest" Tucker's conversation on the "theory of Rent, Colonel Thompson, and Mr. Malthus; the Value of Public censure and eulogy . . . Philadelphia ale, American politics and a hundred other things."[20]

Despite such evidence as this, the image of Tucker as a brilliant, witty, and beloved professor of philosophy has been exaggerated. A principal source of the idealized view is Professor George Sherley's sketch of Tucker in the *Virginia University Magazine*. This account, which was relied upon by many later writers, including Bruce and Jay B. Hubbell, is based on information given to Sherley by Tucker's granddaughter in the presence of Tucker's two surviving children and is more legendary than accurate.[21] Tucker may daily have ridden a large white horse down the College Avenue, followed by his dog "Metaphysics," as Sherley reports, but it is highly unlikely that students "never lost sight of the reverential respect" due the eccentric but jovial teacher, or that they called out "Yonder goes dear old Tucker on *Money and Banks*."[22]

Several unfavorable opinions of Tucker's personal traits have survived. His aloofness from those he considered his social inferiors drew the ire of a visiting Vermonter, John Adams Kasson, who came to Virginia as a tutor, carrying Tucker a letter of recommendation. The third Mrs. Tucker, Kasson wrote his brother, was "a vain, affected, and disagreeable woman," while her husband was merely "vain and selfish." Both, however, were rude, "*malgré* their affected display of silver plate and fashion."[23] Dunglison, the closest of Tucker's

19. Bruce, *History of the University of Virginia*, II, 33.

20. Harriet Martineau, *Retrospect of Western Travel* (London, 1838), I, 206, 207-208.

21. "Our University, II: George Tucker, Professor of Moral Philosophy in the University of Virginia, 1825-1845," *Virginia University Magazine*, XIX (June, 1880), 560; Bruce, *History of the University of Virginia*, II, 22-23; Hubbell, *The South in American Literature, 1607-1900* (Durham, N.C., 1954), p. 245.

22. Sherley, "George Tucker," p. 560.

23. Quoted in Younger, *John Kasson*, p. 414. Another indication that the Tuckers' style of living antagonized certain students and visitors is seen in a letter by Robert Lewis Dabney, in which he contrasted the dress of Mrs. Tucker with the frontier simplicity of his Aunt Polly. Dabney saw, he said, "a very venerable lady, the wife of one of the professors who has all the honours of age upon his head, & who is herself not so young as she once was formerly, having had herself three husbands, besides the present, walking out this cold windy day in light salmon slippers, with stockings to correspond" (R. L. Dabney to C. W. Dabney, Oct. 25, 1840, Dabney Papers, University of Virginia Library).

friends, asserted that Tucker was "at all times ever since I knew him exceedingly sensitive" and that he took expressions of professional differences of opinion as indictments of his honesty or ability.[24] And some of those who had occasion to work with him, especially in his old age, noted that he was inordinately proud of his scholarship and that he had a "crochety & rather presuming temper."[25]

Nor did Tucker's competence escape criticism. The eccentric John Randolph of Roanoke, whose hostility toward his foster father, St. George Tucker, may have biased him against Tucker, wrote Francis Walker Gilmer that Tucker's appointment to the faculty would have been a mistake if moral philosophy "was anything but an empty name."[26] Certain of the students and faculty who had an opportunity to observe Tucker's teaching testified that he was an ineffectual and boring lecturer. An outspoken and temperamental colleague, George Blaetterman, is said to have told Tucker to his face that his lectures were nonsensical.[27] The testimony of Robert Lewis Dabney, a student who was to become one of the South's militant defenders, echoed Blaetterman's opinion from the students' point of view. After failing one of Tucker's "pestilent examinations," Dabney complained to his brother: "This year the director . . . is old Mr. Tucker, who I should think, if I believed in the transmigration of souls, contains the spirits of all the pettifoggers that ever were born. . . . The old granny has a whole raft of whimsical notions about the terms in common use, and requires us to come to them. Consequently, those who have not heard his lectures on rhetoric or found out his hobbys some how or other, stand but a poor chance."[28] In philosophy, Dabney said, Tucker was "dull and uninteresting," and with the textbook "written in a very diffuse obscure style . . . the matter is confusion twice confounded, by the time daddy Tucker has stumbled & stuttered, & grumbled over it."[29]

24. See Robley Dunglison to Henry S. Randall, Nov. 18, 1858, University of Virginia Library.

25. Henry S. Randall to Hugh Blair Grigsby, Nov. 26, 1856, in *The Correspondence Between Henry Stephens Randall and Hugh Blair Grigsby 1856-1861,* ed. Frank J. Klingberg and Frank W. Klingberg, University of California Publications in History, XLIII (Los Angeles and Berkeley, 1952), p. 68.

26. John Randolph to Francis W. Gilmer, March 31, 1825, Bryan Papers, University of Virginia Library.

27. Bruce, *History of the University of Virginia,* II, 160.

28. R. L. Dabney to C. W. Dabney, March 12, 1842, Dabney Papers, University of Virginia Library.

29. R. L. Dabney to C. W. Dabney, Oct. 13, 1840, Dabney Papers, University of Virginia Library. The textbook which Dabney objected to was probably either Thomas

With only a few opinions, the disinterestedness of which is uncertain, it is impossible to judge accurately Tucker's effectiveness as a teacher, though it may be assumed that the awkward speech habits that afflicted his legal career may have persisted to impair his lecturing. That he was intellectually active and productive, however, is attested by his writings during his professorship, which are impressive both for quantity and for variety of subject matter. During his first year at the University, Tucker's duties, as he complained to Joseph C. Cabell,[30] kept him from writing for publication; but in a few years, as teaching became easier, he began to write again, seemingly both to supplement his salary and to gratify what he always termed his "propensity for fame." Within a period of eighteen years, he published one satire, three books on economics and statistics, a then-standard biography of Jefferson, as well as two pamphlets, one intended to defend his study of Jefferson against an anonymous attack in a New York church journal, and the other a memorial to a friend. Together with his colleague, the versatile Dunglison, he founded and edited the *Virginia Literary Museum* (1829-1830), a magazine in which he published an enormous body of writing, including his last fiction. He contributed a substantial chapter to George Long's *America and the West Indies,* and, as in the past, he continued to send essays, many unsigned, to newspapers and magazines.

Among the most numerous and interesting of these publications are those in which Tucker discussed contemporary political and economic problems and revealed how limited was his faith in the workings of a democracy. The disillusionment which he felt on viewing his first democratic election in 1796 steadily increased, so that by the late 1820's the former near-Jacobin had become an ultra-conservative Whig, convinced that only men of property with a tangible, taxable interest in government should be allowed to run the nation.

Brown's *Lectures on the Philosophy of the Human Mind* or Dugald Stewart's *Elements of the Philosophy of the Human Mind.*

30. Tucker to Joseph C. Cabell, Feb. 25, 1826, Cabell Deposit, University of Virginia Library. Tucker complained about the inequality among the professors' salaries and argued that in the time spent preparing his lectures he "could get and have got" more by writing for the magazines. The inequality in the pay of the professors came from the difference in the number of students attending the various schools. Each professor received a basic stipend of $1500 and collected from each student enrolled in his school an additional $20. In 1826, tickets for enrollment were sold to only twenty-eight students in moral philosophy, but to one hundred in classical languages and to about eighty in mathematics and modern languages. Enrollment figures for the years from 1825 to 1845 are given in *A Catalogue of the Officers and Students of the University of Virginia* (Charlottesville, Va., 1880).

To Tucker, Andrew Jackson's election to the presidency in 1828, symbolic of the triumph of democratic demagoguery, seemed to signal the possibility of class warfare. Tucker saw Jackson as a nineteenth-century "Tiberius" who would, in his thirst for power, ignore the sacredness of property, the foundation of all good government.

Tucker's reaction to the ascendancy of Jacksonian democracy took several forms. On the one hand, he tried to make sure that Jackson would never receive the support of Virginia. Well aware that "the General's" popularity in the South was highest among the poor whites,[31] Tucker, as a supposedly disinterested observer of politics discussing proposed changes in the Virginia Constitution, argued pseudonymously that slaveholders should have the right to cast votes for three-fifths of their slaves, that the secret ballot—which destroyed the "manly independence" of voters—should be eliminated, and that no more than one half the free men should be given the franchise.[32]

More immediately, Tucker served as a local booster for Clay and from Charlottesville worked in unison with his friend and Clay's official campaign manager, Senator Josiah S. Johnston of Louisiana, for Clay's nomination for the presidency.[33]   Tucker, who so thoroughly distrusted Jackson as to fear that the President's agents were intercepting his letters, also suspected his erstwhile friends and believed that William Wirt's candidacy on the Anti-Masonic ticket was a bit of political skulduggery intended to insure Jackson's triumph in New York.[34] As late as 1834, Tucker, still fighting for a lost cause, pleaded with Joseph C. Cabell to work for the nomination of Clay, claiming that if the Old Dominion supported him, Clay would "without a question" win the presidency in 1836. But, he pointed out ominously,

31. Clement Eaton, *Freedom of Thought in the Old South* (Durham, N.C., 1940), p. 28; Charles Henry Ambler, *Sectionalism in Virginia from 1776 to 1861* (Chicago, 1910), p. 166.

32. See the series in the *Literary Museum* signed "V" and entitled "The Constitution of Virginia": Letter II, No. 8 (Aug. 5, 1829), 121-124; Letter III, No. 14 (Sept. 16, 1829), 209-212; Letter IV, No. 15 (Sept. 23, 1829), 234-236; Letter V, No. 16 (Sept. 30, 1829), 241-247. For a discussion of Tucker's authorship, see below, Pt. II, pp. 97-99.

Some of Tucker's suggestions were also contained in a letter to James Madison in which he proposed that Virginia not follow the lead of Pennsylvania and Maryland in granting near-universal suffrage. See Tucker to Madison, Sept. 19, 1827, Madison Papers, Library of Congress.

33. See Tucker to Josiah S. Johnston, Dec. 8, 1831, Johnston Collection, Historical Society of Pennsylvania.

34. Tucker to Josiah S. Johnston, Oct. 19, 1831, Johnston Collection, Historical Society of Pennsylvania.

if Clay failed again, Van Buren, Jackson's protégé, would win over any other Whig, even Daniel Webster, Tucker's second choice.[35]

Tucker also became a propagandist for the second National Bank, writing a number of articles under the pseudonym of "One of the Sovereign People" in the pro-Bank Washington *National Intelligencer*, in which he denounced Jackson's audacity in withdrawing the government funds from the Bank and defended Nicholas Biddle's "right" to use the Bank's money and influence as he saw fit to direct the campaign against Jackson.[36] One of Tucker's anonymous essays, this time published in the *American Quarterly Review*, was discovered to be his and led to accusations that Tucker was one of Biddle's hirelings, a claim which Tucker in his autobiography denied, insisting that he received no more than the usual fee of two dollars a page for writing it.[37] But his article was so favorable to the Bank that he received the personal thanks of Biddle, who planned to reprint and circulate two thousand copies of it.[38] Long after the Bank crisis was history, Tucker, unlike many Whigs, remained loyal to Biddle and continued to praise him for protecting Bank stockholders, whom Tucker described as being made up of retired businessmen, planters, "salaried officers, or widows or orphans."[39]

More indicative of Tucker's theoretical economic opinions during the period of his professorship are those works in which, in expressing his continuing belief in the inevitability and desirability of an industrial economy, he supported Clay's "American System"—itself an adaptation of that portion of Hamilton's theory of economics which Tucker always favored. In his acknowledged works on political economy and in pseudonymous magazine pieces, Tucker not only praised factory work and the disinterested benevolence of bankers and factory owners, but also defended the protective tariff and painted a vision of America as one "great Flanders" with federally subsidized

35. Tucker to Joseph C. Cabell, Sept. 5, 1834, Cabell Deposit, University of Virginia Library.

36. The articles, variously titled "The President's Late Act," "The President's Bank Manifesto," and "The President's Late Manifesto," appeared on Oct. 9, 12, and 16, 1833. For Tucker's authorship, see Tucker to Gale and Seaton, Oct. 12, 1833, Miscellaneous Papers, New York Public Library, in which Tucker suggested that because Jackson's agents might be stealing the mail, the Bank hire its own carriers.

37. "Autobiography," p. 41. The article, entitled "The Bank of the United States," appeared in the *American Quarterly Review*, IX (1831), 246-282.

38. Nicholas Biddle to Tucker, April 1, 1831, Biddle Papers, Library of Congress, quoted by Joseph Dorfman, *The Economic Mind in American Civilization, 1606-1865* (New York, 1946), II, 883 and n.

39. See *Theory of Money and Banks Investigated* (Boston, 1839), p. 307.

but privately managed and promoted canals and railroads carrying produce to all the states. When in the 1840's the specter of Jackson finally passed into the background, Tucker's optimism about the future of the United States increased. Nevertheless, he continued to deprecate the giving of equal political rights to poor and rich, though he thought it more than possible that the more intelligent wealthy citizens could adequately control the rabble.[40]

Tucker's hopes and fears for the future contributed greatly to his desire to visit England, a nation in which he believed one could see, in its factories, great estates, and crowded cities, the future of the United States. Many other factors, of course, had a part in his aim. He wished to view the country from which his ancestors had emigrated to the New World; and, always interested in meeting and observing the great and influential, he wanted to know the best of English society and to compare English and American manners and customs. Lastly, Tucker still hoped for a foreign post, once the Whigs, under Clay's leadership, gained control of the White House, and he felt that a trip abroad would help prepare him for such an eventuality.[41]

In 1839, with comfortable returns from his investments in land and business stocks and with a three-month leave of absence from the University, Tucker sailed from New York to Liverpool aboard a British steam packet.[42] He took a quick look at Chester and the Shakespeare country and then settled down in London, anxious to meet English society. He acquired comfortable lodgings in Charing Cross, only to be shaken by the dictum of Sir Robert Inglis and his friend Andrew Stevenson, America's representative in the Court of St. James's, that his lodgings were "not the most eligible." After locating more respectable rooms on St. James's Street and joining the Travellers' and Athenaeum clubs, he began his visits in earnest, sending messages and delivering letters of introduction.

Tucker was only moderately successful in his quest to mix with the great in England, though he did meet some interesting people in his brief stay. He delivered letters of introduction to Samuel Rogers, the poet, and to Lord Holland, only to learn later, to his great distress, that he had mixed up his letters. He breakfasted with Charles Babbage, the statistician, and, during a meeting of the British Association

40. Tucker's Whig concept of the idea of progress and his fears of mob rule are discussed below in Pt. III, Chap. XII.

41. Sherley, "George Tucker," p. 561.

42. Unless otherwise noted, all of the information about Tucker's trip abroad is taken from his "Autobiography," pp. 42-46.

in Birmingham, shared a crowded hotel room with Henry Hallam, the historian and critic, and Thomas Tooke, the economist, whom he found "very amiable as well as sensible." Lord Brougham appeared to Tucker to be rude and haughty. In London at a dinner of the Society for the Diffusion of Useful Knowledge, Brougham presided at Tucker's table, studiedly ignoring the Virginia visitor in order to direct attention toward his own accomplishments. Perhaps the most pleasant of Tucker's new acquaintances was the Earl of Leicester, at whose family estate Tucker spent two luxurious days, discussing politics and agriculture with the eighty-five-year-old Whig and his young wife.

On the whole, Tucker found England distasteful. He showed but qualified praise for British institutions, admiring the succinct and sensible debates in Parliament, but finding the procession of Queen Victoria to be a "gorgeous exhibition . . . more fit to amuse a child than one of my age." The crowded cities of Liverpool, Birmingham, and London amazed him, and he took great pleasure in merely watching throngs of obedient Englishmen going to and from their work. He appreciated, too, England's "beauty & high cultivation, the country, the magnificence of the fine country seats," and the "opulence which no other nation has ever reached." Yet British reserve and the manners of society were not pleasing to him. In the higher classes he found, indeed, "the same mixture of ease, frankness & courtesy which characterizes our Southern gentry & especially of South Carolina," but there existed so much deference among the various ranks and so many artificial distinctions that a stranger, unless he were known to be an American, could not find any easy conversation. Only Sir Robert Peel's police were friendly enough to answer his questions. Tucker came to "the conclusion that there were more churls in England than in all Europe besides."

Tucker's visit to England, combined with his growing interest in Malthus' population doctrines, motivated him in 1841 to begin a novel, in which he embodied within a highly conventional framework a discussion of the blessings and perils of the densely populated world of the future. Although he completed a draft of the novel, he never tried to publish it. But many of the speculations which it contains he included in *The Progress of the United States in Population and Wealth* (Boston, 1843), chapters of which appeared in *Hunt's Merchants' Magazine* from 1842 to 1843. The book was not a financial success—Tucker had to print it at his own expense—but it, along with the recommendation of Robert Walsh, helped gain him membership in the Statistical Society of Paris, an honor Tucker greatly appreciated.[43]

The last five years of Tucker's professorship were years of general discontent. Throughout his life, he prized very highly evenings spent in conversation with polished, serious men. He always remembered his life in Williamsburg and Richmond as one of enlightened and polite discussion, and he lived among his associates in Charlottesville an existence well-filled with the social amenities. But, in the forties, society at the University no longer held the charm for him that it once had. Most of his old friends had died, and of the new appointees to the faculty, only his relative Henry St. George Tucker joined him in mild protest against the religious enthusiasm that engulfed the campus. The two old men declined to give up drinking wine and refused to support a temperance society which had the backing of the majority of the faculty, the administration, and many students.[44] Moreover, Tucker was an old man who, as many of his friends admitted, could be extremely testy, especially when his income or his honor was threatened. He always objected to the differences in salary among the professors, believing rightly enough that his work was as valuable as that of any other teacher on the staff, and over the years he had continually argued that his salary should be increased to equal those of his colleagues.[45] In 1842, then, he was enraged when the administration, ignoring the terms under which he was hired, notified him that his basic annual salary would be reduced from fifteen hundred to one thousand dollars. He spent long hours collecting proof that Jefferson had in fact and intention hired him for life at a guaranteed annual salary of fifteen hundred dollars, and he wrote to Joseph C. Cabell, still a member of the Board of Visitors, that he would never have accepted the professorship at a salary of one thousand dollars, that, indeed, he almost had not accepted it at all. Yet Tucker, it seems, was willing to negotiate. He had long held an inclination for city living, believing that the denser the population, the greater the potential for genteel and cultured society.

43. "Autobiography," p. 50.
44. Bruce, *History of the University of Virginia,* III, 130-131.
45. See, for example, Tucker to Joseph C. Cabell, June 22, 1837, Cabell Deposit, University of Virginia Library. Cf. Tucker's letter to Cabell on Feb. 25, 1826. The cause for differences in faculty salaries is outlined in note 30, above.

He made clear to Cabell that, should he be allowed to continue to teach at his present salary, he would retire in a few years to Phila-delphia—to a world of men of letters and science.[46]

46. Tucker to Joseph C. Cabell, July 25, 1842, Cabell Deposit, University of Virginia Library. Tucker was hired for life at a guaranteed yearly salary of $1500. For terms of the appointment, see Joseph C. Cabell's letter to Tucker, Dec. 29, 1824, Cabell Deposit, University of Virginia Library.

CHAPTER V

RETIREMENT IN PHILADELPHIA

IN 1845 TUCKER, seventy years old and with investments that returned him from three to four thousand dollars a year, moved from his residence on the University Lawn to lodgings in Philadelphia. The Pennsylvania city which he had admired since 1795, when he first came to America, was an important cultural center. There he could have access to well-stocked libraries, attend the meetings of the American Philosophical Society, and enjoy the company of his old friend, Robley Dunglison, who was teaching at the Jefferson Medical College.

Despite such attractions, however, Tucker at first found Northern living considerably less enjoyable than life in the South. To the Virginia gentleman, accustomed to the conveniences of a slave economy, the problems of finding and keeping servants in the North was a great irritant. Just before leaving Charlottesville, Tucker emancipated his five household slaves, but he took two of them to Philadelphia as servants—a woman and her granddaughter, who was to be bound until she was eighteen. Writing in 1858 in his auto-biography, Tucker doubted the wisdom of his generosity, seeming to believe that in the nineteenth century, whites and blacks alike were better served by the slave system. Two of the males he freed died without having "abused their new privilege," but the third was suffering from Tucker's kindness. In 1858 he was still living in Charlottesville, expecting at any moment to be separated from his wife and children, still in slavery, by the execution of a law which compelled free Negroes to leave the state. The inconsiderate action of the two females that Tucker brought to Philadelphia represented to him the violation of trust which Northern zealots promoted. The ex-slaves, he felt, should have reciprocated the "feeling and sentiment" which had led him to free them; yet both broke their pledges to remain as servants and soon after arriving in Philadelphia fled to New York, "invited by some black abolitionist, to secure their wages."[1]

Nor did Tucker find social life in the Northern city so much to his liking as he expected. Although he was wined and dined, he said, by many of the city's leading citizens, he judged that Philadelphia society, while polite, was "not particularly intelligent."[2] He listened to lectures, visited Peale's Museum, paid social calls, attended dinner clubs, still finding society "not so natural or elevated" as it might be, or as it was in Europe.[3]

But Tucker's dissatisfaction diminished as his activity increased. Released from teaching responsibilities, he found time to write and lecture on a variety of subjects. He presented papers on economics and philosophy before the American Philosophical Society, of which he had been a member since 1837;[4] became in 1845 a member of the National Institute for the Promotion of Science;[5] joined the American Association for the Advancement of Science and urged its members to set up a section on "Political Economy & Statistics";[6] engaged in an extended literary duel with Alexander Everett over the significance and interpretation of Malthusian population theory;[7] and wrote or refurbished articles for various Philadelphia magazines and news-papers.

He wrote a four-volume *History of the United States,* a census study to supplement his 1843 edition of the *Progress of the United States,* and a study concerned with the bank panic of 1857. In his *Political Economy for the People* (Philadelphia, 1859), a summary of his late social and political beliefs, he still predicted the eventual death

1. "Autobiography," manuscript copy, Tucker-Harrison-Smith Papers, University of Virginia Library, p. 51.
2. Tucker to Maria R. F. Tucker Rives, Jan. 17, 1846, Tucker-Harrison-Smith Papers, University of Virginia Library.
3. Tucker to Maria R. F. Tucker Rives, Feb. 11, 1847, Tucker-Harrison-Smith Papers, University of Virginia Library.
4. Leonard C. Helderman, "A Social Scientist of the Old South," *Journal of Southern History,* II (1936), 155 and n.
5. See National Institute for the Promotion of Science *Proceedings* (1845).
6. *Proceedings* (1848), I, 134-135.
7. "The Malthusian Theory, Discussed in a Correspondence Between Alex. H. Everett, and Prof. Geo. Tucker, of the University of Virginia," *United States Magazine and Democratic Review,* n.s. XVII (1846), 298-302, 379-389, 438-441; XXII (1848), 11-18.

of slavery, but at the same time presented the stock arguments on its benefits—to whites and Negroes alike,[8] praised the work of Adam Smith, straddled the fence on the issue of the tariff, and, finally, argued against laws prohibiting usury.[9] His last publication was a book, *Essays, Moral and Metaphysical* (Philadelphia, 1860), containing much of what he had said in the 1822 *Essays*.

Work in imaginative literature had ceased long before he moved to Philadelphia. His associations were now largely with historians and scientists. He became an intimate friend of Hugh Blair Grigsby and corresponded with him and Henry S. Randall about American history. Tucker embarrassed both Dunglison and Grigsby with his claims that Randall was misappropriating materials from his *Life of Jefferson*. Randall was outraged, and, even after he received an "explicit retraction of & apology for all offensive expressions,"[10] found it hard to forgive his accuser. Randall told Grigsby that he referred to Tucker's *Life of Jefferson* and corresponded with Tucker not because he was helpful, since "his authority was of no more real use to me than is a fifth wheel to a carriage," but because they had mutual friends. Tucker trying to understand Jefferson, Randall explained, was "ice trying to understand fire!"[11]

If Tucker had in his old age "a spirit of pugnacity becoming earlier years,"[12] the members of his family seem never to have felt its effects. He exchanged enjoyable visits with his daughters and vacationed with them at summer resorts in Virginia and New York. An examination of his active correspondence with his children and grandchildren from the beginning of his stay in Philadelphia makes it clear that Tucker was a devoted parent whose affection was returned by his offspring.

The great bulk of Tucker's letters, however, even personal letters to his family, reveals a constant preoccupation with his private finances.[13] As comfortably fixed as he was with profitable invest-

---

8. Pp. 84-86.

9. Pp. 142 ff.

10. Henry S. Randall to Hugh Blair Grigsby, Nov. 26, 1856, *The Correspondence Between Henry Stephens Randall and Hugh Blair Grigsby 1856-1861*, ed. Frank J. Klingberg and Frank W. Klingberg, University of California Publications in History, XLIII (Los Angeles and Berkeley, 1952), p. 68.

11. Henry S. Randall to Hugh Blair Grigsby, Dec. 4, 1856, *Correspondence Between Randall and Grigsby*, pp. 70-71.

12. Hugh Blair Grigsby to Henry S. Randall, Nov. 12, 1858, *Correspondence Between Randall and Grigsby*, pp. 147-148.

13. See, for examples, Tucker to Edmund Fontaine, Sept. 30, 1848, and undated letter, Henry E. Huntington Library, on selling some Louisa Railroad stock and buying

ments in the Rhode Island and Louisa railroads, steamboat stocks, Chicago lots, and Virginia land, Tucker never forgot his past difficulties and embarrassments. As he told his granddaughter—urging her to consider property when she married—"reason," "wisdom," "true religion," and "moral prudence" all combined to prove the truth that wealth was important for comfort and peace of mind. Drawing upon his experience to give weight to his advice, he said that, except for the loss of friends, "a want of prudence in money matters had contributed nine-tenths of the pain & vexation" of his life.[14]

After the death of his wife in 1858, Tucker, whose vitality had never flagged, continued to visit the South each winter to escape the rigors of Pennsylvania weather. On one such trip in December, 1860, he set off to visit Judge Hopkins of Mobile, Alabama, traveling through Richmond, Charleston, Columbia, and Savannah. From Savannah on January 24, 1861, after the secession of Georgia, he wrote that such a solution "seems to be a poor remedy for an unpopular president." Surely the need for "a wise provident government" would bring the Southern states back to some sort of a union under a modified constitution.[15] But as he stayed longer in the South he saw that the people "seemed to be crazed in the fancies of imaginary evils and their strange remedies."[16]

At this stage of his life, Tucker's loyalties, like those of so many, were divided. As a young man he was in many ways a typical Southerner, professing allegiance to the defense of Southern womanhood and the *code duello*. Gradually, though, because of his economic theory, which reflected his belief in the necessity and value of a commercial-industrial society, he became more and more at odds with his Southern, agrarian environment. Expedience always competed with "honor" as his standard. Nationalism instead of particularism was the basis of his politics. Despite an emotional attachment to the South, he was not able to understand why a compromise could not be worked out to settle sectional problems.

---

shares of stock in steamboats. Letters also indicate an interest in getting the state of Virginia to finance or pay for building a railroad tunnel—to benefit "the whole west" and the people and the railroad.

14. Tucker to Maria C. Harrison, June 9 and Oct. 2, 1850, Tucker-Harrison-Smith Papers, University of Virginia Library.

15. Tucker to Eliza L. C. Harrison, Jan. 24, 1861, Tucker-Harrison-Smith Papers, University of Virginia Library.

16. Tucker to Robley Dunglison, quoted by George Sherley, "Our University, II: George Tucker, Professor of Moral Philosophy in the University of Virginia, 1825-1845," *Virginia University Magazine*, XIX (June, 1880), 571

Tucker was spared the ordeal of seeing the states at war. While he was in Mobile watching the loading of a ship on which he was embarked to visit his family in Virginia, he was struck on the head by a bale of cotton. He was nursed in the house of friends for three days, then conveyed to Virginia to the home of his daughter, Mrs. George Rives, where he died after a lingering illness of three months. Except among his family and close friends, his death passed almost unnoticed. The Richmond *Enquirer* published an obituary on April 13, 1861, but made the error, often repeated by historians and bibliographers, of confusing him with Henry St. George Tucker. In Philadelphia, Robley Dunglison, who was his intimate for thirty-seven years, composed a sketch of his life, which was published in the *Transactions* of the American Philosophical Society for 1862.

PART II

TUCKER AS MAN OF LETTERS

CHAPTER VI

EARLY OCCASIONAL WRITINGS

INTRODUCTORY

GEORGE TUCKER's contribution to American letters has never been thoroughly examined, though his writings have been praised by several recent critics. These writers rank Tucker as a significant figure in American literature and assert that his works are worthy of revaluation. In 1936 Leonard Helderman claimed that Tucker's novels and satires exemplify "the pioneer striving of the American genius" and show a considerable imaginative power.[1] In the *Literary History of the United States,* John D. Wade, referring to Southern literature of the early nineteenth century, stated that Tucker was "the most notable author in the South" and that his career reflects "the state of literary culture in Maryland, Virginia, and the Carolinas during the 1820's."[2] More recently, Jay B. Hubbell called Tucker "one of the best and one of the least known Southern writers of his time" and lamented that, although his writings in economics have been rediscovered, "his literary work is still neglected."[3]

As these critics have noted, Tucker's literary career was typical of his age and culture in several respects. Like many of his contemporaries, he began writing for local newspapers, usually as a member of a temporary literary group; he defended, as in the nationalistic Philadelphia *Port Folio,* American culture against British attacks;

1. "A Social Scientist of the Old South," *Journal of Southern History,* II (1936), 155-156. See also Helderman's "A Satirist in Old Virginia," *American Scholar,* VI (1937), 484.
2. *Literary History of the United States,* ed. Robert E. Spiller, *et al.,* rev. ed. (New York, 1953), p. 306.
3. *The South in American Literature, 1607-1900* (Durham, N.C., 1954), p. 243.

he was motivated to write his first novel by the success which Cooper achieved in following Scott; and, most important of all, he was forced, because of economic and social reasons, to regard literature as an avocation rather than a profession. His poems, satires, essays, and novels were done in moments taken from his studies, his social activities, and later, from his onerous duties as a lawyer and politician or his more pleasing responsibilities as a professor.

Tucker's imaginative writings fall naturally into three groups, each reflecting characteristics of a period of his life. (1) From the time of his immigration to the United States in 1795 through his years under the influence of the Richmond literati, Tucker dabbled in literature, wrote occasional poems and verse satires, joined several short-lived literary societies, and contributed frequent topical essays to local newspapers. (2) From 1814 to 1824, after he had established himself as a lawyer and politician in south-central Virginia, Tucker developed more serious literary ambitions. He was the probable author of a satire on Virginia manners and morals, and he published his first novel and most important literary work, *The Valley of Shenandoah.* (3) During the twenty years of his professorship, from 1825 to 1845, Tucker published a well-known satire, *A Voyage to the Moon,* several short stories, and in 1841 completed an unpublished novel. Much of his writing in this period, however, dealt with the general economic and intellectual problems of the kind that he treated fictionally in *A Voyage* and "A Century Hence." After 1841, Tucker abandoned belles lettres altogether, devoting his attention exclusively to unadorned history, philosophy, and economics.

FROM BERMUDA TO RICHMOND

Tucker exhibited an early, though casual, interest in writing, especially in writing poetry. His first literary attempt, a Latin ode written when he was eleven years old on St. George's Island, Bermuda, was returned to him by his tutor with the comment that he would do well to practice writing in English before trying to compose in a classical language.[4] Later, in Williamsburg, at the home of St. George Tucker, he received just such practice and acquired some facility in composing extemporaneous verse. An early poetic account of a fire was refused for publication in a Richmond paper,[5] and not

4. "Autobiography," manuscript copy, Tucker-Harrison-Smith Papers, University of Virginia Library, p. 4.
5. *Ibid.,* opposite p. 12.

until 1797 did Tucker appear in print, when the Bermuda *Gazette* published his "In Memoriam," an elegy commemorating his uncle, William Hall.[6]

During his attempt to establish a law practice in Richmond in the early 1800's, Tucker published some poetry in local newspapers under various pseudonyms. In the collections of family papers are preserved a few poems attributed to Tucker by his descendants and the curator of manuscripts at Colonial Williamsburg, which may perhaps be representative of the kind and quality of his early work. "To a Young Lady on Her Birth Day"—signed "Agrestis" and published in the Virginia *Argus*—celebrates Clarissa's anniversary and her approaching marriage, and it may be addressed to Tucker's second wife, Maria Ball Carter, on the announcement of their engagement:

> May nothing wayward long delay
> Our wish'd for hymeneal day,
> When each fond heart to each will prove
> Th' extatic joys of mutual love;
> And whilst our days in peace glide on
> As blissful as they first begun,
> May friends and books and converse sweet
> Within our humble dwelling meet:
> With alll [*sic*] that Thomson's verse exprest,
> All that wedded love e'er blest;
> And when life's current gently flows
> And *passion* sinks in soft repose,
> May *mem'ry's* retrospective ray
> Both cheer and warm life's winter day.[7]

Another poem, "Written in a Garden," signed "A.B.," appeared in the Virginia *Gazette* on June 9, 1804. It is an elegy in which the poet, reflecting upon the transiency of life, compares the brevity of Clara's life to that of the rose and expresses his lasting grief:

> Flow on my tears, you yet bestow
> The only joy my heart can know,
>   While life's dull lamp shall burn;
> For wrapt in gloomy reverie,
> Deluded fancy seems to see
>   Her angel form return.

6. *Ibid.,* opposite p. 13.
7. Tucker-Coleman Collection, Colonial Williamsburg.

> Blest vision! who canst yet recall
> What bound me to this earthly ball,
>   Thy airy footsteps stay—
> A blank save thee, the world shall seem,
> And I in shadowy raptures dream
>   My ling'ring life away.[8]

St. George Tucker, who liked to think of himself as more than a gentlemanly dabbler in poetry,[9] was not opposed to Tucker's writing and by exchanging verses through the mails with his young relative even encouraged him. But St. George was anxious that Tucker utilize his literary talents to promote his professional career. Worried by Tucker's indolence and aware that the publication of a serious prose composition would do more to enhance his legal reputation than would the publication of poetry, he urged that Tucker devote his time and energy to writing on some "weighty subject." Tucker objected that he had "neither time, inclination or ability" to do as St. George wanted; if he ever did write such a piece, he added, it would be "by stealth, without the privity even of my nearest friend."[10] Several months later an uprising of slaves in Richmond led Tucker to write and publish a pamphlet which is of little intrinsic interest to his belletristic career, but which seems to have played an important part in gaining him the recognition of contemporary writers. Despite its anonymous publication, the *Letter . . . on . . . the Late Conspiracy of the Slaves* (1801) was widely known to be his and, Tucker believed, served to introduce him to Richmond as a man of letters.[11]

TUCKER, WIRT, AND *THE BRITISH SPY*

By 1803 Tucker's reputation as a skillful writer, perhaps strengthened by unrecovered publications in local newspapers, was such that some Richmond citizens supposed him to be the author of the anonymous essays appearing in the Virginia *Argus* as "Letters of the British Spy," which follow the stock device of having an outsider, here a British citizen, report on the manners of a society he observes for the first time. Being mistaken for William Wirt, the real author

8. Tucker-Coleman Collection, Colonial Williamsburg.

9. See William Stevens Prince, "St. George Tucker As a Poet of the Early Republic" (Yale University diss., 1954), pp. 164-165, who argues that St. George Tucker was a serious poet because he carefully revised his work and published much of it.

10. Tucker to St. George Tucker, Aug. 14, 1800, Tucker-Coleman Collection, Colonial Williamsburg.

11. "Autobiography," p. 16.

of the "Letters," at first troubled Tucker on several counts; but, as he reported to St. George, he quickly found a satisfactory solution.

Without doubt you have met with the British Spy in your travels. For a long time the town was divided, as to the authorship, between Wirt & myself. I don't know whether I was most flattered by the supposition, or mortified that it was not true. But as I was both unwilling to receive praise I was not entitled to, and to be suspected of sentiments which I did not entertain, I appeared on the subject of the 2*d* letter in the form of "an enquirer." If this has by chance met your eye, inform whether I have not attacked a theory to which you are partial, or whether when you were corresponding with the Massachusetts literati, you contrived a formal theory of your own. This same Mr. Spy is certainly an elegant fellow, tho' . . . my individual taste inclines me to prefer *Attic* simplicity & conciseness to the pomp and occasional redundancy of the *Asiatic* manner.[12]

In his letter to the "British Spy," also published in the *Argus,* Tucker objected to Wirt's uncritical acceptance of the Count de Buffon's opinion that the earth's features were to be accounted for "by a natural operation of the ocean that covered it."[13] Tucker called attention to the fact that "the theory of this celebrated naturalist has long been deemed both improbable and inadequate," and he enumerated several more recent geological explanations whose propounders had the benefit of more years of observation and were able to see contradictions in Buffon's hypothesis.[14] Instead of defending his position on scientific grounds, Wirt, who later admitted that he knew almost nothing about Buffon or geology, somewhat unfairly accused Tucker of rejecting Buffon's theory in favor of newer ones because of intellectual shallowness and a desire for popularity. "While we are children," Wirt wrote, "it may be well enough to lie passively on our backs and permit others to prepare and feed us with the pap of science; but when our own judgments and understandings have gained their maturity, it behooves us . . . to take a position from which nothing shall move us but reason or truth, not novelty and fashion."[15] Tucker's reply—published in the *Argus* on October 19, after the last of Wirt's ten letters had been printed—contained nothing appreciably new and received no answer. Tucker repeated his assertions about Buffon's faulty hypothesis, refusing to retract or modify his statements

12. Tucker to St. George Tucker, Sept. 30, 1803, Tucker-Coleman Collection, Colonial Williamsburg.
13. *The Letters of the British Spy,* 9th ed. (Baltimore, 1831), p. 73.
14. *Ibid.,* pp. 84-85.
15. *Ibid.,* pp. 41-42 n.

because, he said, his "esteem for truth" exceeded even his "esteem for the British Spy."[16]

Tucker's criticisms of Wirt, though of slight literary merit, strengthened his reputation as an essayist in Richmond literary society. Even Wirt, who was at first embarrassed and piqued by Tucker's attack, acknowledged his competence in a back-handed manner by writing his friend Dabney Carr that Tucker, "poor fellow," was a "better philosopher & writer than . . . lawyer or orator."[17]   Moreover, Tucker had the pleasure of knowing that his work would be included in Wirt's volume, *The Letters of the British Spy,* which went through ten editions and many reprints.[18]

ESSAYS IN THE RICHMOND *ENQUIRER*

In less than a year after his encounter with Wirt, Tucker made a more formal appearance as an essayist.   This time he joined nine others in writing a series of papers for the Richmond *Enquirer,* newly founded by Thomas Ritchie as a "model party paper" to support Jefferson's administration.   With the intention of giving Ritchie's periodical "some éclat at the start, [James] Ogilvie, a democratic Scotchman and an enthusiast in French politics and philosophy, proposed an association called 'The Rainbow,' consisting of ten persons, who were in rotation to write two papers apiece for the Enquirer."[19] In addition to Ogilvie, Tucker, Wirt, and Ritchie, the society included several other distinguished Richmond citizens: Meriwether and Skelton Jones, editors and founders of the Richmond *Examiner;* the

16. *Ibid.,* p. 125.   The dates of Tucker's letters in the *Argus* remain in doubt. Jay B. Hubbell, "William Wirt and the Familiar Essay in Virginia," *WMQ,* 2nd ser., XXIII (1943), 138-139, merely states that Tucker's letters were reprinted without numbering in *The British Spy.* Malcolm Lester says Tucker's two letters appeared in the *Argus* on Sept. 7 and Oct. 4, 1803, but neither date is correct. In *The British Spy,* Wirt's second letter, which prompted Tucker's inquiries, has a footnote answering "An Enquirer" and is dated in the collected text as Sept. 7, 1803, but it appeared in the *Argus* on Sept. 7 and Oct. 4, 1803, but neither date is correct. In *The British Spy,* appeared in the *Argus,* but it does not appear on Sept. 7.   In the printed text, it is referred to by Wirt in a footnote to Letter II and is printed in whole after Letter IV. Tucker's second letter, which Lester says appeared on Oct. 4, 1803, really is in the Oct. 19 issue of the *Argus.* See the bibliography to Lester's "George Tucker: His Early Life and Public Service, 1775-1825" (University of Virginia M.A. thesis, 1946).
    17. Quoted in Hubbell, "Wirt and the Familiar Essay," p. 139.
    18. According to Frank P. Cauble, Tucker's first letter to the *Argus* appeared in the first collected edition of *The British Spy,* and both of his letters appeared in the second and in all succeeding issues of the volume.   See "William Wirt and His Friends, A Study in Southern Culture, 1772-1834" (University of North Carolina diss., 1934), p. 116 and appendix.
    19. "Autobiography," p. 13.

brothers William and Dr. John Brockenbrough, the former a politician and later a judge on the Virginia Supreme Court of Appeals, and the latter a president of the Bank of Virginia; Peyton Randolph, the son of Edmund Randolph, a clerk in the Supreme Court of Appeals; and George Hay, the most famous Republican lawyer in Richmond.[20] A total of twenty-five essays on various political and social topics, a few by men not original members of the "Rainbow Society," were published in the *Enquirer,* and the first ten pieces were later republished in book form. Tucker is unquestionably the author of two essays, "On the Illusions of Fancy" and "On Luxury,"[21] and he probably wrote a third, in which dueling is defended as a worthy institution.[22]

LIGHT VERSE AND SATIRIC LETTERS

Although the correspondence between Tucker and St. George between 1800 and 1806 indicates that Tucker frequently ridiculed some of his contemporaries in Richmond, his only recorded satire during this period is a rather clumsy piece of verse, the immediate motivation

20. Hubbell, "Wirt and the Familiar Essay," pp. 136-152, has the fullest and most accurate account of the founding and history of the association. See also Cauble, "William Wirt and Friends," whose information is abundant but who confuses St. George, Henry St. George, and George Tucker.

21. "Autobiography," p. 21. Hubbell ("Wirt and the Familiar Essay," pp. 140-143) examined Tucker's autobiography and used it to identify correctly Tucker's contributions as those signed "X." Basing his judgments on internal evidence and on inscriptions in the fly-leaves of copies of *The Rainbow; First Series* (Richmond, Va., 1804) in the Library of Congress and the Duke University Library, Hubbell assigns twenty-two of the twenty-five essays to the ten members of the "Rainbow Society" as listed by Tucker. Assuming that the pseudonyms used in the first series were used by the contributors as signatures for all their works and that unsigned papers belong to George Hay, Hubbell assigns two essays to each of the members, with the exceptions of John Brockenbrough, who wrote but one, and Ogilvie and Tucker, each of whom he believes composed three. Three additional essays, signed "C," "G," and "B," he does not identify. A copy of *The Rainbow* in the possession of the Virginia Historical Society, signed by George Hay (one of the members) and given to a Joseph L. Bryan, lists the names of the contributors of the first ten essays as they are deduced by Hubbell. However, Hubbell fails to mention that his attribution is contradicted by a confusing statement in Tucker's "Autobiography": "We went through two numbers to each, & the contributors stopped with Wirt whose pen had been the most exercised and the most successful" (p. 21). If Tucker's memory is to be trusted, only twenty of the twenty-five essays were written by members of the "Rainbow Society" and Wirt, not Ogilvie, signed his work "O" and wrote the first number of the first series and the only number of the third series; and the authorship of all the essays as Hubbell has assigned them is doubtful. For another, probably less accurate discussion of the "Rainbow" essays, see Cauble, "William Wirt and Friends," pp. 168-210.

22. Hubbell also believes this to be Tucker's work (see "Wirt and the Familiar Essay," p. 144 and n.). See Pt. III, p. 213n., for a brief discussion of Tucker's authorship.

of which was Mrs. Tucker's forty-dollar loss in a card game. Imitating Christopher Anstey's *New Bath Guide,* Tucker satirized the acquaintances with whom he and his wife played the game of loo.[23]   As "Hickory Cornhill," a backwoods bumpkin recounting his impressions of Richmond ladies, Tucker said:

> Though their dresses were made of the finest of stuff,
> It must be confessed they were scanty enough
> Yet that nothing thus said should their husbands avail,
> What they take from the body they put in the tail.
> When they sit they so tighten their clothes that you can
> See a lady has legs just the same as a man.

Of the effect of the game upon genteel living and refined conversation, he wrote:

> When I could but admire that choice occupation
> Which call'd forth such bright and refin'd conversation
> "Is diamond the trump?   Then I vow I can't *stand.*"
> "I must also throw up"———"Let me look at your hand."
>
> *   *   *   *   *   *
>
> "Play on, Mrs. Clutch, for I know 'twas a stump"
> "Ace of spades."———"I must take it; you're off with a trump."
> "No indeed———but I've noticed, whenever you stood,
> If I was before you, I always was loo'd."[24]

This slight poem received as much attention as anything else Tucker ever wrote. As the editor of the *Southern Literary Messenger* said when he reprinted it in 1838, some liked its moral and some claimed to see a truth of resemblance to real people in it, as well as "a certain spice of *espièglerie.*"[25] At the time it provoked "An Answer to Hickory Cornhill," a poem which Tucker said was "much reprehended for its indelicacy."[26]

> What is meant when a lady declares she can't stand,
> And will throw up—I hope nothing else but her hand?
> 'Tis true that when wives ev'ry duty neglect,
> And sit gaming all night, they ought to be check'd.

23. "Autobiography," p. 22.

24. "A Letter from Hickory Cornhill, Esq., to His Friend in the Country," Richmond, Va., *Enquirer,* Jan. 9, 1806.

25. IV (1838), 327-328.

26. Tucker to St. George Tucker, Jan. 19, 1806, Tucker-Coleman Collection, Colonial Williamsburg.

Or their husbands will find that their cash is all fleeting,
Or favours received which are not worth repeating!—
Their spouses may take both a *cross-hop* and jump,
And their horns may grow out to be more than a stump.[27]

For several years after Tucker left Richmond and settled in what was then western Virginia in 1808, his interest in and contact with the social and literary events in the capital continued to involve him in the literary ventures he had participated in as a resident. Two satirical letters to the Richmond *Enquirer,* though published in 1811, bear more similarity to his Richmond writings than to the more significant work he was soon to begin, and they are treated, therefore, with his early writings.

These letters were printed as parts of a series of twenty-eight essays published in the *Enquirer* from December 22, 1810, to December 24, 1811, and collected with five more essays into book form in 1814 as *The Old Bachelor*.[28] Wirt—the "Old Bachelor" or, as he was sometimes called, "Dr. Cecil"—served as the editor of the series and probably wrote most of the essays, though St. George Tucker, Dabney Carr, Louis Hue Girardin (a French schoolteacher), and others also contributed. The fifteenth number, published on March 5, 1811, was made up of three letters addressed to "Dr. Cecil," two of which were Tucker's.[29] Both ridiculed Virginia manners and thus differed considerably in tone and purpose from most of the *Old Bachelor* essays, which were designed to defend American institutions against British libels,[30] and were, if not sentimental justifications of American manners and morals, either extremely temperate criticisms of, or explanations for, America's weaknesses in literature and politics.

In his first letter, in the form of a complaint by "Richard Vamper," Tucker satirized the affectations of Richmond merchants who insisted upon being addressed as "Esquire." If this term, "Vamper" argues, is to apply to those of real distinction, he, like the other shopkeepers, can claim cause for its use, since he is a descendant of a long line of

27. "An Answer to Hickory Cornhill, Esq., from His Friend in the Country," Richmond, Va., *Enquirer,* Jan. 16, 1806.

28. The fullest discussions are Hubbell, "Wirt and the Familiar Essay," and Cauble, "William Wirt and Friends."

29. In a letter to Dabney Carr on Feb. 27, 1811, Wirt wrote that "the letters from Vamper and Schryphel" are "from G.T." See John P. Kennedy, *Memoirs of the Life of William Wirt, Attorney General of the United States,* rev. ed. (Philadelphia, 1850), I, 274.

30. See Peter H. Cruse's biographical sketch of Wirt in *The British Spy,* 10th ed., rev. (New York, 1832), p. 63.

shoemakers and, moreover, has five distant relatives in Congress. In a dialogue between "Rosalie" and "Dr. Cecil," probably written by Tucker and printed directly after the letter, "Rosalie" objects that the letter is too personally directed toward some citizens and receives from "Dr. Cecil" an admonition, much like the apology Tucker sent to the Richmond *Enquirer* defending "Hickory Cornhill's" comments on loo playing: "If the errors exist, which this letter implied (taking it ironically) I have no mercy or feeling for them. They deserved to be hissed out of pure and virtuous society.[31]

Legislators and vainglorious women as well as merchants are lampooned in the second letter, from "Peter Schryphel," a widowed and orphaned German farmer from Pennsylvania who recounts his experiences in Richmond during a convention of the Virginia General Assembly, a period of high social life in Richmond. The naïve young man's hand is shaken by "amicable and philanthropic" politicians. He is praised for his taste in dress by Richmond tailors, who try to sell him additional articles of clothing by arguing that "Lawyer Lounge" or "Dr. Calomel" have purchased similar items. Two old matrons who hate to see "young men so *hum-drum*" insist that he enjoy himself by sitting down to a game of loo, and "Miss Ogle" and her equally mercenary girl friends flirt with him, for it is whispered about town that he is a "Dutchman—very rich—lives in Richmond— Mr. Bell's New House."[32]

To allow a gullible back-country farmer to ascribe benevolence to self-interested merchants and to praise rural politicians for their philanthropy and friendliness was, in effect, to deny the thesis underlying Wirt's efforts and to support the British contention that Americans were a culturally backward and mercenary group of provincials. Certainly the "Vamper" letter does not evidence Tucker's anti-aristocratic tendencies, as Jay B. Hubbell thinks,[33] so much as his discernment and derision of middle-class pretensions. In any event, Wirt complained to Dabney Carr shortly after receiving the letters that Tucker's satire was too cold and analytical, "the irony . . . too deli-

31. *The Old Bachelor* (Richmond, Va., 1814), pp. 93-94. In his "Autobiography," p. 21, Tucker wrote that when his pseudonymous articles for the press were "of a satirical character, I commonly resorted to irony." For Tucker's apology for "Hickory Cornhill," see "A Card of Apology to All Whom it May Concern," Richmond, Va., *Enquirer*, Jan. 16, 1806.

32. *Old Bachelor*, pp. 94-97.

33. "Wirt and the Familiar Essay," p. 151.

cate."[34]   Satire and ridicule were obviously out of tune with a work whose purpose, said Wirt, was "virtuously to instruct, or innocently to amuse" so as "to excite the emulation of the rising race" by holding up to it as models the giants of the post-Revolutionary War period.[35]

34. Kennedy, *Memoirs of Wirt,* I, 280, in reprinting Wirt's letter of March 23, 1811, does not give Tucker's name, but Hubbell ("Wirt and the Familiar Essay," p. 151) is correct, I think, in saying the contributions of Tucker are the only ones which could be described as too ironical.

Hubbell, "Wirt and the Familiar Essay," p. 150, says that two letters from "Stephen Micklewise" and "Romeo" in the twentieth number, which appeared in the *Enquirer* on March 29, 1811, and two letters from "Diogenes" and "Susannah Thankful" in the twenty-seventh number, which appeared in the *Enquirer* on Dec. 7, 1811, may be Tucker's, but he gives no reasons for his belief and cites Peter Carr and St. George Tucker as other possible writers.   Of the four letters, only those from "Diogenes," which supports British claims of Virginians' laziness, and "Stephen Micklewise," in which "Micklewise" chides his wife for extravagance, seem to me to be the possible work of Tucker.

35. *Old Bachelor,* No. 11, p. 63; No. 12, p. 69.

CHAPTER VII

FICTIONAL CRITICISMS OF VIRGINIA

BETWEEN 1814 AND 1824, a period during which Tucker was working harder than he ever had before to achieve success in law and politics, he also composed his most significant literary works, which are especially notable as indicating his growing desire to become a professional writer. Early in this decade, in 1814 and 1815, he sold to the *Port Folio* twelve essays on "various subjects of taste, morals, and national policy." These papers, which are examined in Part III of this study, though dealing with subjects similar to those Tucker had treated earlier, are more carefully thought out and better written than his contributions to the Richmond newspapers as a member of Wirt's literary coterie.

Tucker's success in selling his writing to a national magazine seems to have suggested to him the possibility of escaping from the routine world of business, law, and government to the more exciting and profitable one of letters. Partly as a result of the success of these essays, Tucker composed his best book, *The Valley of Shenandoah* (1824), a novel of rural Virginia. But before *The Valley*, he probably wrote *Letters from Virginia* (1816), a satire on Virginia manners and morals—a volume whose authorship has been carefully guarded and which must be discussed at length in the context of Tucker's literary and political career.

LETTERS FROM VIRGINIA

Letters from Virginia, Translated from the French was published anonymously in Baltimore in 1816, when Tucker was a newly-elected representative to the Virginia General Assembly from Pittsylvania

County. Using the familiar scheme of allowing an unprejudiced foreigner to comment on contemporary affairs and manners, the author satirized Virginia by means of twenty-three supposedly recently-discovered letters written by a French traveler. The Frenchman, who was persecuted by Napoleon for his attachment to the royal house of Louis XVI, found shelter in England. From there he came to Virginia not only to view the scenes where his "dear and lamented father," later executed on the guillotine, "poured out his first blood at the shrine of liberty,"[1] but also in the hope of "seeing a true republic, where the laws are made and administered by the best men, only to promote the happiness of the people."[2]

The French "Traveller" describes Virginia cities and discusses, as the "translator" announces in the preface, the "morals, manners, [and] literature" of the Old Dominion. He visits Williamsburg and concludes that it has "little to recommend it to a stranger. . . . Indeed, if it wasn't for the College, and the Court," and the lunatic hospital, it would hardly be worth seeing.[3] He finds Norfolk to be a dirty town, its houses constructed in a "slovenly style," and its crowded streets so crooked that "even Hogarth, with all his passion for the 'waving line,' " would have condemned them.[4] In Richmond, "the fountain head of law, wealth, and fashion," public taste, manifested by the homes "built of course [*sic*] bricks, blackened by being burnt with coal," is even worse.[5]

"Traveller," the young aristocrat, deplores the importance which Virginians attach to oratory and their readiness to select leaders on the basis of the ability to harangue a crowd. Since oratory is the only road to fame in Virginia, young men are urged by their elders to practice the arts of the public speaker, of which there are four classes. The *"Political Spouter,"* especially prevalent in every court-yard and tavern, is represented with feet cocked up on the mantle before he *"lets out,"* unwinding himself in "long discourses upon liberty, the rights of man, the freedom of the seas, general suffrage. . . ." *"County Court Lawyers"* achieve eminence by following the advice of their successful predecessors:

When you rise at the bar, only remember to speak as fast as possible, to shew your fluency. No matter about the choice of words, (tho', to be

1. Letter XII, 105.
2. Letter I, 10.
3. Letter XIV, 122.
4. Letter III, 18-19.
5. Letter XXI, 198-199.

sure, the longer and rounder the better,) but take the first . . . that come
to hand, and be careful you don't stop. . . .   But above all things, be sure
and speak long enough.

"Fourth of July Orators" or, as he also calls them, "the *Orators of the
Human Race,"* "set up once a year, (generally in very hot weather,)
to proclaim their independence with a loud voice, and abuse the
British *con amore."*   Lastly there exist the *"Slangwhangers"* or
"Stump-Orators" who are "passionately fond of the word *Republican"*
and browbeat voters before polling places.[6]

Although "Traveller" claims to have strong "republican partiali-
ties,"[7] he is critical of the leveling tendencies of a democratic society
and considers many of its citizens to be pretentious and vulgar. He
sees the folly of the democratic ambitions of his valet, La Rose.
Having affianced himself to the daughter of a Richmond silversmith,
La Rose tells his master that he must resign his post, since his future
father-in-law refuses to marry his daughter to a servant, a disgraceful
office in a land of freedom, but will take La Rose into his shop and
make him a silversmith instead. "Traveller" accepts La Rose's advancement with a mixture of amusement and chagrin and forbears
from disillusioning him. "Liberty, fortune, & a pretty girl," he
philosophizes, "who would not leave a poor master for these?"[8] In
all the cities in which "Traveller" visits he finds large numbers of
middle-class republicans who consider themselves "the most enlightened people in the world," yet are credulous enough to admire low-
class foreigners, most of whom are French, posing as exiled aristocrats.[9]

Certain classes in the Old Dominion, those with true claims to
gentility, however, escape all criticism. In Williamsburg there are,
for example, several families "peculiarly courteous and engaging"
because "they still retain the air of the *old Court,* which they have
derived from their ancestors, unconsciously, and almost in spite of
themselves."[10] They have the manners reflecting their higher status,
as do a few families in Norfolk who "are at once easy and polite;
familiar, and yet sufficiently elegant."[11] In Richmond, the same "true

6. Letter XXII, 203-211.
7. Letter XXIII, 214.
8. Letter VII, 44.
9. Letter XXIII, 218-219.
10. Letter XIV, 122.
11. Letter III, 21.

old Virginia breed" is contrasted with the self-styled higher classes, "who indeed are chiefly of foreign extraction."[12]

One of the longest pieces in the *Letters* is, on the surface, a discussion of the causes of racial inferiority and is centered around Jefferson's opinion on slavery as expressed in his *Notes on the State of Virginia.* Jay B. Hubbell, who calls Letter XI "an able, lawyerlike refutation of Jefferson's suggestion . . . that the Negro's intellect is inferior to that of the white man,"[13] fails to see that the argument about Negro inferiority is used as a vehicle for a personal attack upon Jefferson. In his *Notes on Virginia,* Jefferson advanced it "as a suspicion only, that the blacks, whether originally a distinct race, or made distinct by time and circumstances, are inferior to the whites in the endowments of body and mind."[14] "Traveller" finds the hypothetical nature of Jefferson's conjectures "hardly sufficient to excuse him in the eye of reason or of heaven, for this libel."[15] Jefferson's opinion must be the result of prejudice, "Traveller" argues, since in the same volume Jefferson himself stood on opposite ground to refute the claims of the Count de Buffon and the Abbé Raynal that the backwardness of Indians and of white settlers in America was due to inherent inferiority. In any event, he says, Jefferson's inexcusable remarks have caused masters to mistreat their slaves.[16]

"Traveller" then comments upon certain of Jefferson's statements, refuting them reasonably where he can, but resorting to ridicule and insult where reason does not suffice. Jefferson, for example, to help prove that whites were more beautiful than Negroes, cited the blacks' "own judgment in favour of the whites, declared by their preference of them, as uniformly as is the preference of the Oran-ootan for the black woman over those of his own species."[17] "Traveller" rebuts:

As to our author's [Jefferson's] remarks, upon the comparative beauty of the two races, I must certainly agree with him in taste, (tho' I own I was a little surprised at his decision after the stories I have heard of him.) I will never give up the lilies, and roses, and blushes of the whites, for the dull mask of the blacks. Nor shall I very readily consent to exchange our flowing hair for their woolly heads. I am not quite so satisfied, however, as he seems to be, about making my own judgment the

12. Letter XXI, 200-201.
13. *The South in American Literature, 1607-1900* (Durham, N.C., 1954), p. 250.
14. *The Works of Thomas Jefferson,* ed. Paul Leicester Ford (New York and London, 1904), IV, 58.
15. Letter XI, p. 74.
16. P. 73.
17. *Works of Jefferson,* IV, 50.

standard of taste for all the world. Their preference of the whites, (in their amours I suppose he means, by his allusion to the obscene fable of the Oranootan,) can hardly be regarded as a concession of the points in our favour, as it may be very naturally ascribed to pride, and ambition to associate with superiors; for La Fontaine tells us, there is always a little grain of ambition in love. Nor is this supposed preference of theirs by any means universal, (whatever Mr. J's own experience may have been.)[18]

In concluding the discussion of beauty, "Traveller" says:

After all, whether the blacks are uglier or handsomer than the whites, can prove nothing as to their inferiority in the endowments of the mind, unless we are to take it for granted that beauty and genius always go together, a proposition for which Mr. J. ought not to contend.[19]

Jefferson believed that the Negroes' reason and imagination were inferior to those of Indians or whites, and though he admitted that the blacks were backward partly because of the lack of opportunity to learn, he pointed out that environment was not alone responsible because some of them had been educated and many were so situated "that they might have availed themselves of the conversation of their masters."[20] In support of his hypothesis that nature and not condition caused the Negroes' inferiority, as exemplified in their lack of achievement in the arts, Jefferson contrasted their accomplishments with those of the slaves of Augustan Rome, whose bondage was much harsher than that of American slaves.[21] "Traveller" doubts that the conversation of Virginia planters "is so strongly saturated with intelligence." Admittedly, the slaves have not "started up philosophers and poets from the work bench; but neither have their masters."[22] And really, he concludes, despite Jefferson's assumption to the contrary, there can be no comparison drawn between the slaves in America and the slaves in Augustan Rome, for it is unfair to compare Terence's environment even with "the philosophical atmosphere of Monticello, which shall be considered (for the sake of argument) as the seat of genius, the garden of taste, and, if you choose, the mountain of the muses into the bargain."[23]

18. P. 75.
19. P. 76.
20. *Works of Jefferson*, IV, 52.
21. *Ibid.*, pp. 52-55.
22. Pp. 85, 86.
23. P. 97.

This attack upon Jefferson in the *Letters* seems to me to present a major problem for which some explanation must be given before the satire can be further discussed as belonging in the canon of Tucker's work. Most of the critics who attribute the volume to Tucker ignore the assault on Jefferson and assume at the same time that Tucker was a life-long admirer of Jefferson and a supporter of his social, political, and economic policies.[24] Only Jessie Bernard, who shares the conviction that Tucker was ardently pro-Jefferson, asserts that the allusion to Jefferson's alleged association with Negro women destroys any possibility of Tucker's authorship, since Tucker, she says, would never have defamed anyone, and especially Jefferson, by "scandalous innuendo."[25]

Joseph Dorfman, on the other hand, who has surveyed the economic and political controversies which concerned Tucker and his contemporaries, attributes the volume to Tucker and explains it in the context of Tucker's consistent pro-Federalist bias. In addition to the disparagement of Jefferson in Letter XI, the book contains, Dorfman believes, "attacks on the policies and views of Jefferson."[26] Dorfman cites two passages in which the embargo in particular is attacked. In Letter VI, "Traveller's" friend, a sensible Virginian educated at Yale College, says that Virginians, whose "genteel laziness" prohibits them from engaging in commerce, have much to learn from Yankees—the "most enterprising people in the world." To "good people," it seemed that by evading the rules of the embargo to save the West Indies from famine, the resourceful and independent New England traders had acted as the agents of a wise Providence.[27] Letter XVIII, addressed to "Traveller's" fiancée, is a fantasy provoked by a reading of Stith's *History of Virginia,* envisioning a sale of women imported from England as much-needed wives for the settlers in the early seventeenth century. After describing the equal readiness of the men to buy and the women to be sold into marriage, "Traveller" mentions the current condition of the marriage market in Virginia, which is much less favorable to women:

24. Leonard C. Helderman, "A Satirist in Old Virginia," *American Scholar,* VI (1937), 481-497, and his "A Social Scientist of the Old South," *Journal of Southern History,* II (1936), 148-174. See also Hubbell, *The South in American Literature,* pp. 250, 255.

25. "George Tucker: Liberal Southern Social Scientist," *Social Forces,* XXV (1946-47), 134.

26. *The Economic Mind in American Civilization, 1606-1865* (New York, 1946), II, 542.

27. Letter VI, 38.

You must know that the embargo, and other restrictive measures of government, have fallen very heavily upon the ladies, by impoverishing their lovers at home, and cutting off supplies from abroad. There are . . . great murmurs among these fair malcontents, against the president and congress; for I believe they are nearly all *federalists,* that is, as the word imports, friends to *union*.[28]

It seems to me that such comments are neither as important nor as effective ingredients of the *Letters* as Dorfman thinks. Allusions to the embargo in Letter XVIII are a minor part of a comic allegory, and Letter VI is intended not so much to deprecate Republican policies as to satirize avaricious Yankees, who "love money a little better than their own lives," and especially to criticize the unprofitable gentility of Virginians.[29] Yet, the slaps at the embargo bolster the attack on Jefferson by recalling his personal backing of a political measure which, in 1816, when the *Letters* was written, was widely believed to have been an unwise and inept solution to the nation's problems.

In any event, it is clear that Dorfman's view of Tucker as an opponent of Jefferson is generally correct, and that the hostility toward Jefferson in the *Letters,* the aspersions on the embargo, and the damning allusions to Napoleon as a destroyer of liberty—all representative of Federalist attitudes in the early 1800's—though they do not prove Tucker's authorship, certainly do not militate against it. For in the early nineteenth century, Tucker was sympathetic with many of the Federalists' policies, greatly distrusted the French, and was, especially in the years from 1811 to 1819, strongly opposed to Jefferson's governmental policies. In a pseudonymous pamphlet published in 1811, which was instrumental in Tucker's gaining the job of commissioner of a company whose purpose it was to improve foreign trade and stimulate the sale of Virginia crops, Tucker alleged that Jefferson's purchase of the Louisiana Territory was crippling the nation's, and especially Virginia's, economy.[30]   Further indications of Tucker's

28. Letter XVIII, 168. See also, for example, Letter XIX, in which "Traveller" recounts how he fell asleep and dreamed of meeting with "Federalist" girls who desire union but whose "intercourse" has been curtailed by the embargo.

There is some distortion in Dorfman's summary of the *Letters* because he telescopes Letters VI and XVIII: "The Embargo and other restrictive measures, declared 'Traveller,' were passed 'to starve the English out of home and house,' but their operation has been to impoverish the Americans. The critics are 'nearly all *Federalists,* that is, as the word imports, friends to Union.' " Dorfman, *Economic Mind,* II, 543.

29. Letter VI, 38, 39-40.

30. *A Letter to a Member of the General Assembly of North Carolina on the Navigation of the Roanoke and Its Branches* (Richmond, Va., 1811), pp. 19-20. Tucker

antipathy toward Jefferson and his administration are contained even in Tucker's somewhat official biography of Jefferson. Though composed with the help of Jefferson's heirs and close associates and with the purpose of "placing his virtues & his services in a true light before his countrymen, and at the same time drawing a veil over his errors & defects to which I was not blind,"[31] it is no adulatory study. Tucker criticized Jefferson's invocation of the embargo—whose adverse economics effects, said Tucker, its proponents did not thoroughly comprehend—and Jefferson's dislike of banks, cities, and tariffs. He also reproved Jefferson for his ungentlemanly action in imprisoning the Governor of Detroit, Henry Hamilton, later Governor of Bermuda and Tucker's benefactor, and for Jefferson's distrust of Tucker's Federalist friend, John Marshall, during the prosecution of Aaron Burr.[32]   Indeed, Tucker's friend and contemporary, Hugh Blair Grigsby, wrote that on close examination of Tucker's work, "we find that in comparing Hamilton and Jefferson together, he awards the palm of genius to Hamilton."[33]

---

may have been opposed to the embargo and the non-intercourse acts because of their depressive effects on trade in Bermuda, where his father and other relatives made their livings by trading with the United States. In 1810 Tucker's brother Henry came to Virginia penniless, and Tucker supported him through medical school (see Tucker to St. George Tucker, Oct. 21, 1810, Tucker-Coleman Collection, Colonial Williamsburg). During this period, Tucker's father suffered great economic misfortunes possibly caused by America's foreign policy (see Tucker to St. George Tucker, June 3, 1810, Tucker-Coleman Collection, Colonial Williamsburg).

31. "Autobiography," manuscript copy, Tucker-Harrison-Smith Papers, University of Virginia Library, p. 40.

32. *The Life of Thomas Jefferson, Third President of the United States, with Parts of His Correspondence Never Before Published, and Notices of His Opinions on Questions of Civil Government, National Policy, and Constitutional Law* (Philadelphia, 1837), I, 128-131; II, 71-74, 158-160, 229-231, 265-268, 333-339, 380-383. See also Dorfman, *Economic Mind*, II, 881. Particularly interesting are Tucker's references to Jefferson's distrust of John Marshall for attending a dinner given by the Federalists for Aaron Burr, over whose trial for treason Marshall was presiding. Tucker, who in his autobiography (p. 28) praised Marshall and represented him as having "the simplicity of a child," said that Jefferson was unfortunately carried away by party rage to attack Marshall as being prejudiced. Tucker himself attended the dinner, given by Mr. W[ickham], and said that Marshall never spoke to Burr during the evening (*Life of Jefferson*, II, 231).

For a comment which may refer to Jefferson's attack on Marshall, see Tucker to St. George Tucker, Oct. 21, 1810, Tucker-Coleman Collection, Colonial Williamsburg: "From what I have lately heard of a certain great man, some of his private transactions have lowered him still more in the public estimation than his utmost outrages on the dignity of a judge or the decency of a gentleman have ever done."

33. Review of Henry Randall's *The Life of Thomas Jefferson*, cited in *The Correspondence Between Henry Stephens Randall and Hugh Blair Grigsby 1856-1861*, ed. Frank J. Klingberg and Frank W. Klingberg, University of California Publications in History, XLIII (Los Angeles and Berkeley, 1952), p. 13.

Moreover, there is evidence that Tucker had some personal reservations about Jefferson. In his reminiscences he related that Jefferson, unlike the genial Madison, "was occasionally somewhat dictatorial & impatient of contradiction."[34] Early in life Tucker, who was himself charged with being intolerant of disagreement, may have had an opportunity to discuss with Jefferson the writings of Buffon and Raynal—whose theories provide the background for the discussion in Letter XI in which Jefferson is attacked—and to have been rebuffed by the Republican leader. Tucker admittedly held little regard for the *Notes on Virginia* and remarked in his *Life of Jefferson* that Jefferson blundered badly in "conceding the natural inferiority" of the blacks, since in so doing he gave to the followers of Raynal support for their belief that humans in America degenerated.[35] The opportunity to take Jefferson to task for his scientific theories, for his political policies, and for what Tucker considered to be his high-handedness, without the risk of incurring his or his friends' anger, may have appealed strongly to Tucker.

The anti-Jefferson sentiments expressed in the *Letters,* then, offer little argument against Tucker's authorship. On the other hand, his membership in the Republican party and his fear that his reputation as a businessman and lawyer might suffer if he were known to be an author would help explain why Tucker never mentioned the *Letters.* The Republican party was to send him to Congress in 1819 to serve for three terms. After 1825, he had absolutely nothing to gain by claiming the work and could have done so only with great embarrassment, since he owed his appointment at the University of Virginia to Jefferson's good will and, in addition, received favors from many of Jefferson's friends.

Evidence in the *Letters* to suggest that Tucker did not write the volume is unconvincing. Letter X is a discussion of the "slovenly diction" and lack of invention in the poetry of Richard Dabney, a Virginia writer whom Tucker nowhere else mentions. More important, one essay disparages Thomas Moore, one of Tucker's favorite writers, as "the little museling [that] flew over this state . . . almost without lighting, and upon his return to England, sat down to write a libel on it in prose and rhyme."[36]

34. "Autobiography," p. 40.
35. *Life of Jefferson,* I, 179. Early in life Tucker was very much interested in the writings of Buffon and Raynal (see *Life of Jefferson,* I, 179 n.).
36. Letter VIII, p. 48.

On the other hand, there is a considerable amount of internal evidence which, though not conclusive, leads me to concur with the great majority of those who have examined the satire[37] and to assume that Tucker wrote the *Letters*. Tucker held many of the prejudices and enthusiasms manifested in the *Letters*. Like the French visitor, for example, he expressed a strong dislike for Virginia frontier oratory, partly because of jealousy—for Tucker's political and legal career was retarded by his inability to speak well in public—but mainly because he thought public speaking as practiced in Virginia put the "English language and common sense . . . to the rack" and was offensive to "the man of taste"[38] and because he associated frontier oratory with republican political demagoguery. Tucker also shared "Traveller's" tastes in society, praising the true aristocrats of Virginia, especially of Williamsburg and Norfolk, and satirizing middle-class merchants, as in *The Valley of Shenandoah* and in his "Peter Schryphel" contribution to *The Old Bachelor*.

Other evidence of Tucker's authorship is to be found in the similarities in arguments and reasoning between the *Letters* and the works either acknowledged or established as his. The claim set forth in Letter III that a canal "to communicate with the waters of the Roanoke . . . would enable North Carolina to pour her riches into the lap of Norfolk"[39] certainly recalls Tucker's sanguine proposal in *A Letter . . . on the Navigation of the Roanoke and Its Branches*. The explanations for the literary backwardness of Virginia in Letter XVI, summarized in "Traveller's" statement that "there are still no large cities, no learned clergy, no liberally-endowed colleges, no well-furnished

37. Helderman, "Satirist in Virginia," pp. 481-497; "Social Scientist," pp. 148-174; Malcolm Lester, "George Tucker: His Early Life and Public Service, 1775-1825" (University of Virginia M.A. thesis, 1946), pp. 79-81; Hubbell, *The South in American Literature*, p. 250; Dorfman, *Economic Mind*, II, 542-544. The Catalogue of the Library of Congress reads: "Attributed to George Tucker by Sabin, the Brinley Catalogue, British Museum, Halkett & Laing, & Mr. Polock, the well-known Philadelphia antiquarian and dealer, who knew Tucker personally. The 'Letters' have also been attributed to William Maxwell (by the Phil. Lib. Co.) and to James Kirk Paulding (by [Patrick Kevin] Foley)." Neither the Philadelphia Library Company nor Foley gives reasons for their attributions (see Foley's *American Authors 1795-1895: A Bibliography of First and Notable Editions Chronologically Arranged with Notes* [Boston, 1897]). Amos L. Herold is probably correct in believing that bibliographers have confused *Letters from Virginia* (1816) with Paulding's *Letters from the South* (1817). See Herold's *James Kirk Paulding: Versatile American* (New York, 1926), p. 160.

38. "On Style," *Essays on Various Subjects of Taste, Morals, and National Policy* (Georgetown, D.C., 1822), pp. 161-162.

39. P. 21.

libraries,"[40] are generally like those made elsewhere by Tucker when discussing national literature.[41]   Many of the comments upon the Negro also resemble Tucker's.   For example, despite his fluctuating attitudes toward slavery, Tucker for most of his life was convinced, as was "Traveller," that the Negro was not inherently inferior in mentality to the white man.[42]   And the sentimental depiction in Letter V of a band of chained slaves being sold south to the Carolinas is similar to Tucker's description of a slave auction in *The Valley*.[43]

Tucker must have been well aware that the *Letters* followed the same form as Wirt's *British Spy*, the florid style of which he had so strongly objected to and must have intended to avoid.   Speaking of style in the preface, the "translator" of the *Letters* said he was against "all . . . fuss and parade":

> As to the style, I don't know what great judges will think of it, but to me it appears light, familiar, and various.   The writer is sometimes gay, sometimes sentimental, sometimes philosophical, always pleasing.   His work indeed abounds with negligences and familiarisms, which I had some thoughts of retrenching, and supplying their place with something a little more elegant of my own; for I hope the reader will believe that I understand how to write long winding sentences of the most fashionable and soporific construction.   I have not done it, however . . . because I even conceit a beauty in this pleasing defect of his style.   It is like the morning dress of a Quaker girl, the more charming for its simplicity and neglect.[44]

Although the effusive style is generally avoided, some of the letters lapse into what Tucker had called Wirt's "*Asiatic* manner."   In a fashion inconsistent with the satiric tone of most of the book, "Traveller" was sometimes willing to cease criticizing Virginia society in order to ingratiate himself with readers who enjoyed over-written sentimental scenes.   In Letter XVII, for example, "Traveller" visits the graveyard at Jamestown, thinking of Pocahontas, the Ceres of America.   Smitten with melancholia as he meditates upon the transiency of life, he pleads for all to seek solace in religion.

40. P. 141.

41. See "On American Literature," *Port Folio*, 3rd ser., IV (1814), 44-59.

42. See *Letter to a Member of the General Assembly of Virginia, on the Subject of the Late Conspiracy of the Slaves with a Proposal for their Colonization* (Baltimore, 1801), pp. 5-6; and George Long, George R. Porter, George Tucker, and Wilhelm Wittich, *America and the West Indies, Geographically Described* (London, 1845), pp. 223-244.

43. See the discussions of slavery in these works in Pt. III, Chap. XI, pp. 182-183, 188-192.

44. P. vi.   Compare Tucker's similar statements in essays "On Style" and "On Simplicity in Ornament" in *Essays* (1822).

Despite several letters which deal thus sentimentally with the recent past, the volume is essentially a satire, the merit of which has been greatly overrated.[45]   The critical attitudes toward Virginia manners, men, and customs undoubtedly constitute the most valuable and interesting portion of the volume. Yet most of what is said is not effective, because Tucker, though he avowed a "passion for going behind curtains to see things as they are," seldom gave enough attention to any one topic to get below its surface. With the possible exception of the letter on Jefferson, the commentary voiced by "Traveller"—himself an unbelievable creation with a personality devoid of charm or interest—is not only superficial but lacks the saving graces of spontaneous wit and lively humor. Tucker relied so heavily on stale literary convention to enliven his letters that his criticisms, when not simply asserted in the mode of the journalist, all too frequently appear as though they could have been written without their author's ever having been in Virginia. For example, in order to satirize the indolence and vanity of Virginians, he embodies the defects in an Addison-like caricature of "Harry Whiffler," the lazy son of a planter, who, having run "thro' the whole circle of *vices*" at William and Mary and having failed as a lawyer, sets himself up as an author in Richmond, libeling prominent men and defending Napoleon as an Imperial Republican.[46] Like most of the other sketches in the *Letters,* this piece is of some importance in studying Tucker's development as a writer since it shows his continuing criticism of certain aspects of the society in which he lived, but it is not successful satire. In the *Letters* he was working in a form in which he had great interest but, unfortunately, only a modest talent.

MONEY AND LITERATURE

The question of literary backwardness in America was of great concern to Tucker and his contemporaries, who filled the magazines with explanations for their country's inferiority. Tucker's own situation in the early decades of the nineteenth century typifies that of the aspiring writer who had to weigh against the uncertain rewards of literary fame and fortune the stigma which the mere attempt to write might attach to his social and professional reputation. On May 28, 1813, Tucker wrote to St. George, who since 1800 had worried about

45. Hubbell, *The South in American Literature,* pp. 250-251; Helderman, "Satirist in Virginia," pp. 481-497, and "Social Scientist," p. 14.
46. Letter IX, pp. 52-58.

Tucker's inability to succeed as a lawyer or to free himself from debt, that his progress in the law, though not spectacular, was far greater than he "ever expected, or even dared to hope."[47] Less than eight months later, he proudly confided in St. George about a series of essays which he contributed to the *Port Folio,* for which he received two dollars a page. But he asked that St. George not reveal his identity as author, not only because the essays "would lose more than they would gain from my name," but also because Tucker, like many writers of his period, knew that his name, too, might suffer if he were known as a writer. There are, he told St. George, "hundreds of very prudent & knowing people who are very well convinced that a man who writes for the public cannot be a lawyer or a man of business."[48]

St. George understood Tucker's desire for anonymity, since he himself had been dabbling in literature for a number of years and had necessarily considered the effects such an avocation might have upon his career. William Wirt, an eminent lawyer and well-known essayist, from time to time had exchanged "effusions" with St. George and had encouraged him to write a play about the patriots of the American Revolution.[49] But Wirt himself hesitated to appear before the public as a dramatist, and in 1812 he asked St. George what effects the writing of a drama might have upon his professional character. St. George answered that Dwight's *Conquest of Canaan* had advanced him in his own section, that Humphreys, Washington's aide, had been promoted because of his literary work. But Barlow's poetry did not result in a promotion—"yet we now see him an Envoy abroad. Should he fail in his embassy," however, "I shall not be surprised to hear it said, it might have been predicted from his poem."

To apply this to a man of any profession, if the author be a person who has inspired an exalted opinion of his talents, and the poem be given to the world in such a manner as to appear merely as a *jeu d'esprit,* the effusion of a leisure moment, and without any view to profit or emolument, or as an offering at the shrine of party,—I think, in such a case, the public would regard it favourably, and as an evidence of a variety of genius and talent capable of embellishment beyond the professional walk.[50]

47. Tucker to St. George Tucker, Tucker-Coleman Collection, Colonial Williamsburg.

48. Tucker to St. George Tucker, Feb. 3, 1814, Tucker-Coleman Collection, Colonial Williamsburg.

49. William Wirt to St. George Tucker, Jan. 29, 1812, Tucker-Coleman Collection, Colonial Williamsburg.

50. John P. Kennedy, *Memoirs of the Life of William Wirt, Attorney General of the United States,* rev. ed. (Philadelphia, 1850), I, 308-309.

St. George, it seems, passed on this same advice to Tucker, urging him to devote more time to law and less to "childish amusements." But Tucker was reluctant to abandon his favorite avocation:

I fancy to myself that if I were released from my present drudgery of practicing the law I could pass my time very agreeably in those intellectual exercises of which you speak too unworthily in calling them childish amusements—I know of no way in which a man can pass his time more suitable to the character of a rational creature. Perhaps however I should in time grow weary of the sameness & languish for more bustle and variety. Certain it is I never passed my time so much to my satisfaction before tho' I literally lead a life of labour, exposure & discomfort.

In an attempt to placate the old judge, who, no doubt, thought his young relative might be returning to his indolent ways, Tucker closed the long letter by appealing to St. George's national pride and by suggesting that he "contribute something, particularly in the practical way to the Port folio—since it has laid aside all tincture of party politics, I think it a very respectable journal—& deserving of encouragement as a national work."[51]

If disagreement existed between the elderly judge and Tucker about the advisability of writing, Tucker's silence indicates that St. George had convinced him of the injudiciousness either of spending his time or of risking his reputation as a writer. Furthermore, though with proper incentive Tucker could and did write under pressure, his time was fully engaged from 1816 to 1824 with political and financial problems. He was a member of the Virginia General Assembly from 1816 to 1819 and a representative in Congress from 1819 to 1825, and he was occupied in paying off debts and increasing his property holdings. Except for some light society verse done in 1820 while he was in Washington[52] and a memorial volume for his favorite child, from 1816, when *Letters* was published, until 1824, Tucker composed only four essays, which, with those written for the *Port Folio,* he published in book form as *Essays on Various Subjects of Taste, Morals, and National Policy* in 1822.[53]

During his last years in Congress, however, Tucker's financial situation caused him, for the first time in his career, to try to earn a

51. Tucker to St. George Tucker, May 23, 1815, Tucker-Coleman Collection, Colonial Williamsburg.

52. His wife Maria wrote to him that she was pleased "that you are exercising your poetical talents once more—You disappoint us all by not enclosing the verses you wrote for Miss Morton." Maria B. Tucker to George Tucker, Dec. 3, 1820, Tucker-Harrison-Smith Papers, University of Virginia Library.

53. Preface, p. x.

large sum of money by his pen. As early as 1815, in analyzing the reasons for the disparity in literary achievement between America and England, Tucker wrote that in England authors came "from the *redundancy* of educated men"—that poverty made men poets.[54]   Although no such harsh economic law was operative in Tucker's case, by 1824 his long-accumulated debts, increased by the burden placed upon him by the financial collapse of his father-in-law, made his situation almost a critical one.[55]   It was natural that Tucker finally turned to writing to augment his income, even made an attempt to become a professional writer.   Some ten years earlier, he had expressed a desire to earn his living by writing, and by 1824 he had grounds for believing that his talents as a writer were worth capitalizing upon. Although it is not known how much money he received for his 1822 *Essays,* certainly his confidence must have been bolstered by its favorable reception.   He may have seen Edward Everett's comments in the influential *North American Review* in 1823, describing the volume as "a purely literary banquet";[56] and he surely was flattered by the remarks of James Madison, who, in thanking Tucker for his gift of the book, praised it as "containing much valuable matter" and as providing an effective answer to "charges of our national . . . backwardness."[57]

With such encouragement for his past work, Tucker determined to try writing fiction, perhaps believing that though he cut only a mediocre figure as a lawyer and legislator, he might achieve fame and fortune as a novelist.   The financial successes of Scott and, especially, Cooper, it seems, first awakened him to the rewards he might reap.   In explaining his reasons for postponing his decision on accepting the professorship of moral philosophy at the University of Virginia, he wrote to Joseph C. Cabell:

I have for more than a year . . . indulged the hope that I might pursue the business of authorship as a profitable calling.   I have (but this is a secret) actually essayed the public favour in a novel just published in New York and should it meet with anything like the success which has attended Cooper, I should think my prospects of profit much greater than any professorship could hold out.   He has made about $5000 by each of his novels—and the Valley of Shenandoah, my new work, was written in

54. *Essays* (1822), pp. 45-46, 47.

55. For a more detailed account of Tucker's finances, see above, Pt. I, pp. 21-22, 26-28.

56. XVI, 45.

57. James Madison to George Tucker, July 15, 1822, Madison Papers, Library of Congress.

two months. The situation to which you invite me, would almost put a stop to my efforts as an author, or would confine them in a channel in which I have already found that little reputation is to be acquired & no money.[58]

The two-volume novel, *The Valley of Shenandoah,* composed in a brief two months in 1824—from July 1 to August 31—represented a bold attempt to win recognition as a novelist.

THE VALLEY OF SHENANDOAH

The Valley of Shenandoah is Tucker's most important literary work and his chief contribution to American letters. With the anonymous *Tales of an American Landlord,* "a dreary religious novel" also published in 1824, it is the first attempt to depict Virginia life in fiction.[59] In his only published novel Tucker combined with some exemplary moral instruction a survey of Southern manners and institutions. Although he suggested ideal patterns of social and moral behavior based upon the values of an aristocratic plantation society, Tucker commented realistically upon much of that society, criticizing pointedly the landed aristocracy for their inability to manage and hold onto their estates. At heart a cultural historian, interested in analyzing the impact of social and economic forces upon man in society, Tucker included in *The Valley* a mass of sober sociological and economic information in order to explain the development of Virginia life.

While Tucker began *The Valley* under the handicap of never having attempted fiction, he held several advantages which may have contributed to his belief that he was eminently qualified to write a novel to help satisfy the appeals which were then frequent for a national literature making use of an American background. First of all, the variety of Tucker's experience must have increased his hopes for success. Few American and certainly no English writers, Tucker correctly assumed, could have the knowledge of the South which he possessed. He had lived a life both of indolence and of hard work, had firsthand acquaintance with the finest and richest aristocratic families in Virginia, and had, on the other hand, lived among the poor working groups of Scotch-Irish and Germans. Direct observation provided him with the knowledge necessary to set the locale—Virginia, two decades after the Revolutionary War—and it allowed him, as he

58. Tucker to Joseph C. Cabell, Jan. 1, 1824 [1825], Cabell Deposit, University of Virginia Library.

59. Jay B. Hubbell, *Virginia Life in Fiction* (Dallas, Tex., 1922), pp. 21-22.

wished, to incorporate into his work the manners, habits, and character of the Virginia people.[60]

A second and greater asset which Tucker possessed was his concern with and knowledge of economics. A scholarly interest in theoretical economics, already manifested in the publication of essays on banking and other important economic subjects, was complemented by much practical experience in the everyday problems of business and law. He was personally acquainted with the difficulties of running plantations, and, having been employed as a banker and debt collector and having appeared in the courts as plaintiff and defendant, attorney and litigant, he was aware of the magnitude and significance of the economic changes constantly occurring in Virginia. Not long before Tucker wrote *The Valley*, his wife's parents, the Charles Carters, became bankrupt, and the proud family had to sell their goods and slaves at public auction. Carter's economic collapse, which affected Tucker's career to a degree, provided an immediate source for *The Valley*, which tells the story of the ruin of an old aristocratic Virginia family.[61]

The tale of Virginia life begins as Edward Grayson brings James Gildon, his companion at William and Mary College, to "Beechwood," his home in the Shenandoah Valley. Gildon, who has been urged by his father—an avaricious New York merchant—to marry a Virginia heiress, is captivated by Louisa, Edward's innocent and beautiful sister, and succeeds in winning her love. The Graysons tactfully inform Gildon that the recently deceased Colonel Grayson, a Revolutionary War hero, has left them almost impoverished. But Gildon is confident that he can persuade his father to accept Louisa, and he persists in his suit, though he never declares himself, thus rousing Mrs. Grayson's suspicions that he might be "one of those odious and contemptible beings, which are called male coquettes." Edward is too occupied with his own problems to guide his sister effectively. His love for the incomparable Matilda Fawkner is continually frustrated by Matilda's mother. The descendant of a Dutch grazier and one-time overseer for Edward's grandfather, Mrs. Fawkner brought her fortune to her marriage to her social better and is anxious for Matilda to marry someone with money. Although Matilda's affection for Edward is constant, they are forced to postpone marriage until Edward receives

60. "Autobiography," p. 37.

61. In his preface Tucker said that many of the characters and events in *The Valley* were based on persons and happenings in real life. See *The Valley of Shenandoah; or, Memoirs of the Graysons* (New York, 1824), I, vi.

his law degree and achieves success and enough financial independence to support his family and to marry.

The gathering at "Beechwood" breaks up as Louisa goes to visit her uncle Colonel Barton. Gildon, supposedly en route to New York to seek permission to marry her, meets Frank Barton, Louisa's cousin, and wrangles an invitation to the Barton estate, where he seduces Louisa. After he has departed in earnest, Louisa discovers first that she is pregnant and later that Gildon, who has succumbed to his father's threats of economic boycott and to the charms of a rich New York coquette, has "released" her from their engagement.

Although Edward never learns of his sister's seduction, the mere rumor that Gildon spoke of Louisa "in terms of levity" sends him to New York to challenge his old college friend to a duel. After a long but unsuccessful siege, Edward satisfies his "most fastidious" honor by posting notices of Gildon's cowardice in New York coffee houses and prepares to return to Virginia. But chance brings them face to face. In the ensuing fight, Edward draws a gun and is stabbed to death by Gildon.

After the initial shock of Edward's death the Virginia ladies face their fates. Matilda determines to devote herself to God, turns Catholic, and enters a convent at Georgetown. Louisa pays for her sins by dying after a two-year illness, which apparently also causes her to miscarry Gildon's child. Mrs. Grayson lives on alone, "the Lady Bountiful of the neighborhood, a monument of the efficacy of religion in enabling us to bear up against the ills of this life." As for Gildon, he is acquitted of criminal charges by a jury but "condemned to lasting infamy by the public." Deserted by all, he plunges "into the excesses of pleasure and dissipation" and dies, we are told, "a confirmed sot."

Through a lengthy discussion of the causes for Louisa's fall, Tucker fulfilled his explicit intention of supplying "to youth the wisdom and experience of age."[62] Louisa herself provides a competently summarized bill of particulars when she recognizes her folly as "the wretched consequences of imprudent love, of disingenuous concealment, and disobedience to the best of parents!"[63] Her "softness, gentleness, timidity and affection," Tucker explained, were corrupted by reading such a novel as "Mrs. Radcliff's [*sic*] Mysteries of Udolpho," from which she gained "false and exaggerated conceptions

62. *The Valley*, I, v.
63. *Ibid.*, II, 185.

of human life—of the elevated and transcendent virtue of lovers—the raptures of sentimental love, and the necessity of loving to fulfill the destiny of every human being, at least of every young person."[64]

By contrasting Louisa's attitudes toward life with those held by the more admirable Mrs. Grayson and Matilda, Tucker emphasized that happiness in love and life is achieved only by prudently regulating the passions. Mrs. Grayson, who is introduced early in the novel reading "some work of rational piety,"[65] is the perfect model for moral conduct. In her home, love between man and woman, on the latter's part, anyway, is much like a form of religion. For her, "the image of her husband was always associated with a feeling of religion and devotion to which, indeed, pure and virtuous love in woman is very nearly allied."[66] Mrs. Grayson, who doubts the honor of Gildon's intentions toward Louisa from the beginning, struggles to quench her daughter's passion. Noticing Louisa's "suffused cheek and fluttering manner" after Gildon has asked her for a locket in the Graysons' sitting room, she quickly sets to work:

She . . . asked her daughter to play a favourite hymn, in which the Deity is fervently besought to inspire us with good resolutions, to pity our weaknesses and to uphold us in our wavering course—for she was habitually fond of church music, and since her husband's death had never been seen to take pleasure in any other.[67]

When Mrs. Grayson sees that "humility and contrition" have overcome her daughter, she pulls Louisa from the room, tucks her into bed, and reads to her Tillotson's "excellent sermon on the regulation of the passions; for she preferred his vigorous sense, and rational devotion to the more polished compositions of the present day."[68] The temporary effect of this teaching is seen during family worship in the Episcopal Church, when Louisa finds her eyes wandering to meet the glance of Gildon. Conscious of the impropriety of her act as well as of "the terrestrial character of her thoughts," Louisa concentrates upon the hymnal and prayer book until "the predominating feeling of her bosom gained the ascendancy." The combination of heightened emotion and earthly love so overpowers her that she reaches

64. *Ibid.*, I, 91.
65. *Ibid.*, I, 2.
66. *Ibid.*, II, 139.
67. *Ibid.*, I, 309.
68. *Ibid.*, I, 309-311.

a kind of Platonic ecstasy: her love becomes purified, "refined from its earthly dross," and she thinks of her lover as an image of God.[69]

Matilda, who handles her relations with Edward more efficiently than Louisa does hers with Gildon, is the epitome of good sense and clear thinking. She always obeys her parents, yet is able to convince her lover that modest behavior does not preclude affection or pity. As logical as she is righteous, she berates Louisa for lamenting that Gildon may not return from New York by pointing out that his absence indicates "either that he never loved you, or that he sacrifices his love at the shrine of avarice and ambition, in either of which cases, he deserves not your regard."[70] Indeed, Matilda is as sensible and unromantic a female as can be imagined throughout most of the book until the close, after Edward's death, when she accepts "transubstantiation, the worship of saints, and other catholic tenets, that are repugnant to the common understandings of men" and, waiting six months to prove herself prepared for the convent—since "alas, we can never be indifferent to the opinion of the world in our conduct, however conscience may approve of what we do"—she takes the veil forever.[71]

Tucker's second aim in *The Valley* was to delineate in the vein of Scott the manners, customs, and habits of the Virginia people. It seems clear that the Scott whom Tucker had in mind when he composed *The Valley* was not the Scott of those romances dealing with the distant past, not the Scott of *Ivanhoe,* but the Scott of the *Waverley* series, who was concerned with recent and local history. Tucker was drawn to write this sort of historical novel partly, of course, because Cooper proved that such works could be highly profitable for an American. But also Tucker's serious interest in historical writing—later to be demonstrated by a biography of Jefferson and a detailed history of the nation—contributed to his desire to write a social history. *The Valley,* more than anything else Tucker ever wrote, fulfilled his requirements that good history acquaint man with "the progress of society and the arts of civilization; with the advancement and decline of literature, laws, manners, and commerce."[72] In his record of post-Revolutionary society, Tucker emphasized those parts of it which he knew most thoroughly and brought into sharp focus

69. *Ibid.,* I, 312-313.
70. *Ibid.,* II, 190.
71. *Ibid.,* II, 314, 315-316.
72. "Discourse on American Literature: Delivered Before the Charlottesville Lyceum, December 19, 1837," *Southern Literary Messenger,* IV (1838), 85.

the ways of life and the attitudes of people completely different in their national origins as well as in their social and economic status.

One of the most interesting of Tucker's contributions to an understanding of this period of Virginia social history is his lengthy discussion of the races in the state. The Scots from Northern Ireland and the Germans, called Dutch, represented by the Steener family, inhabit the region west of the Blue Ridge.[73] The Germans, most of whom have come down to Virginia from Maryland and Pennsylvania, are a "painstaking, plodding, frugal people." They are without taste or talent for literature and the arts, ignore education and public affairs, and cast their votes purely from selfish motives or because they have been flattered. They amass property slowly but certainly and, though of phlegmatic temperament, are constantly in the courts. In short, "they are the drayhorses of society," good for "coarse but useful labour."[74] The Scotch-Irish, on the other hand, are as ardent, impassioned, bold, and imaginative as the Germans are dull and slow. "When bent on . . . gain or ambition, they manifest great enterprise and perseverance; but are often idle, indolent, and improvident." Extremely individualistic and brave, they serve as "the advance guard of civilization," and after conquering the Indian, they distinguished themselves in arts, politics, education, and religion. The Scots have considerably more "pride and intolerance" than have other Presbyterians and exert great forcefulness in politics. When they settle in large groups, as in Pennsylvania, they retain their hatred for the English and their democratic spirit and politics; but when dispersed, as in Virginia, where Americans classify all as either "French" or "English," they ally themselves with the Federalist party, which they support with great skill.[75]

In *The Valley,* though Tucker can appreciate the obstinate pertinacity of the Germans, his sympathies are clearly closer to the Scotch-Irish, whose virtues and vices he fuses in the character of M'Culloch. A former Jacobin, M'Culloch has been driven into the Federalist ranks by the outrageous attacks upon "the old general" and the horrors of the French Revolution. He has lost much of his once prospering property and is forced to consider moving from his beloved Virginia to Kentucky—that *"el Dorado* of all bad managers"—where his family will "feast on bear-hams and buffalo hump." Even his home evidences the "liberal thoughtless disposition" and "bad management" that lie

73. *The Valley,* I, 47-48.
74. *Ibid.,* I, 49-54.
75. *Ibid.,* I, 54-57.

behind his financial distress. A rickety fence, supported by props, sur-
rounds his unpainted house, whose broken windows are stuffed with
pillows and old coats, and in his front parlor, unmatched and shabby
furniture sits incongruously upon an expensive, luxurious rug.[76]

In contrast to both the Scotch-Irish and the Germans are those
Virginians descended from English stock who inhabit chiefly the
eastern portion of the state. Tucker was concerned not with analyzing
their national characteristics but with depicting them as America's
true aristocrats. Drawing upon his own remembrances of Williamsburg during this period, Tucker described a group of fifteen or twenty
well-to-do families living in idyllic contentment. In the evenings,
they discuss literature, politics, and science and entertain one another
by composing *bouts rimés* and playing charades. Here, said Tucker,
were the

advantages of wealth, without parade or rivalship, learning without
pedantry or awkwardness, frankness without rusticity, refinement without
insincerity or affectation, luxury unattended with gaming or any excess,
and a free intercourse between the sexes, with the most perfect innocence
and purity of manners.[77]

On the same side of the Blue Ridge and of the same stock are the
wealthy planters, typified by Colonel Barton, Mrs. Grayson's brother,
who represents higher classes everywhere, yet is uniquely a product of
Virginia plantation life. In one concise paragraph, Tucker described
him as one of those

more fond of hospitality than show; great epicures at table; great lovers
of Madeira wine, of horses and dogs; free at a jest . . . ; with a goodly
store of family pride, and a moderate portion of learning; never disputing
a bill, and seldom paying a debt, until, like their Madeira, it had acquired
age; scrupulously neat in their persons but affecting plainness and simplicity in their dress; kind and indulgent, rather than faithful husbands,
deeming some variety essential in all gratifications of the appetite.[78]

Tucker made it clear that gentility was a quality independent of
wealth, at least in Virginia's fluid economic situation. The Graysons,
for example, originally rich planters from the eastern seaboard, have
lost their wealth but not their birthright. All their neighbors, including even the loan sharks who are taking their property, give them
due obeisance, remembering their aristocratic descent and their regal

76. *Ibid.,* I, 41, 44, 58, 168-169, 170.
77. *Ibid.,* II, 52.
78. *Ibid.,* II, 105-106.

life at court before the American Revolution. Mrs. Grayson, though "mild and gentle as a dove, possesses," says her son, "a loftiness and pride of character" which ensures her superiority over the Steeners.[79] Like his father, Edward Grayson himself displays "that air of mingled frankness and courtesy . . . so difficult for any one to catch who has not been bred a gentleman." He has "the most scrupulous and fastidious honour" and, though somewhat haughty to those who do not recognize their inferiority, he is "all mildness and consideration" to those who are "acknowledged inferiors."[80]

As a part of his discussion of Virginians, Tucker commented finally upon a fourth race, the Negroes. As much as any novelist of the South, Tucker knew that the institution of slavery provided the underpinning of Virginia plantation life. He described closely slaves' cabins and their ways of life, their loyalty to the whites, whom they emulate and love. He affirmed that the blacks are happy in their bondage and that they are an integral part of a complicated social system which, despite a few unattractive features, is well worth preserving.[81]

Drawing upon observations gathered during his first years as an immigrant in the new nation, Tucker discussed the schisms between Federalist and Jeffersonian Republican, incorporating with his treatment of local politics intelligent and informed commentary upon Virginia's legal system. He treated tolerantly the moderate republicanism of Edward and Gildon, but he firmly denounced those extremists who cite the "fluent, ardent, and specious" doctrines of Godwin's *Political Justice* to attack Washington.[82] Tucker lauded the rectitude and dignity of the courts and sympathized with convivial and hard-working lawyers, exposed as they are to the "grossness and vulgarity," the "knavery and frauds" of "ill-mannered, low-minded" rural clients who hang upon the words of uneducated frontier orators.[83]

Humor and satire in the novel reinforce the delineation of a society in the process of change. The *nouveaux riches* are ridiculed for their ignorance and pretensions. Neither Major Fawkner's "Dutch" wife nor a wealthy, over-confident South Carolinian fop can appreciate the moral code of the Graysons. Frederick Steener, Ma-

79. *Ibid.*, I, 117.
80. *Ibid.*, I, 3, 11.
81. For a full discussion of slavery in *The Valley,* see below, Pt. III, pp. 188-192.
82. *The Valley,* II, 27-28.
83. *Ibid.*, I, 224-226, 229.

tilda's cousin, however, is good-naturedly portrayed in his bungling poor taste. Educated at Lexington and therefore lacking the polish of William and Mary graduates, Steener, much like Squire Western, is more interested in hunting and eating than in good conversation. Described as "stout, square-built, full faced" and indifferent to women, at least "to that portion of the sex which is best worth knowing," he is without grace of any kind. Much to his Aunt Fawkner's dismay, he plans to marry Susan Tidball, an innkeeper's daughter, because "she was a fine hearty girl, and would not require nursing, like your chalk-faced chits, who cut themselves in two, like so many wasps."[84] Steener's letter to Susan, a mixture of stilted rhetoric from his aunt's *Complete Letter Book* and such a statement of his own as "if I knock under to a woman, it must be a young one,"[85] might well have been cited by Tucker as an example of the incongruous combination of elements for his essay "On the Ludicrous."[86]

Although in *The Valley* Tucker clearly met his expressed intentions—to impart moral instruction and to delineate life in late eighteenth-century Virginia—he failed to write a good novel. The weaknesses in his work are many. Despite obvious efforts to reproduce speech habits, especially of rustics and slaves, more often than not Tucker failed to write idiomatic dialogue. For the most part, his characters are stock creations who exist either to illustrate the moral lessons Tucker wished to inculcate or, more importantly, to serve merely as representative models of their society. Among the major figures, Gildon alone is complex enough to be interesting for his own sake, and even in his delineation, Tucker did not portray him through dramatic action or speech and was too often content to assert what he was supposed to be—"one of those mixed and imperfect characters, which though seldom found in novels, are very commonly met in real life."[87] When describing the emotions of his cast as under great strain, Tucker resorted to the conventions of those very sentimental romances whose unreality—albeit on other grounds—he frequently condemned. Lovers are overcome by slight shows of affection and reflect their agitated feelings in sighs, blushes, and sobs. When Matilda conveys to Edward through Louisa a locket containing one of her dark curls, Edward "experienced that delight which can be known only to those whose feelings have been refined and sublimated

84. *Ibid.*, II, 62-63, 64.
85. *Ibid.*, II, 81.
86. *Essays, Moral and Metaphysical* (Philadelphia, 1860), pp. 203-217.
87. *The Valley*, I, 173.

by sentimental love. . . . He kissed the little present again and again, with the most rapturous joy, and it was some time before he would forego the luxury of his feelings. . . ."[88]

As a result of his understandable attempts to appeal to a wide audience and to survey as much of Virginia life as he could, Tucker introduced into his chronicle more elements than he could bring together successfully. In order to make use of his own experiences on a trip to New York in 1796, for example, Tucker caused Edward, then in hot pursuit of Gildon, to while away several days in Philadelphia, calling upon General Washington, inspecting a model jail, and touring Congress and local museums.[89] Sometimes Tucker's lack of selectivity results in more serious flaws, as in his failure to maintain a desirable uniformity of tone in certain scenes. Thus, Mrs. Grayson's close brush with death is developed without cause into a satire, bordering on burlesque, when Tucker ridicules the medical profession by allowing three farcical doctors—Selby, Blodget, and Manifee (or Minorfee)—to argue for their pet "depleting remedies" over her sick bed.[90]

One of Tucker's greatest difficulties stemmed from an inability to move gracefully from the story of the Graysons' decline to those sections of the novel which, best remembered by cultural historians,[91] are devoted to discussing Virginia social history. Almost all of the digressions, some of which are almost irrelevant to the plot, are introduced awkwardly into the story as answers to innumerable questions posed by Gildon, who, like Tucker's anticipated audience, knew little about the region. For example, before Tucker began his long essay upon the characteristics of the Germans and the Scotch-Irish, given in the form of Edward's answer to Gildon, he announced, with the heavy hand evident throughout the book, that Chapter IV "may seem very dull prosing to some of my readers," who may therefore thumb through it without losing the thread of the narrative, "though we would modestly hint, that sometimes the mountain, whose waste and barren surface exhibits neither flower nor leaf, often contains valuable materials to those who will take the trouble of searching a little deeper for them."[92]

88. *Ibid.*, I, 307.
89. *Ibid.*, II, 247-250.
90. *Ibid.*, II, 149-152.
91. See, for example, Shields McIlwaine, *The Southern Poor White from Lubberland to Tobacco Road* (Norman, Okla., 1939), pp. 20-21.
92. *The Valley*, I, 48.

To catalogue further weaknesses in Tucker's novel would serve little useful purpose, since the defects are readily apparent and are much the same as the faults committed by other fledgling novelists of this period in America. It is worth while, instead, to examine the novel in relationship to the philosophical concept which strongly influenced almost all of Tucker's writings—the idea of the gradual progress of society. In 1822, two years before he composed *The Valley,* Tucker published a volume of essays expressing an optimistic acceptance of the economic and social changes in the United States, heralding them as sure indications of the nation's emergence as the most powerful and cultivated country on the globe. Although a part of Tucker's early optimism can be written off as characteristic of the nationalism of the period—some of the essays having been composed shortly after the War of 1812—Tucker's belief in the beneficence of progress was deep-seated and life-long.

The Valley, unlike the essays, is not a tract praising the nation's progress, for the hero and his family fall—victims of economic change. But the whole study of Virginia life in the 1790's rests upon the assumption that the laws which control the progress of a society are unalterable and impersonal. *The Valley,* indeed, provides the clearest picture Tucker ever presented of a society in the process of inevitable economic and social evolution. The novel is built around the effects which alterations in economic fortune have upon the Grayson family. To emphasize the Graysons' decline as well as the flux of society, Tucker constantly juxtaposed the past and the present by causing Granny Moll, an ancient and loyal slave, or sometimes Edward Grayson himself, to call up visions of the idyllic past when the Graysons lived in regal but unostentatious quiet near Williamsburg as the intimates and equals of General Braddock and Lord Botetourt. In contrast to the old Virginia families, beaten in the economic struggle and fleeing west to new farms, are the new orders that are playing a more and more important role in society: the Steener family who have achieved wealth and social respectability despite their descent from indentured servants, an ex-overseer who is now able to buy the Graysons' slaves for his own cotton plantation in Georgia, the loan-shark Hatchett, and the overseer at "Beechwood," who is accumulating rich farmland in the Tidewater.

In emphasis, *The Valley* is essentially different from any other of Tucker's works in that it reflects not his enthusiasm for change but his acute recognition of the price exacted as a result of social and economic evolution. Here Tucker is not the prophet of progress who looks hopefully to the future and extols the material benefits of a complex society, but the traditionalist who looks nostalgically to the past, lamenting the loss of much that is good. Simple good taste and gentility, as represented by the Graysons, are being replaced by the crude social standards and boorish manners of ex-servants and second- or third-generation Americans. Yet Tucker's disturbance at what he depicts as having occurred is, even in this novel, partially balanced by a belief in the justice of economic laws. His opinion thus modified is reflected in the conclusion at which Edward arrives as he explains to Gildon the causes for the fall of Virginia's aristocrats:

All this is perhaps as it should be, but the change often furnishes subjects of melancholy contemplation to those who can feel for the fallen, and with a good deal of blame on the reckless course of expense they have pursued, and contempt for their deplorable incapacity for business or labour, and their silly pride, there is mingled a lively pity for their humiliation and distress.[93]

By attempting to attribute the shifts of fortune to specific causes, Tucker hit upon the underlying theme of the novel—the effects which generations-old economic incompetency has upon Southern and primarily Virginian life. This theme, which comes close to pulling together many of the dissimilar elements of the story, evinces Tucker's intention to yoke into meaningful relationship the story of the Graysons' fall from opulence and happiness to poverty and despair with the social and economic analyses which make up so much of the novel. In Colonel Grayson's wasteful extravagances and in his consideration for all except his family are the seeds of the sentimental tragedy that descends upon his heirs. It is indeed to escape from the demands of the "thoughtless hospitality" which her husband had been accustomed to extend to others and from "the idle, social habits of her neighbors" that Mrs. Grayson moves from "Easton" to "Beechwood." The Colonel, a tender, generous, and respected man, was, as Edward tells Gildon, too good-natured, too trusting, too gullible. He placed too much faith in his agents, was too lenient in disciplining his slaves, sentimentally stood surety for the debts of friends, and squandered money in waste lands in the hope of quick profit.[94] In slaveholding states, Edward explains, landowners, brought up as they are in ease and idleness and with refined tastes, spend their income before they get it, partly be-

93. *Ibid.*, I, 112-113.
94. *Ibid.*, I, 1, 65.

cause they insist upon living beyond their means and partly because they foolishly believe the sanguine statements of overseers. Since they find that they can borrow money easily, using their slaves and land as security, they are able to delude themselves and sometimes their creditors about their mismanagement. Such lax attitudes are especially prevalent among the aristocrats, the first settlers of the Old Dominion, who find they cannot compete against the more frugal, industrious, or avaricious parvenus who are gradually taking over their farms.[95]

Though Edward can thus elaborate on the faults of his class, he, ironically, does not benefit from the knowledge himself. When he visits "Easton" to look over the slaves and property before selling them, Edward is easily gulled by the "adroit politician" Cutchins, the overseer of "Easton" for his father before him and for himself. Cutchins evades Edward's questions on crops and slaves, and it is only after an old slave explains the situation to him and after Cutchins becomes rude that Edward realizes how much profit the overseer has siphoned off the Grayson land to buy an estate and slaves of his own.[96]

The Graysons' errors are shared by others, even, sometimes, by those outside their class. In the Tidewater, Colonel Barton lives in luxury, and he and his son Frank make a splendid living from their estates, but this is solely because they have honest overseers. Frank Barton's habits as an inveterate loo player and idler will surely, Tucker made clear, lose him his property.[97] And Hatchett, the money-lender, is about ready to seize all of the goods of the admirable M'Culloch.[98]

Indeed, throughout the book, the possession or lack of money determines the destiny of the characters. Had the Graysons retained their wealth, Louisa, Gildon, Edward, and Matilda would have been happy. The point is driven home by Tucker through the amassing of details of a new economic force, personified by the Steeners, Hatchett, and Cutchins, and illustrated by the consequent passing of the Graysons. It is dramatized in the auctions of slaves and household goods and examined through pages and pages of dull discussions on the fertility of soil, the relative advantages of slave and free labor, and the virtues and vices of overseers. The moral to be gained from the sad story of the Graysons, summed up by Edward and reiterated by Tucker time and time again, is that prudence in money matters

95. *Ibid.*, I, 109-113.
96. *Ibid.*, II, 39-44.
97. *Ibid.*, II, 100, 112-113.
98. *Ibid.*, II, 160-161.

is the first of all virtues.[99] The novel, then, may be read as a parable urging the remaining "true old breed" of Virginians to mend their ways, to avoid being ruined by the ironclad laws of economics, and to "progress" with the rest of the nation.

Tucker's debut as a novelist was not successful. Harpers offered him five hundred dollars for the manuscript if he would remain in New York to supervise its printing, explaining their low bid by saying that they would have to pay a translator fifty dollars to decipher the handwriting. Tucker refused, because, he said in 1858 when the novel was no longer important to him, a book that one had to pay someone to read was not worth bothering about. Tucker's determination to sell the novel elsewhere, though understandable when it is remembered that he felt he needed a large profit and could not afford to linger in New York, was unfortunate. Charles Wiley, with whom he signed a contract calling for a division of profits and expenses, soon failed in business, and Tucker received for his pains only several hundred copies of *The Valley*. Tucker, who had been postponing his decision whether to try to earn his living as a novelist or to become professor of moral philosophy, finally accepted the academic post, still hopeful, however, he said in 1858, of trying another novel "in the same line, in which I would bestow that labour which I was now satisfied was indispensable to success."[100] At the time, nevertheless, Tucker's hopes for *The Valley* to sell remained high, for in 1827 he traveled again to New York to arrange for a second edition, which was published in 1828 by Orville A. Roorbach but which seems to have been no more marketable than the first.[101]

Tucker reasoned that *The Valley* failed because of its unhappy ending and because "its catastrophe was offensive to Virginia pride," a conclusion which, however incompletely accurate, exerted an obviously adverse effect upon his later works. For Tucker never again wrote a serious story whose outcome was to so great an extent de-

---

99. *Ibid.*, II, 39.

100. "Autobiography," p. 37.

101. Tucker to Maria Tucker, Aug. 24, 1827, Tucker-Harrison-Smith Papers, University of Virginia Library. Tucker did not mention the second New York edition in his "Autobiography," but he did write that *The Valley* was "reprinted in London and was translated into German" (p. 37). Samuel Allibone, *Critical Dictionary of English Literature and British and American Authors* (Philadelphia, 1876), III, 2464, repeats this information. Hubbell, *The South in American Literature*, p. 245, says mistakenly, so far as Tucker's knowledge is concerned: "Although Tucker did not know it, a second edition was published in New York in 1828 besides one in London and still another in Germany." I have been unable to substantiate either foreign publication, but a copy of the New York 1828 edition is in the Library of Congress.

termined by the logic of the characters' situations. It is possible, of
course, that even if *The Valley* had sold well, Tucker might not have
written another in the same vein, for, to a degree impossible to determine, the book was influenced in its conception and writing by a
multiplicity of personal calamities which never again so overwhelmed
him. His wife, it will be recalled, died in 1823 after a long and
painful illness. Tucker's anguish was great. Her loss, he said, was
like "that which parts the soul from the body." He reproached himself at the time for having burdened her with overwork on the frontier
to help him to achieve success,[102] and in *The Valley,* it seems, he
attempted to do her justice by portraying her as Mrs. Grayson. Following hard upon her death was the fearful recognition that all of his
and his wife's sacrifices in distasteful rural Virginia threatened to go for
naught because he could not raise the cash to pay his many pressing
creditors. And associated with his own troubles and probably of
particularly great force at this time were those of his wife's parents,
whose depressed economic situation seems to have given Tucker the
germ for his story. Clearly enough, the novel reflects that it was
written, as Tucker told St. George, in a "melancholy hour,"[103] the
intensity of which never occurred again, for after 1825 Tucker re-
covered his good spirits and lived a life relatively free from misfortunes. In any event, probably because he never felt so deeply
again and was unwilling to write a work which might not be
popular, he made sure that all his subsequent efforts ended, at the
expense of all probability, as happily as possible. Instead of pro-
gressing as a writer of fiction, which perhaps he might have done,
Tucker seriously deteriorated.

102. Tucker to St. George Tucker, Feb. 27, 1823, Tucker-Coleman Collection,
Colonial Williamsburg.

103. Tucker to St. George Tucker, April 25, 1825, Tucker-Coleman Collection,
Colonial Williamsburg.

CHAPTER VIII

PROFESSORIAL WRITINGS

A VOYAGE TO THE MOON

DURING THE FIRST YEAR of his professorship of moral philosophy, Tucker's academic duties consumed most of his time and energy, and he made no attempt to write fiction. But he was always one to make use of every bit of information he acquired, and, after two years in Charlottesville, he discovered that the preparation he had made for his lectures provided him with material for a new book. In 1827 he published in New York under the pseudonym of "Joseph Atterley" *A Voyage to the Moon.* Unlike *The Valley,* a complete financial failure which seems to have been ignored by the press and probably was not read by many people, *A Voyage* was relatively successful. It earned Tucker one hundred dollars, was reviewed favorably in two important magazines,[1] and was sold to one thousand readers.

In his new work, Tucker continued the vein of satire begun in his contributions to the *Old Bachelor* and carried on in parts of *The Valley* and, perhaps, in *Letters from Virginia,* but he composed *A Voyage* in a different form and largely for different purposes. Tucker's earlier satirical writings, intended to expose the foibles of Virginians, dealt with the everyday happenings of his fellow citizens. *A Voyage,* though it contains some criticism of the manners of Tucker's contemporaries, is primarily concerned with ridiculing "the errors of the day in science and philosophy"[2] and takes place in a fantastic, other-worldly setting. An old Brahmin, who has discovered in a metallic substance the principle of repulsion from the earth, persuades Joseph Atterley, the narrator of *A Voyage,* to accompany him on a trip to the moon. In order to

1. Anonymous, *Western Monthly Review,* I (1828), 674-676; [Robley Dunglison], *American Quarterly Review,* III (1828), 61-88.

2. "Autobiography," manuscript copy, Tucker-Harrison-Smith Papers, University of Virginia Library, p. 39.

give some air of plausibility to Atterley's extraordinary adventure, Tucker carefully described the journey in outer-space and straight-forwardly narrated the facts of Atterley's life and the events preceding and following his trip.

Much of the satire in *A Voyage* is too general and pointless to merit detailed recording—especially the part intended to prove that, though the Lunarians have customs foreign to those of earthdwellers, they have the same "passions and propensities."[3] Tucker described, for example, the follies of female moon dwellers who cover themselves like birds with feathered coats and wear simulated bills, decorate their bonnets with live insects, and, if they are young and vain, wear glass crystals to cover their bosoms.[4]

Also of a general nature is Tucker's ridicule of certain aspects of religion. While visiting an acquaintance, Atterley notices his host's daughter descending the stairs backwards, an art which he at first takes to be "a mere girlish freak, or perhaps a piece of coquetry." Only later does he discover that "about the time the earth is at the full, the whole family pursued the same course . . . because it is one of the prescribed forms of their church."[5] In the country of Morosofia, Atterley is provided with proof that "although religion cherishes our best feelings, it also provides a cloak for the worst." He watches a family at dinner eat unattractive parts of food, only to obey the impulse of nature and eat the best when they think themselves to be unobserved.[6]

Of more lasting interest is the satirical treatment of the professions. On the moon, cases at law are settled through the matching of hired prize fighters who are close friends outside the ring. Although ordinarily the judgment is given to the fighter with the greatest "strength and wind," the judges often assign victory on rules and precedents "known only to themselves, if known at all."[7]

Lunar medical treatment, Tucker made clear, is like that practiced on earth. In a scene reminiscent of the treatment of Mrs. Grayson's illness in *The Valley* but perfectly in keeping with the comic and satiric tone of *A Voyage*, Tucker derides both the pretensions of physicians and the absurdity of their remedies. Dr. Shuro, while attending to a

3. *A Voyage to the Moon: With Some Account of the Manners and Customs, Science and Philosophy, of the People of Morosofia, and Other Lunarians* (New York, 1827), p. 37.

4. *Ibid.*, pp. 96-97.

5. *Ibid.*, p. 120.

6. *Ibid.*, pp. 98-100.

7. *Ibid.*, pp. 175-177.

victim already weakened by natural discharges, justifies his wishes to bleed him and perform other evacuations. Fuming at those physicians who follow the "empirical" method, he cites his essay on the morbid action, in which he has illustrated that "disease is an unit, and that it is extreme folly to divide diseases into classes, which tend but to produce confusion of ideas, and an unscientific practice." Dr. Shackrack has completely different notions about medicine and about what Shuro has called the "beautiful simplicity" of his theory; he would "stimulate" everyone. "Pour in the *stimularetia* and *irritentia,* and my life for it, the patient is saved." Dr. Dridano, called in consultation to resolve the dispute, explains the errors of both the other attendants. The body, he says, is a mere machine in which various fluids get obstructed. He would call a session of maturer doctors to convince his colleagues "whether we shall blister, or sweat, or bleed, or salivate"—any one of which remedies would be beneficial. When Dr. Shuro accuses him of stealing his theory, Dridano denies the imputation: "You use several remedies for one disease: I admit several diseases, and use one remedy." As they shout and wrestle about the room, the Brahmin cures the old patient, and the doctors, after collecting their fees, rush off to publish their cures in learned medical journals.[8]

If such broad humor found a sure audience among those familiar with nineteenth-century physicians, other parts of the satire were not so readily appreciated. One anonymous reviewer, who claimed to see the influence of Swift in *A Voyage* and even praised Tucker for showing more learning and less grossness than Swift, complained that Tucker had so carefully concealed "the hidden and allegorical" meanings in his satire that it was not worth the difficulty of digging them out.[9] He was obviously referring to those portions of *A Voyage* in which Tucker, by satirizing the philosophers and scientists on the moon, really attacked their counterparts on earth, hoping, he said, to illustrate "the errors of the learned, and 'the follies of the wise.' "[10] Although Tucker did allude obscurely to contemporary thinkers and to philosophic and scientific theories, some of both seem to be identifiable.

At the school of Lozzi Pozzi [Pestalozzi] students carry instead of books sticks of various dimensions, each marked with a number. By juggling the sticks, they solve problems in all assigned courses. In

8. *Ibid.,* pp. 155-162.
9. *Western Monthly Review,* pp. 674-676.
10. *A Voyage,* p. 16.

grammar, for example, "the rules of syntax were discovered by pieces of wood, interlocking with each other in squares, dovetails, &c. after the manner of geographic canals."[11]

Wigurd, possibly William Godwin, a "voluble, earnest, and disputatious" little man whose philosophical opinions are more irregular than immoral, invites several "enlightened and congenial minds" to a dinner, during which each guest is forced to eat what he does not wish, although Wigurd claims he gives each his choice. Wigurd spouts his opinions on morals and legislation and asserts that all who oppose him are fools, biased by their petty interests or duped by their prejudices. The company discuss philosophy, the foundations of which Wigurd tests by utility or truth, according to his convenience.

If any custom or institution which he had denounced, was justified by his adversaries on the ground of its expediency, he immediately retorted on them its repugnancy to sincerity, truth, and sophisticated nature; and if they . . . resorted to a similar justification for our natural feelings and propensities, he triumphantly showed that they were inimical to the public good. Thus, he condemned gratitude as a sentiment calculated to weaken the sense of justice, and to substitute feeling for reason. He, on the other hand, proscribed the little forms and courtesies, which are either founded in convenience, or give a grace and sweetness to social intercourse, as a direct violation of honest nature, and therefore odious and mean. He was thus able to silence every opponent.[12]

Among the moon's inhabitants are Glonglims, a species born without intellect and cared for by the government until, by a mysterious influence which the moon exerts upon the earth, an earthly inhabitant loses a portion of his understanding to his counterpart on the moon, who then conforms to the earthman in thought and action.[13] The most striking representative of this breed of people, who are characterized by a wildness in the eyes, is a "lively, flippant little personage . . . one of the most distinguished literati of the country," by the name of Reffei [Francis Jeffrey]. On hearing Atterley extol the odor of the rose, Reffei tries to prove to him that his "popular prejudice" misleads him and that

the chief part of the gratification . . . arises from some past scene of delight, of which it reminds you; as, of the days of your innocence and

11. *Ibid.*, pp. 164-167.
12. *Ibid.*, pp. 112-114, 117-118.
13. *Ibid.*, p. 38.

childhood, when you ran about the garden—or when you were decorated with nosegays—or danced round a may-pole, (this is rather a free translation)—or presented a bunch of flowers to some little favourite.

Atterley is convinced of the truth of this "ingenious" theory until the smell of a rose temporarily causes him to revert to his old belief, at which point, however, he recalls Reffei and "mentally added thanks to divine philosophy, which always corrects our natural prejudices."[14]

Despite its essentially satiric character, *A Voyage* contains long, purely expository discussions of such topics as the causes for differences in habits, customs, and manners of various races and the errors in Ricardo's theory of rents. It ends with an Oriental tale recounting the Brahmin's romantic past, his ardent love for Veenah, frustrated by the machinations of an inherently evil Batty Mahn who causes her death by suttee. Why Tucker concluded his intellectual satire in this fashion can best be explained, perhaps, by his hope to appeal to that portion of his readers who had no taste for satire, philosophy, or economics. If this is so, his judgment would seem to have been acute, for the anonymous reviewer who found the philosophy so indigestible praised the sentimental romance as the best of the book. "It is simple, natural, pathetic, and affecting."[15]

A Voyage has considerably more polish than any of Tucker's previous publications, and its writing indicates that a good deal of care was lavished upon it; yet problems of structure which so bothered Tucker in *The Valley* were rather side-stepped than conquered in this work, for its modest plan of organization called for no more than a casual linking together of anecdotal essays within a contrived framework. Largely because of the topical nature of most of the subjects treated in the book, the satire has now lost much of its point, and the volume is significant chiefly for the light it throws on some of the interesting social and intellectual issues of the early nineteenth century. It indicates, further, that Tucker's acceptance of the chair of moral philosophy did, as he predicted,[16] turn his literary interests away from the concerns of his fellow Virginians which he had explored somewhat successfully in *The Valley*.

14. *Ibid.*, pp. 206-208. See below, Pt. III, pp. 121-124, 156-157, for Tucker's treatment of Jeffrey's use of associational psychology to explain the origins of the beautiful.

15. *Western Monthly Review,* p. 676.

16. Tucker to Joseph C. Cabell, Jan. 1, 1824 [1825], Cabell Deposit, University of Virginia Library.

VIRGINIA LITERARY MUSEUM

ATTRIBUTIONS OF AUTHORSHIP

During his fourth year at the University, Tucker joined with his colleague, Dr. Robley Dunglison, to found *The Virginia Literary Museum*,[17] a weekly magazine whose purpose—as stated in the prospectus printed in the first issue on June 17, 1829—was "to communicate the truths and discoveries of Science to the miscellaneous reader, and to encourage a taste for polite literature." Contributions were to be made by faculty members, whose minds would be "kept in a state of active inquiry" by their lectures. Along with essays on "Moral or Physical Science, Philology and Polite Literature" were to be included histories of Virginia and other states, with an account of their peculiarities in customs, manners, language, and progress.[18] Perhaps to encourage practical and political support, the magazine carried official University announcements and copies of examinations given by teachers in the various departments. As Dunglison explained to Madison some four months before its first issue, the magazine thus would save the University money and would keep its name constantly before the public.[19]

Since all the articles in the *Literary Museum* were signed with various pseudonyms, establishing the authorship of the papers is extremely difficult. Except for four or five short articles and the poetry, all of the work was done by those within the University.[20] Most of the poems, all those signed "D.C.T.," were done by Dabney Carr Terrel, who died before the magazine began publication,[21] though Tucker, as "Mercutio," published a humorous poem in twelve stanzas called "The Tariff," "suggested by the remark recently made by Mr. Webster in his celebrated speech in the Senate."[22] Most of the

---

17. *The Virginia Literary Museum and Journal of Belles Lettres, Arts, Sciences &c.*, was printed by F. Carr in Charlottesville, Va., and issued on Wednesday of each week. The price was $5.00 per year.

18. No. 1 (June 17, 1829), 1. All fifty-two issues of the *Literary Museum* are numbered Volume I.

19. Cited in Philip Alexander Bruce, *History of the University of Virginia* (New York, 1920), III, 346.

20. "Q," "To the Public," No. 52 (June 9, 1830), 817-818.

21. Bruce, *History of the University of Virginia*, II, 249.

22. No. 35 (Feb. 10, 1830), 559-560. J. W. Wayland, "The Virginia Literary Museum," *Publications of the Southern History Association*, VI (1902), 9, assigns this work to Tucker. Webster is reported by "Mercutio" to have said: "It was the tariff! tariff! tariff! everything began with it and ended with it! He believed if there was *any word to rhyme with it,* all their sonnets would be on the same subject." I have found no quotation exactly like this in Webster's speeches as recorded in the National

members of the University faculty made occasional contributions,[23] but Dunglison and Tucker, the editors, both emphasize in their unpublished autobiographies that, since their colleagues took little interest in the magazine, the two of them wrote almost all of the 831 double-columned pages of the *Literary Museum* during its one-year life.[24] Tucker nowhere specifically states what he wrote, but it is possible, by eliminating what Dunglison wrote and by examining the contents of the remaining articles and comparing them with Tucker's acknowledged works, to determine his contributions with some accuracy. Dunglison signed his "necessarily numerous, and . . . varied" articles "Zy, *, D, zy, Ψ, xy, wy, Yy, β, Δ, Γ, Θ, z, φ, Y, Σ, and Zephaniah Stump."[25] Dr. Samuel D. Gross, a friend and colleague of Dunglison at the Jefferson Medical College, lists the following representative but incomplete list of titles as coming from Dunglison's pen:

Fashions and Dress in England at the commencement of the Seventeenth Century; Onomatopoeia; Modern Improved Systems of Road-making; Certain ceremonies connected with the Dead; Anthropology; Blondel and Richard the Lion-Heart; English Provincialisms; Penitentiary Discipline; Universities; Legends of the English Lakes; Superstitions; Americanisms; Early German Poetry; Etymological History; Sanscrit Language; Ancient and Modern Gymnasia; Cradle of Mankind; English Orthoepy; Canals of the Ancients, and Jeffersoniana.[26]

Edition of his addresses. But the reference is probably to one of the following of Webster's replies to Senator Robert Y. Hayne of South Carolina, as cited in *The Writings and Speeches of Daniel Webster,* ed. J. W. McIntyre (Boston, 1903): "First Speech on Foot's Resolution" (Jan. 20, 1830) in V, 248-269; "Second Speech on Foot's Resolution" (Jan. 26 and 27, 1830) in VI, 3-75; "Last Remarks on Foot's Resolution" (Jan. 27, 1830) in VI, 76-80. The poem in the *Literary Museum* is neither an attack nor a defense of the tariff, but the effect of the verse is to minimize the significance of the issue in national affairs.

23. Tucker, "Autobiography," p. 41. Bruce, *History of the University of Virginia,* II, 249, says Bonnycastle, the only contributor he mentions outside of Tucker, Dunglison, and Terrel, wrote a sketch called "Story of the Blue Ridge." A note in a volume at the University of Virginia Library states that Charles Bonnycastle signed his work "PZ" and that Robert M. Patterson used the pseudonym "Trevor."

24. Tucker, "Autobiography," p. 41. Tucker says he and Dunglison edited the magazine on separate weeks. See also Dunglison, "Autobiographical Ana," manuscript copy, Library of the College of Physicians and Surgeons of Philadelphia, I, 24.

25. "Ana," I, 24. Dunglison's handwritten list of the pseudonyms he used correlates closely, though not completely, with signatures I have found in the *Literary Museum:* Zy, *, Z. Y., Ψ, X. Y., XY., Xy., Wy., Yy., β, Δ, Γ, Θ, Z., φ, Y, Σ, and Zephaniah Stump.

26. "Memoir of Robley Dunglison, M.D., LL.D.," *Summary of the Transactions of the College of Physicians of Philadelphia* n.s., IV (Feb., 1863-May, 1874), 299. Jay B. Hubbell, *The South in American Literature, 1607-1900* (Durham, N.C., 1954), pp. 967-968, mistakenly lists the series of articles called "Americanisms" as "probably by

Tucker's non-fictional contributions seem to have been written under the initials "V," "Q," "K," and, probably, "C.C." All of the essays so signed deal with subjects which Tucker taught or in which he was interested, and these, as well as the tales and sketches written under these pseudonyms, have striking resemblances to his published works and his unpublished novel. On July 20, 1829, Madison, in a letter to Tucker asking for a back number of the *Literary Museum,* enclosed his subscription fee of five dollars and an original draft of the Constitution of Virginia, to be published in the magazine when its pages were "not otherwise appropriated."[27] A copy appeared without accompanying initials in the fifteenth number along with the fourth essay of a series of papers printed from July 22 to September 30, 1829, all signed "V," which discuss proposed changes in the Constitution to be considered by the convention meeting in Richmond. The arguments presented for and against one point, for example— whether county court magistrates should be selected by the legislature from legally trained candidates or be chosen by influential families— are exactly those debated by lawyers Trueheart and Hardy in *The Valley*[28] and establish "V" as one of Tucker's pseudonyms.

As definitely his are those papers signed "Q," many of which are almost exactly like his signed articles. Printed under this initial are "The Siamese Twins," in which, in expressing his reasons for wanting to interview Chang and Eng, he used even the same phraseology found in his accounts published after his meeting with the twins.[29] A second selected example which illustrates the close tie between his acknowledged work and the pieces in the *Literary Museum* signed "Q" is

Tucker." M. M. Mathews, *The Beginnings of American English: Essays and Comments* (Chicago, 1931), p. 99; and Gross, "Memoir of Dunglison," p. 299, are correct in assigning the series to Dunglison, since the articles are signed "Wy," a pseudonym used by Dunglison, who, "a close student of philology and general literature" (Russell H. Chittenden, "Robley Dunglison," *DAB,* V, 512-513), also wrote in the *Literary Museum* upon the dialects of Ireland, Man, Yorkshire, and Cumberland.

Dunglison did the "Jeffersoniana," though Tucker, as "V," published a note to the first issue (No. 1, 14-15), defending the utility of reading Hume on history despite Jefferson's strictures on Hume's partiality to the Stuarts, and, as "V," wrote "Jefferson's Memoir and Correspondence," No. 4 (July 8, 1829), 49-51, and No. 5 (July 15, 1829), 68-70.

27. Madison to Tucker, July 20, 1829, Madison Papers, Library of Congress.

28. "The Constitution of Virginia, Letter V," No. 16 (Sept. 30, 1829), 244-245. The discussion in *The Valley of Shenandoah; or, Memoirs of the Graysons* (New York, 1824) is on I, 200-210.

29. No. 34 (Feb. 3, 1830), 529-531. See below, Pt. III, pp. 162-163, for Tucker's interview with the Siamese twins; and see Tucker's letter to Joseph C. Cabell, March 18, 1832, Cabell Deposit, University of Virginia Library.

"Political Economy: Ricardo's Theory of Profits," an attack on one phase of Ricardian economics which Tucker was to elaborate in his treatise *The Laws of Wages, Profits and Rent Investigated* (1837).[30]

Except for one article signed "V," all those in a series entitled "On the Policy of Encouraging Manufactures" are under the initial "K."[31] They contain the same arguments for admitting factories in the South which Tucker presented in his classes on economics;[32] and his comments on slavery and its moral effects are exactly those expounded in *The Valley, Progress of the United States in Population and Wealth* (1843), and other of Tucker's works.[33] Another article by "K" entitled "Bank of the United States," defending Senator McDuffie's position on monetary policy, is a condensed version of Tucker's "The Bank of the United States" in the *American Quarterly Review,* an article which was reprinted by Nicholas Biddle in his fight against Jackson's anti-Bank campaign.[34]

Seven articles signed "C.C." are on but two topics—Hume's theory of cause and effect and "Education of the People." Tucker's interest in the refutation of Hume's philosophical theories, which will be discussed later,[35] makes his authorship of the essay attacking Hume almost certain. The essays on the education of working people really cover much more ground than their title indicates and contain many of Tucker's established views. The author, "C.C.," citing Bacon, Newton, and Stewart, says that, while he cannot follow the extreme views of Condorcet, he believes the moderns are superior to the ancients "in every department of knowledge, which allows of being progressive."[36] He attacks a General Mercer, who claimed that Adam Smith's *Wealth of Nations,* always a favorite with Tucker, might better be called "an inquiry into the nature and causes of the

30. No. 18 (Oct. 14, 1829), 273-276.
31. No. 2 (June 24, 1829), 17-20; No. 3 (July 1, 1829), 42-47; No. 4 (July 8, 1829), 59-61; No. 5 (July 15, 1829), 77-80; No. 7 (July 29, 1829), 103-107; No. 10 (Aug. 19, 1829), 154-157.
32. See "Lectures on Political Economy," in "Notebook of Robert Lewis Dabney," Dabney Papers, University of Virginia Library.
33. Joseph Dorfman, *The Economic Mind in American Civilization, 1606-1865* (New York, 1946), II, 548, who has examined Tucker's economic writings, says that the essays bear all the earmarks of Tucker's authorship.
34. IX (1831), 246-282. For proof of authorship of the *American Quarterly Review* article, see Nicholas Biddle to Tucker, April 1, 1831, Biddle Papers, Library of Congress, quoted in Dorfman, *Economic Mind,* II, 883 and n.
35. See below, Pt. III, pp. 166-169.
36. "Education of the People, No. 1," No. 16 (Sept. 30, 1829), 249-253. See Tucker's "A Discourse on the Progress of Philosophy and Its Influence on the Intellectual and Moral Character of Man," *Southern Literary Messenger,* I (1835), 405-421.

vices of nations." Further holding the general position of Tucker, who argued also that manufactories and machinery do not increase but only localize poverty, "C.C." said that an attack against Adam Smith really supported the opinions of Rousseau;[37] and in stating the benefits which theoretical sciences confer on the practical arts, "C.C." utilized many of the arguments in Tucker's essay "On Scientific Pursuits" published in the 1822 *Essays*. That the initials "C.C." may be an abbreviation of "Chris: Cruize" lends weight to the evidence that Tucker used "C.C." to identify his works, for "Chris: Cruize" and "C. Cruize"—along with "K" and "Q"—are almost positively pseudonyms that Tucker signed to fictional contributions.

SKETCHES AND STORIES

In the "Introduction" to the *Literary Museum,* Tucker gave as one reason for publishing a weekly instead of a quarterly review the anticipation that a staid review would exclude poetry, fiction, "and other productions of fancy."[38]   According to the University's historian, however, Tucker was opposed in his wish to include fiction in the magazine.   Dunglison, to whom Tucker announced that he would publish some of his fiction, wrote to Cabell:

If there is anything which has detracted more than another from the reputation of Mr. Tucker, it is the fact of his having written works of this character.   Wherever I travel, I hear this objected to him, and find him underrated, for his merits are very far beyond his reputation.   Of these objections, he does not seem aware, although the want of success in the production of what he has issued, ought to have warned him of it.[39]

Dunglison wanted articles "full of solid information" and argued that tales, unless they carried "a useful lesson," were of no benefit at all in forming the young men of a literary institution.[40]   Although Tucker contributed eleven fictional pieces to the magazine, he made them didactic enough to satisfy even Dunglison's rigid requirements.

Two papers, "The Three Talismans" and "The Brothers," totally without literary or social interest, illustrate two commonplace maxims which Tucker sought to teach—that idle minds tend to be corrupted

37. "Education for the People, No. 2," No. 19 (Oct. 21, 1829), 298-300. See Tucker's "On the Future Destiny of the United States," *Port Folio*, 3rd ser., IV (1814), 382-397.

38. "Q," No. 1 (June 17, 1829), 1-3.

39. Quoted in Bruce, *History of the University of Virginia*, II, 22-23.

40. *Ibid.*, II, 346-347.

and that education influences moral character.[41] A third, "Colonel Hazle," which is prefaced with the adage "Economy is the best revenue," is no better written than "The Three Talismans" or "The Brothers," but since in it Tucker concisely sums up an important theme of *The Valley,* it is worth examining.

Colonel Hazle, a portly, gout-ridden Virginia planter who continues to live in luxury despite economic losses, and Tanner Currie, who has over the years acquired most of the Colonel's property, ride together in a carriage. They discuss "the various progress which different states had made in population, wealth and improvement," and try to determine why Virginia, the oldest state in the Union, has a smaller population than either Massachusetts or Pennsylvania. Suggestions are made that slavery has caused both whites and Negroes to be indolent, that the warm climate is detrimental to diligent application, that there is more commerce in the North, and that Northerners have inherited Puritan frugalness through Franklin. Finally the Colonel recognizes the obvious parallel between himself and Virginia and asks Currie, the once improvident tanner, why he has prospered so much while other men, including the Colonel, have lost. Like the answers given by successful men who discussed the problem of acquiring bank stocks in Tucker's sketch "Roads to Riches," Currie's reply is that he has spent less than he has made.[42]

Of five sketches in the *Literary Museum* which deal with Southern life, one called "The Wilderness" recounts an event which took place in the Kentucky wild lands in the life of Mr. O[gilvie], "formerly so well known in Virginia as a supporter of the Godwenian [*sic*] philosophy," whom Tucker knew as the organizer of the Richmond "Rainbow Society."[43] A second short piece, "Maiden's Adventure," by relating how a small stream that ends the James River Canal received its name, clearly fulfills one of the purposes stated in the prospectus to the *Literary Museum*—to collect incidents in the history of Virginia. An old innkeeper tells of a young overseer, banished across the river

41. "K," "The Three Talismans," No. 48 (May 12, 1830), 761-767; "K," "The Brothers," No. 22 (Nov. 11, 1829), 339-344.

42. No. 24 (Nov. 25, 1829), 372-374. "Roads to Riches," by "K," which appeared in No. 4 (July 8, 1829), 55-59, contains as one of its four characters a planter's son, Mr. Heartwell, who, by lending money to friends and neighbors, is about to lose his estate to Mr. Flint, a "tall sallow-looking money lender."

43. "V," "The Wilderness," No. 6 (July 22, 1829), pp. 85-86. Tucker's account of Ogilvie's life is almost as full as that given in the *DAB* (XIII, 645-636), and adds weight for assigning the contributions signed "V" to Tucker, since Tucker seems to be the only faculty member to have known Ogilvie and to have heard his tale.

by Colonel Allen because of his love for the Colonel's daughter. When alerted by an Indian friend, "Old Tarapin Jack," to a tribal raid, the young lover hurries back home to rescue Miss Allen from a swollen stream and, like Leatherstocking, dispatches two pursuing hostiles with a single musket shot. His heroism earns him the affection of the girl and the regard of Colonel Allen, who, we are told, later deeds him his estate.[44]

Three works which deal specifically with midland Virginia are the best of Tucker's writings for the *Literary Museum*. In "The Country Belle" Tucker satirized the romantic female who, lacking good sense, refuses to marry any one of several frugal Virginia men. Instead of laughing at the "propensity" of his leading character, Patty Starkie, to attend gay parties in Richmond and Washington, D.C., which causes her at the age of thirty-five to be without a husband, Tucker emphasized the consequences of her folly. She almost marries a romantic imposter from the North and is saved from this error only to wed her deliverer, Tom Cutts, a local gambler. The tale is patently didactic; Tucker explicitly stated at the end that gamblers don't reform and that Patty, always disobedient to her mother, will rue her mistake.[45]

"The Gold Seeker," at first glance, appears to have been intended to teach "that domestic love can confer happiness, when gold has failed to do so, and that human life is so chequered with good and evil, that if the happiest has its clouds, the most unfortunate is occasionally gladdened with sunshine." But the anecdotal tale of a man who, because of loo playing, loses his position as a hatter in Petersburg and carries his family in search of gold to North Carolina, where the native whites and Negroes cheat him and where he loses his son in a knife fight, has a more calculated purpose. Its intent lies in keeping people from moving south and west from the Old Dominion. A description of a North Carolina family shows that Tucker had as little liking for lubbers as did William Byrd II, the great-grandfather of his first wife. Mrs. Snubbs, proud that her husband is a "squire," sits with her family around a flickering fire, "picking cotton, whilst two or three uncombed, unwashed brats" roast chestnuts. Their cabin is without candles or lamps and is furnished only with one dirty bed and a three-cornered chest, and their food is "ill-cooked, dirty and unwholesome." Tennessee, where the daughter of the family is driven by the

44. "C. Cruize," No. 38 (March 3, 1830), 594-600.
45. "K," No. 40 (March 17, 1830), 632-640.

greedy father, though it is not described, is said to be even worse, a land of malaria, crime, and poverty.[46]

"Julia Moncrief," the longest of the fictional stories about Virginia, expresses the values which Tucker thought to be most worth holding. The titular heroine, whom Tucker described as "one of those favoured beings that are frequently met with in novels . . . on whom nature lavishes her choicest gifts," has been raised in seclusion by her father, whose own upraising has instilled in him "a fastidiousness and delicacy of taste" more suitable to a woman than to a man who must make his way in the world. Participation in the Revolutionary War and marriage to a Virginia belle temporarily alleviated his modesty, but the death of his wife caused him to grow even more delicate and "morbidly sensitive." As a result, he prefers the quiet of the country to the joy and gaiety to be found in the cities and watering places. Julia, however, through the offices of her aunt, obtains leave to attend a ball, where she charms a wealthy South Carolina planter, William Laurens. Less romantically, she dances with her cousin, Henry Clayton, a recent graduate of William and Mary, who, lacking Laurens' business sense, is fond only of "horses, dogs and cockfighting." Alice Spiegle, the gossipy sixteen-year-old daughter of a neighboring land speculator, has been to boarding school and therefore thinks that she can rise above her station and marry the distinguished Laurens. Although Alice shows a degree of cunning and malice surely remarkable in a teen-ager in her efforts to win Laurens' favor, she fails, for Laurens sees immediately the "coarseness of her air, manners and form." Angered by Laurens' rejection, Alice first writes anonymous notes telling him that Julia is betrothed to Henry Clayton and then hires a local jockey to sell the same horse first to young Clayton and then to Laurens. In the ensuing mix-up about the horse, Clayton suspects Laurens of duplicity, challenges him to a duel, and wounds him. The doctor who treats Laurens convinces him of the machinations of Alice Spiegle, and Laurens shortly discovers that Julia not only is free but returns his love. And he forthwith proposes.[47]

The social structure and way of life that "Julia Moncrief" commends are obvious. The Southern aristocrat, William Laurens, and shy, timid, but graceful Julia are at one end of the scale, and Alice Spiegle and the disreputable jockey, whom she must be content to

---

46. "Q," No. 12 (Sept. 2, 1829), 182-189.
47. "K," No. 44 (April 14, 1830), 689-696; No. 45 (April 21, 1830), 706-714.

marry, are at the other. Good society and polite conversation, too, are shown as ingredients of a way of life well worth preserving. Major Moncrief is treated as though he were mentally and physically ill because he refuses to visit the nearby Sweet Springs, which is so highly valued by the Clayton family and by Laurens that the Claytons trek to it each year from eastern Virginia and Laurens all the way from his rich plantation in the Carolinas. Young Henry Clayton comes in for the usual Tucker criticism for his rashness and profligacy, but most of Tucker's ridicule and anger is turned on Alice Spiegle, the jockey, and a despicable and uncivilized "venison-provider" from the frontier, who, while helping Laurens to a doctor after his duel, steals his wallet and flees back into the wilds.

Neither "True Though Truant" nor "The Confessions of a Pirate" has the limited merit of dealing with the South, but both indicate the direction in which Tucker's fiction was to move, for from both of these melodramatic tales Tucker drew material for an adventure in his unpublished novel, "A Century Hence." The longer and inferior story, "True Though Truant," is not signed, but its similarities to "A Century Hence" leave little doubt about its authorship. The tale is one of true love and repented theft, told through letters from a distinguished American visiting in Europe, who acts as guardian for one who he thinks is a runaway boy but who, he discovers "in loosening her vest" after she has fainted, is a girl in disguise.[48]

In "The Confessions of a Pirate," Tucker relates, through letters between a Northern Congressman and a Southern friend, the fate of a young man, the fruit of the Congressman's early liaison with a Creole in Jamaica. Because of poor training, the illegitimate boy becomes in succession a gambler, a pirate, a murderer, and, after his pardon, granted in spite of his atrocious past, a gambler again. "Who does not," Tucker asks rhetorically at the close, ". . . feel the truth of this saying of the wise man—'Train up the child in the way he should go: and when he is old he will not depart from it'?"[49]

In the fifty-second and last issue of the *Literary Museum,* Tucker announced that the magazine was ceasing publication. He explained that the editors encountered many practical difficulties—the impossibility, for example, of reading new books in time to review them for subscribers—and derived little profit from their arduous work.[50] From this time on, Tucker's interests became more and more con-

48. No. 46 (April 28, 1830), 732-736; No. 47 (May 5, 1830), 747-751.
49. "Q," No. 17 (Oct. 7, 1829), 262-270.
50. "Q," "To the Public," No. 52 (June 9, 1830), 817-818.

centrated in the fields of economics, history, and philosophy, and he published no more fiction and only one poem, the "Apostrophe of the Aeolian Harp to the Wind," a short, melancholy piece which appeared in the *Southern Literary Messenger*.[51]

"A CENTURY HENCE"

Sometime in 1841, four years before he retired from the chair of moral philosophy, Tucker composed his second novel and last work of fiction. "A Century Hence: Or a Romance of 1941" is Tucker's attempt to write popular fiction in which he could impart useful moral instruction and expound his vision of the world as he thought it would be after a century of progress. The melodramatic love and adventure story, never published, is told through an exchange of letters by friends and relatives from all parts of the world.

The novel is plotted around the seemingly insuperable difficulties which obstruct the marriage of two young citizens of Centropolis, Missouri—the capital of the United States in the year 1941. Henry Carlton, the son of a distinguished and extremely wealthy United States Senator, and Caroline Maunde, the daughter of Senator Carlton's political and business rival, are in love. General Maunde, who is described as "something of a bashaw," is opposed to the suit of Henry, whose father, he complains, "treated me as an inferior, and is, in grain, a downright aristocrat." Henry, whose "sickly fancy and . . . fastidious taste" make him, at the start of the novel, ill-suited for the "coarse realities of life," has determined that he will never court nor marry any girl whose heart has belonged to another. When he returns home after graduating from the University of Virginia and is misinformed that Caroline has fallen in love with her orphaned cousin, he hastily condemns her as a "selfish cold-blooded coquette" and flies, as his father puts it, "God knows whither."

As a favor to old Senator Carlton, whose pleasure in his wealth and success turns to "gall & wormwood" because of his son's emotional instability, Caspar Bentley, a statistician who is modeled upon Tucker himself, locates Henry and accompanies him on his irrational wanderings over the world, hoping to bring the lad to an appreciation of the "real transactions of life" by appealing to his sense of honor and his

51.1 (1835), 396. This unsigned piece is attributed to Tucker by David K. Jackson, *The Contributors and Contributions to the Southern Literary Messenger (1834-1864)* (Charlottesville, Va., 1936), on the basis of a manuscript letter from T. W. White to Lucian Minor, dated May 15, 1835.

love of glory. Through letters exchanged between old Carlton and Bentley, we receive reports on international politics and economics as well as on Henry's gradual improvement. By helping a wayward British boy, Frederick Steener, return to virtue, and by heeding his father's and Bentley's injunctions, Henry is completely cured and decides to return home after visiting the Far East.

The Maundes, meanwhile, have set off for a cruise on the Pacific, where they are captured by pirates. Henry, whose ship is by chance in the same waters, saves Caroline from the lust of a bearded villain, and her sister and parents from certain death. In gratitude for Henry's intrepid heroism, General Maunde embraces him as a son and forgives the Carltons for their imagined wrongs. He rents a large steamship so that Henry and Bentley can join his family in an extended cruise. Shortly afterwards, once Caroline and Henry have come to an understanding, he sanctions their marriage.

The hero and heroine of "A Century Hence" were intended to appeal to a wide audience. Although Tucker placed Caroline and Henry in a civilization which has kept pace with the century and a half of progress following the post-Revolutionary War period, he gave them many of the manners and habits of Virginians of the ante-bellum South, idealizing them as worthy descendants of genteel aristocrats. Caroline, like her predecessor Julia Moncrief, is a carica-ture of normal humanity, so perfectly innocent and good is she. Al-though she knows that marriage to Henry is impossible as long as her father persists in opposing his courtship, she never attempts to disobey or to reform the old general. She is "a model of prudence & propriety, as well as of delicacy and purity,"[52] the epitome of female passivity and gentleness. Saint-like in her willingness to suffer rather than disturb family calm by disobedience, she forgoes her desire to mix in polite society and spends much time at home, comforting her mother and nursing her sickly sister, interrupting these duties only long enough to embroider "pretty tapestries" or to correspond with her friends. Once Henry gets control over his imagination, he blos-soms forth as a paragon of good sense and social tact. The "noblest of his race," he is a combination of the Southern gentleman who treats all ladies with respect;[53] the gallant youth who will accept a temporary commission in the United States Army to punish the

52. "A Century Hence: Or a Romance of 1941," manuscript copy, Tucker-Harrison-Smith Papers, University of Virginia Library, p. 93.

53. *Ibid.*, pp. 64-65.

"faithless Mexicans";[54] the Beadle dime novel hero who fells lusting pirates with a clean shot through the head;[55] the studious young statistician bent on retiring to his study to devote himself to "letters and philosophy";[56] and, last of all, he is the aristocratic millionaire son of the kindest capitalist of the brave new world.[57]

Tucker's admiration for aristocracy, evident in all his fiction, is seen in part in "A Century Hence" in his delineation of the Carltons and in Henry's comic encounter with the Blotches—a family of vulgar, ambitious middle-class Americans. More forcibly, Tucker expressed his social views by means of Caspar Bentley's letters on English society. Bentley opposes the class system in England and believes that only the "energy of republicanism" can resuscitate the past glories of British aristocracy, but he comments favorably upon this same class in England who "still strive to keep their blood pure and unpalliated with plebeians." Such an attitude, he says, is more galling to the "purse proud upstart" than to the "advocates of natural equality." British lower classes of "1941"—drawn from Tucker's observations of the English workingmen he saw in 1839—and Virginia slaves of 1800 share a similar respect for "quality," for which both are happy to work for "the merest pittance," just to be near it. In a passage reminiscent of one in *The Valley* in which Gildon described old Colonel Barton, Caspar Bentley summarizes the attributes of England's aristocrats: they have "an air of tranquil ease, an absence of all bustle or display, or pretension; a self-possessed simplicity that is very imposing. . . ."[58]

Didacticism is as obvious in "A Century Hence" as it is in Tucker's other fiction. He sought to warn against the dangers of gambling by interpolating into his romance a slightly revised version of a sentimental fictional piece earlier published in the *Literary Museum*,[59] in which a young Englishman degenerates through gaming to piracy, murder, and rapine. More significant, since they reflect Tucker's interest in social psychology, are his admonitions against isolating oneself from the world of affairs. Old Carlton and Bentley worry about Henry's "joint disease of the heart & imagination," the symptoms of which are a refusal to be concerned with the problems of modern

54. *Ibid.,* p. 96.
55. *Ibid.,* p. 116.
56. *Ibid.,* p. 95.
57. *Ibid.,* pp. 1-2.
58. *Ibid.,* p. 50.
59. "Q," "The Confessions of a Pirate," No. 17 (Oct. 7, 1829), 262-270.

life and a disdain for such "normal" loves as expensive riding horses, fine clothing, or "even pictures, mosaics, and other gew-gaws."[60] Henry's cure is gradually effected and he decides to face the "serious duties of life."[61] By the time he rescues Caroline from "a fate worse than death," he is a perfectly adjusted and happy young lover, a suitable marriage companion for Caroline.

Although in "A Century Hence" Tucker wished to inculcate such pedestrian virtues as parental obedience and sociability, his chief aim was to embody his social and economic theories in fiction and thus to give his ideas to as wide an audience as possible. Through the characters' commentary on the world they inhabit, Tucker presented the intellectual core of his novel—his forecast of the "future destiny" of the United States. An understanding of "A Century Hence" hinges upon a recognition that in it, as in many of his essays and treatises on economics and "national policy," Tucker was concerned with interpreting the idea of civilization and progress.

A later chapter will examine in detail Tucker's interpretation of civilization's advancement,[62] but a brief summary of his faith in man's progress is essential here. Tucker's basic assumption was that, by conquering nature and by becoming more civilized or refined, each generation sees an improvement over its predecessor. However, like many of the Scottish philosophers, upon whose social doctrines he founded his own, Tucker disavowed any belief in perfectibilian theories which would accelerate progress by altering the political and social structure of society. On the contrary, he often condemned such "visionary" schemes. His view of the future, moreover, was tempered by the thought that political demagoguery, as witnessed in Jackson's administrations, threatened to destroy the sacred right of property—the foundation of good government. As an early advocate of industrial capitalism, Tucker welcomed the growth of America's population as providing an index to material and social prosperity and established himself, consequently, as a pioneer American critic of the population doctrines of Thomas Malthus. But after 1820 he more and more inclined to accept Malthus' views—partly because he saw in them an

60. "A Century Hence," p. 29. Henry's disease is much like that which afflicted Julia Moncrief's eccentric father. See the above discussion of "Julia Moncrief," pp. 102-103. See also Tucker's statement of 1804 that "hypochondria, delirium, and madness, though remotely caused by corporeal disease, are the *immediate* effects of an imagination stimulated to preternatural vigour" ("On the Illusions of Fancy," *The Rainbow; First Series* [Richmond, Va., 1804], p. 53).

61. "A Century Hence," pp. 60-61, 96.

62. See below, Pt. III. Chap. XII.

excuse for condoning and expanding slavery. From 1837 until the end of his life, Tucker expounded Malthusian doctrines with great vigor, yet never varied from the point of view that only in a crowded nation could the arts flourish and the nation's elite thoroughly enjoy themselves. In "A Century Hence" he drew upon his economic philosophy to present a picture of the complex world of the future, in which both the benefits and the drawbacks of dense populations are seen. Though primarily concerned with discussing the situation of the United States, Tucker included a panoramic view of the world in order to predict the great importance of the young nation and, more importantly, to stress the dangers which lay before America by representing the ills of a Europe already plagued by excess population.

The fruits of progress as set forth in "A Century Hence" are most strikingly seen in technological advances. Because a Professor Johnson has simplified the process of reducing water to its elements, a revolution in travel and industry is taking place. Flying cars hurtle through space, carrying such a man as Henry's father fifteen thousand miles a year to view his plantations and investments.[63] Scientific schemes are formed to harness sun rays for radiant heating and rain water and wind for power;[64] and new plans are under way to make dyes and ersatz foodstuff from waste materials.[65] England, Russia, and the United States are competing in the construction of a gigantic telescope to view the moon,[66] and gas lights illuminate New York City.[67]

Despite such scientific achievements, however, the world is in ferment. The United States is sending General O'Donnell, armed with "flying steam and artillery," to lead the American "Eagles" to victory over Mexico, which threatens to establish an Ozark boundary line.[68] The nation is also involved in wars between Haiti and Cuba and Peru and Chile;[69] and wild Indian tribes in North and South America are fighting.[70] Czarist Russia, with a population of 160,000,000, already the conqueror of Turkey, menaces Europe, North America, and China; and the United States has entered into a Great Western Alliance with headquarters in Paris.[71]

63. "A Century Hence," p. 2.
64. *Ibid.*, pp. 59-60.
65. *Idem.*
66. *Ibid.*, pp. 66-67.
67. *Ibid.*, p. 20.
68. *Ibid.*, pp. 12-13.
69. *Ibid.*, pp. 20-29.
70. *Ibid.*, p. 29.
71. *Ibid.*, pp. 82-83.

While the United States is able to protect itself and seems even to thrive on war, its future internal political and economic stability is threatened by over-population. The problem is not expected to be serious for twenty years, when the population will have increased from two hundred million to three hundred million. At present, there are advantages to the country's dense population. Caspar Bentley, after visiting New York, the "Babylon" of the world, expounds Tucker's theory of "enlightened self-interest" and finds satisfaction in the imposing sight of 1,800,000 people "all obedient to the laws, each one acting in his own sphere & freely following his own inclination so long as that inclination does not clash with the well being of society; each one too, in promoting his own happiness contributing to further the happiness of many others, and thus to bind together the framework of society."[72]

He agrees, too, with Henry's father that a dense population serves the purpose of depressing the cost of labor to a point at which American plantation owners eventually may steal the tea market from China.[73] But he is aware that there exists the increasing danger of an uprising of the "idle, thoughtless, giddy part of the population," led by demagogues.[74] Already in New York, where fifty thousand persons are forced to live in steamboats, peace is maintained and property protected only by keeping a large police force, modeled on the bobbies of London "almost a century ago," on constant alert to quell the hungry mobs.[75] Prudent and intelligent young men like Henry Carlton, who wrote his honors thesis on the "probable fate of China," prepare for the problems of the future by studying statistics and economics.

Bentley observes the situation in Europe and writes home about it. In France and England the increase in population has dangerously augmented "the indigent dependent classes," but the population has not yet reached a point beyond which a plague, a serious war, or a bad harvest would not eliminate the danger of class conflict. The French, Bentley says, meet the population issue squarely by forming "temporary connections," which either tend not to be productive, or, if they are, at least allow parents to send their "fruits" to foundling homes where they die from the lack of "that particular nourishment . . .

72. *Ibid.*, pp. 21, 36-37.
73. *Ibid.*, pp. 1-2.
74. *Ibid.*, p. 37.
75. *Idem.*

minute cares & attentions which only a mother can supply."[76]   Bentley, however, favors over the French plan the British system of postponing marriage until the parties are over twenty-one.

Neither Carlton nor Bentley, who jointly reflect Tucker's own views, believes that the United States is immediately menaced by excess numbers.   As Carlton points out, unlike Europe, America has always had an abundance of food, and her rate of natural increase in population has been declining.   Both agree, however, that the dangers of over-population should be advertised so that even the "meanest" minds will recognize that preventives, such as the English and French have, must be found if America is to avoid Europe's problems.[77]   Recent legislative proposals which Bentley believes are worth consideration are (1) that those who marry females under twenty-eight years of age be taxed—a fairly efficient method since the lower classes, anyway, would postpone marriage, and (2) that the United States revive monastic institutions.   Although Bentley himself grimly suggests "more odious" remedies, he at other times concludes that the only truly effective method of curbing excess population is to "inculcate lessons of prudence & virtue" and leave all to parents to solve.[78]

As in his non-fictional writings, Tucker pointed out that, barring revolutions, the evils of dense populations fall only on the lower classes and are, perhaps, compensated for by the flourishing of the arts. Liverpool may have a hundred thousand beggars, and thousands may have to leave England annually to avoid starvation, but there is no gainsaying the fact that England is the cultural center of the world, with an abundance of excellent poets, sculptors, engravers, and musicians. The best artists in the United States are as good as and perhaps superior to those in England:

But the general state of the arts there is in advance of that with us.   As a proof of it, most of our artists in the imaginative class—our poets, novelists, and dramatists, as well as our writers of natural history—all in short who wish to invoke the aid of vision to illustrate the pictures of their fancy or the real forms of nature find it to their interest to employ English artists for such embellishments.   Nor have we any printed work which can enter into competition with their new editions of Shakespeare, or

76. *Ibid.*, pp. 74-75.

77. These speculations are included in five extra pages added to the end of the manuscript of "A Century Hence," indicating that Tucker, when he wrote the novel, was undecided about some economic and statistical problems.

78. "A Century Hence," p. 25.

Byron, or Scott; or even of our own popular favorites, Jones, Williams, & Brown.[79]

Art produced in the United States seems to be like Hollywood extravaganzas of today.[80] Caroline Maunde, who may be said to represent the ideal of taste and delicacy in the novel, writes to her confidante, Robertini Bender, of a "very pretty novelty" which she, as one of a hundred thousand spectators from Centropolis, witnessed in the park and hopes to see again. By means of steam power and the control of gaseous fluids, there was produced an immense figure of "Apollo drawing the chariot of day. Four horses were in the air and apparently drawing along a light gilded car, whose delicate wheels seemed to touch but not to bear upon the ground. Four figures representing the hours, preceded."[81]

Henry Carlton's father applauds the attempt to revive a taste for "simple tragedy & comedy" but is highly gratified by a colossal musical show put on by a great English touring company;[82] and Washington Graves, Henry's friend, reports on the fine entertainment value of a spectacular mock battle, marking the nation's "last naval victory in the Pacific," in which a huge audience witnessed twenty-four "Columbian" ships trouncing thirty-four Mexican vessels, as gaily decorated balloons controlled by unseen wires floated overhead.[83]

Hubbell speculates that "A Century Hence" was never published because in "the 1840's the market was flooded with ten- and twenty-five-cent reprints of English novels, and American publishers were reluctant to accept manuscripts, even those written by such popular novelists as Cooper and Simms."[84] Although Tucker himself nowhere states why the novel was not published, two reasons other than the unfavorable market suggest themselves. One is related to the fact that at about the time he wrote the novel, he was modifying his economic theory and was not sure exactly how much emphasis he should give to various economic questions. For example, in 1837 and 1843 Tucker predicted on Malthusian grounds the death of slavery

79. *Ibid.*, p. 50.
80. In the Rocky Mountains, however, where the people still "eat, dress & speak as a century ago," only handicrafts are practiced. Washington Graves is delighted with the opportunity to visit these "primitive" people and plans to keep a record of his meetings with them "for the amusement of my friends of Harrison Square" ("A Century Hence," pp. 17, 26-28).
81. *Ibid.*, p. 11.
82. *Ibid.*, p. 27.
83. *Ibid.*, p. 28.
84. *The South in American Literature*, p. 254.

within sixty to eighty years; yet he depicted in "A Century Hence," set in 1941, its continued existence in the deep South.[85] Secondly, Tucker may have believed that the book—a pastiche of pseudo-science fiction, romance, trite morality, and social criticism and satire—could add little luster to his reputation.

Because of obvious weaknesses in plotting, style, and structure, "A Century Hence" must be judged the weakest of Tucker's longer works of the imagination. But, like other of his writings in which didacticism is not limited to trite morality, the novel is of cultural, if not literary, value. Thus, though neither *Letters from Virginia* nor *A Voyage to the Moon* is completely successful as satire, each contains some interesting reflections, the former on the Virginia of the early nineteenth century, and the latter upon the intellectual beliefs of Tucker's age. Like these, "A Century Hence" is of considerable significance in the history of American culture.

In an over-all view of Tucker's imaginative writings, *The Valley of Shenandoah* stands out as his chief contribution to American literature, for, while similarly intended to teach, it succeeds in a way that none of his other works does. Here Tucker was able to dramatize his theme of the effects of economic progress in rural Virginia and to exploit his richest talents. Tucker's gifts, utilized in *The Valley,* were those of the reporter, who can record details of a society, and of the historian, who can appreciate the importance and significance of the past. Most importantly, Tucker was by nature and training a combination of the philosopher-economist and the practical financier, and he added to his chronicle of Virginia a critical interpretation of its society which gave to the book a depth which none of his other works possesses.

In considering Tucker's career as a writer, it seems just to apply the standard which he himself used in evaluating his contemporaries —that "we . . . regard not so much what the writer is, as what, from the intrinsic evidence" of his work, "it appears he might have been."[86] Had Tucker continued to follow the paths which he laid out in his first novel, he could have made a more impressive contribution than he did to the nation's literature. But many factors conspired to work against his growth as a writer. He had to prove to himself that he could make money by writing before he would risk ruining his career;

85. This discussion of slavery, like those concerning some other economic topics, is contained in the five extra pages at the end of the manuscript of "A Century Hence."

86. "On American Literature," *Essays on Various Subjects of Taste, Morals, and National Policy* (Georgetown, D.C., 1822), p. 51.

yet, plagued by indolence and perhaps uncertain of his desire or ability to succeed as a novelist, he waited until heavy debts drove him to make a hasty attempt at fiction. He rested his hopes on the success of *The Valley,* written in a scant two months. Had the novel been profitable, he would have tried to earn his living by his pen. How much he might have improved as a novelist had he devoted all his energy to writing is problematical. Although there is some indication that he did his best writing quickly, additional time might have allowed him to improve his work. The success of *The Valley* might have encouraged him to continue to write about times and places that he knew well. After that novel's failure, Tucker, wishing to find financial security for his family, accepted an academic post which demanded at least as much time as did the practice of law. During his professorship, he wrote a few short pieces dealing with Virginia, but his major efforts in fiction—*A Voyage* and "A Century Hence"—reflect his growing interest in more academic and theoretic, less easily dramatized ideas. A long quest for success as a writer of imaginative literature ended in 1841 in abysmal failure with the completion of "A Century Hence."

PART III

TUCKER AS SOUTHERN THINKER

CHAPTER IX

AESTHETICS AND LITERATURE

AESTHETICS

AN EXAMINATION of Tucker's essays which deal with the subject of taste indicates that his theories were derived from late eighteenth- and early nineteenth-century Scottish and English critics, who, despite many differences, held in common the basic principle that a critic must analyze the effect of a work of art on the minds and emotions of its audience.[1] As Edward Niles Hooker points out, these critics were attempting "to define and to arrive at a standard of taste" for all people, but paradoxically and inevitably they came to conclusions which undermined neo-classic aesthetics and paved the way for "romantic" theories of art.[2] Similarly, Tucker was deeply interested in establishing universal principles of taste from psychological observations of the effects of certain aspects of art upon men, but he refused to accept the controversial theory advanced by Archibald Alison that beauty was due exclusively to the subjective workings of an individual's mind.

Because of the eclectic nature of Tucker's borrowings, his debt to specific writers is difficult to trace. He seems to have been familiar with the ideas of many of the most important philosophers and critics of the neo-classical and early romantic periods, many of whom, of course, mentioned each other's ideas in their writings. Tucker referred to Edmund Burke, William Hogarth, Erasmus Darwin, Archibald Alison, Francis Jeffrey, Lord Kames, Dugald Stewart, Thomas Reid,

1. Gordon McKenzie, *Critical Responsiveness: A Study of the Psychological Current in Later Eighteenth-Century Criticism,* University of California Publications in English, XX (Berkeley and Los Angeles, 1949), 1.
2. "The Discussion of Taste, from 1750 to 1770, and the New Trends in Literary Criticism," *PMLA,* XLIX (1934), 577-578.

Thomas Brown, Alexander Gerard, and David Hume in his essays and lectures. He knew well the *Lectures* of Hugh Blair and *The Philosophy of Rhetoric* of George Campbell, from whose texts, along with those of Kames, Stewart, and Brown, he taught belles lettres and moral philosophy at the University of Virginia.[3] From the writings of these men Tucker acquired the ideas for some of his most interesting compositions.

Two aspects of Tucker's observations must be mentioned at the outset. First, unlike many of the Scottish philosophers and aestheticians whose discussions provided the stimulus and the background for his speculations, Tucker never composed a comprehensive study of aesthetics or literary criticism. Only a few of his essays deal exclusively with problems of taste. Second, Tucker's opinions on aesthetics never changed appreciably over a period of forty-five years. Almost all of his essays on the subject were originally published in 1814 and 1815 in the Philadelphia *Port Folio* and were reissued without significant change in book form in 1822 and 1860.[4]

The first work in which Tucker discussed aesthetics, however, appeared as early as 1804 in the Richmond *Enquirer*. "On the Illusions of Fancy" is, as the title suggests, primarily concerned with the baneful effects which an uncontrolled imagination has upon man's conduct when the suggestions of the imagination are mistaken for those of the memory.[5] But the essay reveals Tucker's interest in psychological criticism and contains the seeds of many of his later writings on taste. In the manner of Alexander Gerard,[6] Tucker briefly described the nature of the imagination and its relation to

3. The aesthetic speculations of these philosophers and critics, who may be considered as "members of a fairly coherent critical tradition" (McKenzie, *Critical Responsiveness*, p. 1), are examined in McKenzie, *op. cit.*, and in Walter John Hipple, Jr., *The Beautiful, the Sublime, & the Picturesque in Eighteenth-Century British Aesthetic Theory* (Carbondale, Ill., 1957).

4. William Charvat, *The Origins of American Critical Thought, 1810-1835* (Philadelphia, 1936), p. 169, says that the *Port Folio* "came under the rule of Blair and Kames" in 1816. Elsewhere (pp. 28, 56, 87-88) Charvat, without citing dates, says that the *Port Folio* reprinted articles from the Scottish *Quarterly Review* and generally followed the tenets of Scottish criticism.

5. *The Rainbow; First Series* (Richmond, Va., 1804), p. 51. Tucker wrote that "hypochondria, delirium, and madness, though remotely caused by corporeal disease, are the *immediate* effects of an imagination stimulated to preternatural vigour" (p. 53). Many British moralists, of course, directed warnings against an unlicensed imagination in ethical problems. See, for example, Dugald Stewart, *Elements of the Philosophy of the Human Mind* in *The Collected Works of Dugald Stewart, Esq., F.R.S.S.*, ed. Sir William Hamilton, Bart. (Edinburgh, 1854), II, 457-467.

6. *An Essay on Taste* (London, 1759), p. 180.

literary criticism. The fancy or imagination he saw mechanically as a "mimic of the senses" which separates or combines those ideas which were imparted by the senses and reposited [*sic*] in the memory" by the universal laws of association—by "*proximity* of time or place, *resemblance* or *contrast.*"[7]   In addition to making this distinction between memory and imagination and to analyzing the workings of the imagination through the association of ideas, Tucker wrote:

> Since eloquence and poetry owe their highest ornaments to the imagination, it naturally becomes one of the principal topics of literary criticism. As it is the object of the orator to persuade, and of the poet to please, the critic considers the fancy merely as an instrument for these purposes, and devises a set of rules from the laws of our nature by which he ascertains the fitness of the means to the end.   He points out where a loose should be given to a native impetuosity of the imagination, and where its unlicensed sallies should be curbed: shews what passages possess the awful grandeur of the sublime and what the attractive loveliness of beauty, and distinguishes those pictures of fancy which are discordant to nature to [*sic*] those which are hit off in the spirit of her finest models.   In a word, guided at one and the same time by the most liberal feelings of the heart and the nicest dictates of reason, he praises or blames the works of the imagination according to the judgment of taste.[8]

Tucker's standard of taste thus is based, like that of most of the early Scottish aestheticians, upon universal laws of association and nature.

Only by implication did Tucker define the qualifications of the proper arbiters of taste in his 1804 essay. Some ten years later in a *Port Folio* paper "On Simplicity in Ornament" (1814), he made clear his awareness that the attempt to formulate a standard of taste upon the psychological analysis of feelings and emotions might lead to the chaos of complete relativity in judgment. He therefore attempted to differentiate between the men of good and vicious tastes by following closely the dicta of Kames and Blair[9] that only the sentiments of cultured men in a "polished" society were to be considered in setting just standards. "In speaking of . . . taste," said Tucker,

7. "On the Illusions of Fancy," pp. 49-50. Tucker's principles of association are the same as those which Aristotle enumerated and which many British critics mentioned.   See, for example, Alexander Gerard's *Essay on Taste,* pp. 167-168; and Dugald Stewart's *Elements of the Philosophy of the Human Mind* in *Works,* II, 261 and n.   A discussion of various principles of association given by the Scottish critics can be found in McKenzie, *Critical Responsiveness,* Chaps. 5, 6.

8. "On the Illusions of Fancy," p. 50.

9. See Hooker, "Discussion of Taste," pp. 580-581; and Charvat, *Origins,* pp. 42, 45-46.

we refer to that of merely a portion of the species. It is not meant to be denied, that what one man calls excesses in variety and ornament, may often give peculiar pleasure to another. The degree of pleasure, which is imparted to every individual, is not only independent of others, it is even independent of his own control: and hence has arisen the maxim *de gustibus non disputandum est.* But taking the sentiments of those whose minds have been most improved by culture, as the standard of excellence, there may be such a thing as a *vicious taste,* and it is this vicious taste alone, which is pleased by excessive deviations from simplicity. When therefore we speak of that middle point, between extreme simplicity and extreme refinement, we refer to the ideal standard which is *capable* of affording the most pleasure, of which the human mind, under the best culture, is susceptible.[10]

In the same essay in which he postulated the differences in taste, Tucker also established the chief principle underlying all his aesthetic speculations—that the perfection of taste in all the fine arts is "found to consist in that middle point between extreme simplicity and extreme refinement."[11] In the progress of taste, he explained, a curious development had taken place. In the early stages of society, man's faculties were too dull and feeble to comprehend variety, but, as they became "disciplined by culture and exercise," they allowed man to appreciate complex patterns in a work of art. Unfortunately, however, artists forgot, first, the limited nature of man's faculties, which can assimilate stimuli only by dwelling on an object for a period of time, and, second, the principle of the association of ideas, which tends to make men connect with simplicity "ideas of modesty, humility, innocence, truth and nature," and with a "parade of ornament" the "disagreeable ideas of pride, self-sufficiency, vanity, and affectation." Since "these various feelings blend themselves with our judgment in all works of taste," all successful music, architecture, gardening, and literature, with the possible exception of prose, which has to become "more multifarious and diversified" as ideas become more complex and numerous, must be without excess refinement.[12]

The most important of Tucker's aesthetic inquiries deals with the nature of beauty and its relation to the sublime. His speculations on these topics make up his most fully developed discussions of aesthetics and, as will be shown later, played an important role in his theory of

10. "On Simplicity in Ornament," *Essays on Various Subjects of Taste, Morals, and National Policy* (Georgetown, D.C., 1822), p. 35.

11. *Ibid.,* p. 27.

12. *Ibid.,* pp. 27-30.

poetry. For forty-five years, in lecture and essay, Tucker discussed the concept of beauty, trying to uphold a clear-cut distinction between aesthetic subject and object and insisting upon the existence of absolute beauty. By a "common sense" investigation of the quality of beauty, he hoped to correct what seemed to him to be the overemphasis which extreme associationist critics placed upon the importance of mental reflection in calling up the emotion of the beautiful.

Tucker's essay "On Beauty," first published in the *Port Folio* in 1815, was designed to refute the "ingenious" theory advanced in Archibald Alison's *Essays on the Nature and Principles of Taste* (1790), a volume to which Tucker's attention was drawn after reading the now-famous essay written on Alison by Francis Jeffrey in the *Edinburgh Review* of 1811.[13] Alison claimed that the "simple perception of an object . . . is insufficient to excite . . . emotions" and assumed that the association of ideas, rather than perception, was the central issue in aesthetic response.[14] William Charvat notes that Alison's theory was "a new departure in Scottish aesthetics. . . . Because of it, the old, necessarily conservative, idea of the intrinsic beauty of objects was undermined, and the conception of sublimity, which is the essence of romanticism, took its place."[15]

As Walter Jackson Bate has observed, however, Alison's radical associationism, which does carry with it the implication of complete relativity in matters of taste, is but the logical outcome of the late eighteenth-century empirical method to determine the essence of beauty.[16] Most psychological critics of the period analyzed beauty as a principle of taste, and many not only catalogued the sources of beauty in an object but also assumed that associated ideas exert an influence on aesthetic appreciation. Among Alison's contemporaries with whose work Tucker was assuredly familiar, for example, Alexander Gerard devoted a full chapter of *An Essay on Taste* (1759) to a discussion of the "sense or taste of beauty" and found that some colors are inherently beautiful because their rays are soothing to the eye; but he also found that, for the most part, "the beauty of colors . . . is

13. Jeffrey's review appeared in XVIII (May, 1811), 1-46. Hipple, *The Beautiful, the Sublime, & the Picturesque*, p. 158, states that Jeffrey "played Huxley to Alison's Darwin" and directed widespread attention to Alison's *Essays.*

14. *Essays on the Nature and Principles of Taste* (Boston, 1812), p. 18.

15. Charvat, *Origins*, p. 5. See Hipple, *The Beautiful, the Sublime, & the Picturesque*, pp. 176-177, for a critical discussion of this traditional interpretation of Alison's work.

16. Walter Jackson Bate, *From Classic to Romantic: Premises of Taste in Eighteenth-Century England* (Cambridge, Mass., 1946), pp. 106-108.

resolvable into association."[17]   In his *Elements of Criticism* (1762), Lord Kames, who, with Dugald Stewart, seems to have been especially influential in molding Tucker's aesthetic theory, acclaimed the beauty of bare, geometric forms, holding that a square, for example, is more beautiful than a hexagon because of its greater simplicity and uniformity.   But Kames also recognized that a certain relativity in taste ensues when simple forms are combined in an intricate design.   He therefore distinguished between "intrinsic" beauty, the result of mere sensory perception, which is "ultimate" and discovered in a single object, and "relative" beauty, which is "accompanied with an act of understanding and reflection."[18]   Dugald Stewart, writing a critique of Alison's theory, elaborately discussed "the more simple and general principles" on which depend the pleasures "of actual sense perception" and gave them a highly significant role in the appreciation of the beautiful.[19]

It was to the more conservative opinions of such writers as Gerard, Kames, and Stewart that Tucker turned when criticizing Alison's ideas.   Like the Scottish theorists, Tucker believed in the efficacy of examining his own consciousness for an understanding of aesthetic experience; and his introspection allowed him to hold that "the greater part of what is called beauty arises not from the visible properties of the visible object, but from the pleasing and interesting trains of thought which such object has excited."[20]   Yet he felt that it was contrary to the "common sense of mankind" to attribute, as did Alison and Jeffrey, all aesthetic gratification to the working of the mind and to deny that there is a direct, sensuous enjoyment in the act of perception.   In reality, Tucker pointed out, the emotion of beauty is aroused by a "direct organic pleasure" which is "sometimes heightened, sometimes diminished, and sometimes entirely effaced by the associations of ideas."[21]   It was his intent to list what properties arouse pleasurable sensations and then to prove why such attributes are enjoyable.

Tucker's first task—to catalogue sources or objects of beauty—was relatively easy.   Reflected light, he said, produces a pleasure which, experienced from infancy to old age, gives value to precious stones and

17. Gerard, *Essay on Taste*, pp. 42-43.

18. *Elements of Criticism* (London, 1824), p. 96.   See Bate, *From Classic to Romantic*, pp. 106-107, who discusses Kames's theory in relation to Alison's.

19. *Philosophical Essays* in *Works*, V, 205-207.   See below, Chap. X, pp. 156-157, for a more detailed discussion of Stewart's probable influence on Tucker's essay "On Beauty."

20. "On Beauty," *Essays, Moral and Metaphysical* (Philadelphia, 1860), p. 143.

21. "On Beauty," *Essays* (1822), pp. 170-171.

explains the beauty which Burke traced to smoothness.[22] Certain colors, especially prismatic hues, are always enjoyable;[23] regular curves and parallel or straight lines have an inherent beauty which is illustrated, for example, by the fact that a "square is more agreeable" than a triangle, "or a circle than a square."[24] Variety, Tucker's last source for beauty, consists of either strong contrasts, as in cut glass, or "gentle, and almost imperceptible variations," as in shells, and every agreeable object which "has a cloud like appearance."[25]

Tucker was aware that to state that some qualities of visible objects are by their nature pleasure-giving is not to prove that such is the case. He set out, therefore, to support his beliefs. He argued that Burke's theory of muted colors was a sophisticated refinement and that bright colors, particularly red, appeal to all people whose "natural feelings" have not been blunted by the "habit of mental speculation."[26] Although Tucker was generally opposed to efforts to elucidate the workings of the mind by physiological theories, such as those set forth by Erasmus Darwin and Joseph Priestley,[27] he now advanced a physiological explanation for the popularity of bright colors as well as for other universal preferences: "the objects of each sense," he suggested, "are agreeable according to the size of the particles impinging on the nerves," and "the senses are susceptible of delight, according to the force of the percussion they can severally support."[28] But probably recognizing that this solution did not explain why all of the qualities he set forth arouse the emotion of the beautiful, Tucker, following the lead of Lord Kames,[29] took the problem completely out of the realm of scientific discussion and turned it over to God. Men enjoy looking at certain objects, especially those which are red, he said, because of

an original law of our organization, stamped on us by the great Author of all things, who, when he ordered that matter should cohere with matter,—that fire should melt wax and harden clay,—that animals should generate

22. *Ibid.*, pp. 172-174.
23. *Ibid.*, pp. 176-182.
24. *Ibid.*, pp. 182-185. Tucker's examples of beautiful forms are given in "On Architecture," *Essays* (1822), pp. 112-113.
25. "On Beauty," *Essays* (1822), p. 185.
26. *Ibid.*, pp. 177-178, 202-203.
27. See below, Chap. X, p. 164, for an example of Tucker's attitude toward Darwin's and Priestley's physiological theories.
28. "On Beauty," *Essays* (1822), p. 201.
29. Kames wrote: "To enquire why an object . . . appears beautiful, would, I am afraid, be a vain attempt: it seems the most probable opinion, that the nature of man was originally framed with a relish [for beauty]." (*Elements*, 3rd ed., I, 259, as cited in Hipple, *The Beautiful, the Sublime, & the Picturesque,* p. 109.)

others in their likeness, also ordained that certain figures, colours and motions should please the human eye.[30]

By suggesting that the Creator so constituted man that he could experience delight upon the perception of certain visual objects and at the same time by assuming that these pleasures could be enhanced, modified, or obviated by the association of ideas, Tucker attempted to compromise between the "vulgar," who considered all the pleasure aroused by visual objects to be due to "natural beauty," and the "learned," who "underrated the pleasures of sense."[31]

If Tucker was something of a trimmer in his position on the nature of the beautiful, yet he took a firm stand on sublimity, stating unequivocally that it is a purely subjective emotion. Though Alison's theory is "erroneous and imperfect" in explaining the nature of beauty, said Tucker at the close of his 1815 essay "On Beauty," it "seems perfectly and undeniably just as it regards sublimity, which is . . . nothing more than the property of exciting in us ideas of power, danger, vastness and the like."[32]

In 1860 Tucker elaborated his discussion of sublimity, insisting that it was a concept totally unrelated to beauty. Almost all metaphysicians, he said, recognize the two divisions in taste, and only Dr. Thomas Brown is illogical enough to allege that the emotions are the same.[33] Instead of discussing such defective theories, however, Tucker intended to distinguish briefly between beauty and sublimity and to examine the contentions of the most reputable philosophers and critics.

Both the beautiful and the sublime, thought Tucker, could be defined largely in terms of pleasure and pain and were to be differentiated, first, by the objects which evoke each emotion, and, second, by the nature of the observer's response to these objects. Beauty is aroused by objects which are "little . . . or at least moderate" in size.[34] At the sight of the beautiful, cares and troubles are dismissed, and the mind is filled with "always agreeable" and sometimes "voluptuous" trains of thought, which can be "traced to pleasing recollections or anticipations, and to images of love . . . or other grateful feelings."[35]

30. "On Beauty," *Essays* (1822), p. 179.

31. *Ibid.*, p. 196.

32. *Ibid.*, p. 206.

33. "On Sublimity," *Essays* (1860), p. 200. In Tucker's mind, Brown's belief that "the same object, when beautiful, may by gradual changes become sublime, would also prove that white and black, day and night, virtue and vice are identical" (*idem*).

34. "Lectures on Rhetoric and Belles Lettres . . . at the Seventh Session, 1830-31," Tucker-Harrison-Smith Papers, University of Virginia Library, Lecture LXV.

35. *Idem.* Cf. "On Sublimity," *Essays* (1860), pp. 193-194.

The sublime, on the other hand, is the product of the "vast, the terrible, the great, and powerful"—including thunderstorms, the ocean, or "exalted virtue in our species."[36] One who witnesses such scenes is gripped by a sense of danger, or fear, or he feels "an elevation of mind." The pleasures of the sublime, which are sometimes greater than those of beauty, are thus frequently combined with disagreeable sentiments or with "qualified pain."[37] Enjoyment rests upon a psychological "law of our nature" that emotional activity is as necessary to man as physical exercise. Added to the "relief from languor," which all observers feel, is the "undefinable sense of inward greatness" which some especially sensitive people experience.[38]

The extreme subjectivism which Tucker had implicitly denounced in all his other aesthetic opinions completely triumphed in his discussion of sublimity. While beauty exists in objects independently of mind, the sublime could be defined only in terms of one's mental reactions to certain stimuli. Since these effects vary so much with the objects that arouse them and the persons receiving them, he thought it was foolish not to admit complete relativity. The theories of Longinus, Burke, Blair, and Stewart, though all true of *some* species of sublimity, are "faulty only in assuming a principle that applies to one, to be applicable to all."[39]

LITERATURE: PROSE

Tucker's earliest and most interesting discussion of prose centers around his use of a concept of cyclic evolution to determine the status and probable fate of English and American writing. His essay "On Style," published in the *Port Folio* in 1814, opens with a paragraph in which he expressed a belief in the rise and consequent dissolution of language, but at the same time posed the contradictory possibility of averting or at least arresting the decline.

Nothing more strongly marks the progress of society from rudeness to refinement than changes in style. As men advance in knowledge, language acquires copiousness; as they become more accurate in their discrimina-

36. "On Sublimity," *Essays* (1860), pp. 196-197.

37. *Ibid.*, pp. 194-195, 197.

38. *Ibid.*, pp. 193-195. Tucker thus explained the reasons for enjoying tragedy or an execution, for drinking alcohol, and for gambling (in which case the subject is impelled by "temporary agitations of his feelings, an increase of sensations, a relief from languor"), pp. 195-196. See also "Lectures on Rhetoric and Belles Lettres," Lecture LXV.

39. "On Sublimity," *Essays* (1860), p. 199.

tions, it acquires precision; and as they increase in sensibility to delicacy and beauty, it acquires elegance and polish.   But there are certain limits to this improvement which it cannot transcend and it yet remains to be decided whether it can long remain stationary in that excellence it has thus gradually attained, or like every thing else that is human, be destined by natural causes to undergo deterioration and decline.[40]

In Europe from the time of the Renaissance, various uses were made of the ancient concept of the eternal rise and fall of cultures, especially in quarrels over the possibility of progress.[41]   Thus, in 1629, George Hakewill, in the manner of Jean Bodin, argued against the primitivistic belief in the decay of the universe and proposed that "there is . . . both in Wits and Arts, as in all things besides, a kinde of circular progress: they have their birth, their growth, their flowering, their failing, their fading, and within a while after their resurrection and reflourishing again."[42]   In the eighteenth century, however, in an age which was generally committed to a belief in progress, the same general cyclic concept of civilization which Hakewill used and which had prepared the ground for the idea of progress was paradoxically applied to literature by Sir William Temple to combat a belief in perpetual progress.[43]   Even earlier, by the mid-seventeenth century, says F. W. Bateson, "the cyclic theory of civilization which . . . Temple popularized later in the century" to attack the idea of literary progress had been applied to language.   Displacing the earlier conception that there could be a "continuous improvement of the language" was the belief, especially strong in the eighteenth century in the works of such critics as Leonard Welsted and Noah Webster, that in all nations language reaches "the climax of its evolution" from which it declines. Great disagreement existed as to exactly when the English language

40. "On Style," *Essays* (1822), p. 157.

41. For the background of this concept and its relationship to literary theory, see Clara Marburg, *Sir William Temple: A Seventeenth Century "Libertine"* (New Haven, 1932), pp. 43-46; René Wellek, *The Rise of English Literary History* (Chapel Hill, N.C., 1941), pp. 41-42, 72-74.

42. Quoted in Richard Foster Jones, *Ancients and Moderns: A Study of the Background of the Battle of the Books,* Washington University Studies in Language and Literature, n.s., No. 6 (St. Louis, Mo., 1936), p. 32.   See Jones, *op. cit.,* pp. 23-42, and J. B. Bury, *The Idea of Progress: An Inquiry into Its Origins and Growth,* new ed. (New York, 1932), pp. 1-97, for a discussion of this concept in the history of the idea of progress.   Also pertinent are Frederick J. Teggart, "The Idea of Progress" in *Theory of History* (New Haven, 1925); and Wellek, *Rise of Literary History, passim.*

43. See Marburg, *Sir William Temple,* pp. 43-53, for the continuity of this concept in literary history.

had reached its "period of perfection," various writers dating it any-where between the Restoration and the end of the eighteenth century.[44]

Throughout the 1700's, this cyclic concept of development was rigorously applied to language and the arts and provided one reason why "theories of progress in aesthetic pursuits were few and qualified," especially in the last half of the century.[45] Following the lead of David Hume, a large number of Scottish and English critics assumed that modern cultures must follow the pattern of Greece and Rome and stated as axiomatic that after literature reaches a certain peak of excellence, it inevitably declines. Widely disseminated, this belief in degeneration was variously explained. Hume himself, drawing the familiar analogy between the life spans of plants and the arts, stressed that great literary achievement in one generation discouraged fol-lowing generations from writing[46]—a theory which seems to have influenced Tucker's discussion of poetry, but not his treatment of prose. Other critics whom Tucker certainly read felt that the self-destruction of the arts came about as artists sought to excel over their predecessors through the use of novelty.[47] Alexander Gerard ex-plained in *An Essay on Taste* (1759) that once literature has reached its height in a nation, later generations of writers "turn aside into unbeaten tracks of nicety and affectation." Gradually, the novelty catches the fancy of the general public and the taste of the generation is debased.[48] In a similar fashion, Archibald Alison in *Essays on the Nature and Principles of Taste* (1790) restated the doctrine of un-seemly and unwarranted innovation as a cause for decline, and Lord Kames, though he suggested other reasons, also argued in *Elements of*

44. F. W. Bateson, *English Poetry and the English Language: An Experiment in Literary History* (Oxford, 1934), pp. 46-47, 49.

45. See John D. Scheffer, "The Idea of Decline in Literature and the Fine Arts in Eighteenth-Century England," *MP*, XXXIV (1936), 156. Scheffer does not relate the idea of the degeneration of fine arts with theories of language and asserts that the idea of literary decline is unrelated to "the idea that the history of man's culture has been characterized by vicissitudes, or by cycles of barbarity and refinement." As Wellek (*The Rise of Literary History*, p. 72) points out, however, Hume used the same cyclic concept as Temple and others; and Scheffer's article really is concerned with the old "biological parallel" of the arts (p. 207 n.). Wellek's argument that Hume "recognized implicitly the 'cycle theory' of Temple" is substantiated by Hume's assertion that the "arts and sciences, like some plants require a fresh soil" in order to flourish and decay again. See "Of the Rise and Progress of the Arts and Sciences" in *Essays Moral, Political and Literary,* ed. T. H. Green and T. H. Grose, new ed. (London, 1889), I, 195.

46. "Of the Rise and Progress of the Arts and Sciences" in *Essays,* I, 195-196.

47. For a discussion of this cause for decay, see Scheffer, "The Idea of Decline," pp. 164, 175.

48. P. 130.

Criticism (1762) that in the fine arts there was a "gradual progress from simplicity to complex forms and profuse ornament" and that literature becomes burdened by an excess of "words, epithets, figures," which indicates its degeneracy.[49]

In his essay "On Style," Tucker summarized eighteenth-century theories of language before expressing his own view of the state of modern prose. Although a few perfectibilians, such as Godwin, argue that style "is still in a state of advancement," the English language, Tucker said, "is generally thought to have passed the summit of its excellence," some critics fixing upon the Age of Anne as its peak, others the "subsequent period of Hume, Robertson, Johnson and Goldsmith," and a very few the time of Dryden. Tucker himself admitted an attachment for the writers of "a century ago" whose "careless effusions" find easier access to the heart than modern works; yet he admired the precision, variety, and regularity of modern prose,[50] which, as he once explained, had to become "more multifarious and diversified" as the "bounds of human knowledge expanded."[51]

Tucker's major concern, however, was not to indicate his preference, but to warn writers of the dangers of degeneration. It was a paradox, he said, that the corruption of language, as witnessed in the histories of Greece and Rome, could be ascribed chiefly to the "perversion of that labour, and the abuse of that taste, by the successive efforts of which it had been perfected."[52] Like the Scottish critics, Tucker argued that in their anxiety to please, modern writers strove for unnecessary novelty and included in their works "new-coined words—strange epithets, and a multiplicity of them—forced conceits—strained metaphors—vain circumlocutions."[53] In short, Tucker believed that prose, like such fine arts as architecture, painting, and music, developed gradually from simplicity to refinement with the advancement of civilization and that, once it reached its peak, it tended to decline as a result of undue innovations in style.[54]

In the tradition of innumerable cisatlantic critics for whom the fostering of a "simple" prose style had been a major preoccupation

49. For a survey of the views of Alison and Kames, see Scheffer, "The Idea of Decline," pp. 167-170, 175-176. Wellek, *The Rise of Literary History*, pp. 73-74, says that Kames, in his *Sketches of the History of Man* (1774), argued against the necessity of decay and for the first time clearly formulated an argument combatting the idea of necessary internal devolution.

50. "On Style," *Essays* (1822), pp. 159-160.

51. "On Simplicity in Ornament," *Essays* (1822), p. 31.

52. "On Style," *Essays* (1822), pp. 157-158.

53. *Ibid.*, p. 158.

54. "On Simplicity in Ornament," *Essays* (1822), pp. 29-31.

since the Colonial Period,[55] Tucker urged American writers to forgo "ornament" for substance. Pointing out that the medium in which they worked already showed traces of that "undue solicitude for novelty and ornament" which signalled the decline of a mature language, Tucker argued that there were in the United States "peculiar circumstances" which tended to hasten the corruption of language. Most Americans, he said, were insufficiently acquainted with the classics or the "earlier English writers." As a result, they encouraged the "false splendour" of recent "novels and romances," as well as the "gaudy and tasteless finery" of New World oratory. In democratic America, where almost anyone could publish in the newspapers, moreover, a multiplicity of writers propagated "the false taste of which they themselves have been the disciples."[56]

But despite the fact that "affectation and false refinement" were evident in much of English and American prose, Tucker's conclusion was not pessimistic. Rejecting the essence of all the theories of degeneration by refusing to accept the inevitability of decline, he asserted that the excellence of English prose could be maintained. He closed his essay by hailing "with pleasure the return of good taste" shown in occasional articles in the *Edinburgh* and *Quarterly* reviews, and by hoping that these works have "not only furnished valuable models of composition, but that they also give an indication that the period of fine writing in our language, may be long protracted, if not perpetuated, notwithstanding the inherent tendency of every mature language, to gradual corruption and decay."[57]

As Professor of Rhetoric and Belles Lettres, Tucker was more interested in making a rhetorical analysis of prose than in speculating on the degeneration of literature. In his lectures dated 1830-31, though

55. See Benjamin T. Spencer, *The Quest for Nationality: An American Literary Campaign* (Syracuse, N.Y., 1957), pp. 7-12, 53-60.

56. "On Style," *Essays* (1822), pp. 161-162.

57. *Ibid.*, pp. 166-167. Tucker's discussion of prose, though restricted to a treatment of diction and style, is undoubtedly a part of the broader conflict between the ideas of primitivism and progress. His disinclination to follow the view that prose must decline seems to be related to his refusal to believe that luxury always leads to the degeneration of morals and art. According to Scheffer ("Idea of Decline," pp. 168-169), one of the external arguments advanced by Kames for inevitable degeneration was that the luxury and decay of a civilization are manifested by excessive novelty in that culture's literature. Tucker's argument—essentially that of Adam Smith and other economists—was that luxury "was a solitary & even indispensable concomitant of civilization . . . and could not enervate a people & only added to the stock of human enjoyment" ("Autobiography," manuscript copy, Tucker-Harrison-Smith Papers, University of Virginia Library, p. 21). See below, Chap. XII, for a discussion of Tucker's attitude toward luxury and refinement.

he continued to advocate perspicuity, delicacy, and especially simplicity in composition, he devoted most of his class discussion to the three styles of prose. The first addresses itself solely to the understanding and makes no attempt to please the imagination or to excite the emotions. Though the remaining two styles also attempt to convince the understanding, they are classified by their predominant appeals, the one to the imagination and the other to the imagination and the feelings. These categories generally seem to be adaptations of George Campbell's "principles in our nature, which, when properly addressed and managed, give no inconsiderable aid to reason in promoting belief" in a speaker's audience. In his *Philosophy of Rhetoric,* Campbell pointed out that the difference between addressing the understanding (judgment) and the fancy (imagination) lies in the distinction between "ratiocination and imagery," in the fact that the fancy is pleased with "the exhibition of a strong likeness, which escapes the generality of people."[58]

Tucker seems to have had essentially the same distinction in mind when he stressed the fact that figurative language must be excluded from works whose function it is to address the understanding. As examples of good style, Tucker cited Hume's essays, Smith's *Theory of Moral Sentiments,* and the works of Buffon, Alexander Hamilton, Albert Gallatin, and James Madison. Locke's *Essay on Human Understanding,* he said, was often considered the perfect example of rational writing, but, while always clear and free of metaphors which would give it a "false hue," it is prose without warmth. Its "proper and intelligible" diction is "often homely, vulgar & undignified." As a proof that Locke's "rough & unharmonious" prose was not a necessary result of his rhetorical purpose, Tucker cited the philosophical writing of Dugald Stewart, in whom

. . . we find the same clearness, the same precision, and often the same exception from figurative language, but always the most elegant & melodious diction. Nothing can be smoother or better turned than his periods, & his words present a succession of pictures to the mind of his readers in which they see his thoughts, coloured indeed, but so coloured as to add to their liveliness & spirit without detracting from their fidelity and truth.[59]

58. *The Philosophy of Rhetoric* (Edinburgh and London, 1808), I, 160, 165-166. Tucker's enumeration, of course, does not exactly parallel Campbell's, who sees the "powers of the mind, the imagination, the memory, and the passions" as handmaids who help reason (judgment) achieve truth (I, 161).

59. "Lectures on Rhetoric and Belles Lettres," Lecture XXIV.

Comprehended in Tucker's second classification are all works on literary criticism, essays on "human manners, & character & conduct," historical studies, and occasionally "didactic & philosophic writing." In this field, Tucker said, the reader's mind is "cheered by the melody of sounds and the lively images of fancy" and is thus "better able to endure the labours of thought." Essayists and critics who are commended are Stewart, Alison, Addison, Goldsmith, Johnson, Irving, and Prescott and, in general, the writers for the *Edinburgh* and the *Quarterly* reviews.

Historical writings, said Tucker, though primarily addressed to the imagination, sometimes appeal to the feelings. The historian must view calamities and human scenes with the eye of the philosopher, for, indeed, history is "philosophy teaching by example," as it shows the effects of various forces upon civil society. For the writer of history, then, "individual actions and characters are important only so long as they are connected with the laws, the religion, the manners, & other great features of civil society." William Robertson, said Tucker, best fulfills this ideal, and his "philosophical history" is consequently of much greater value than is the history of Gibbon, who merely "describes" the past. Voltaire similarly is valuable because, like Robertson, he takes "large views with an eye for the advancement of society," but, said Tucker, he cannot rank with the great writers of history. The arbiters of taste have always placed Robertson in the second or third position, behind either Hume or Gibbon. Tucker thought it beyond the purposes of his lectures to elaborate on the qualities of the writers and was content to characterize their styles: Robertson's modest prose resembles the "unassuming elegance of the lady, Gibbon's the showy attire of the actress"—but Hume's is best of all because it "conveys the idea of indifference to ornament."[60]

Unfortunately, Tucker devoted little space to the style of writing addressed to the feelings, which embraces orations and fiction. The forms in this category, he explained, were among the most difficult to compose, since the writer not only has to enter into the feelings of both his characters and his audience but also has to be especially adept in using language, avoiding long allegories and similes which are more appropriate in works addressed to the imagination, and using only those figures which "comport with a heated or hurried state of mind." As exemplary models for political writing, Tucker listed the works of Junius and Burke. Excellent novelists, he said, were Fielding,

60. Lecture XXV.

Smollett, and Mrs. Frances Sheridan; but he especially recommended Richardson and Goldsmith for "pathos & tender emotions" and Scott for "lofty emotions and strong passions."[61]

LITERATURE: POETRY

Poetic Theory

In poetic theory, as in aesthetics and philosophy, Tucker derived many ideas from the literature of the immediate past. His lectures reveal, in a general way, the influence of those critical and creative writings of the late eighteenth and early nineteenth centuries which stressed the significance for poetry of man's feelings and passions to the neglect of his rational endowments. More specifically, Tucker's theory of poetry reflects his eclectic use of eighteenth-century philosophy to propound a view of the nature and function of poetry. Although he never believed that all of man's experience could be explained in terms of the mechanical operation of the mind, Tucker did hold that the doctrine of associational psychology helped elucidate the nature of poetic creation and communication.

In early lectures on rhetoric and belles lettres, Tucker laid the foundation for his more "philosophical" discussions of poetry by attempting to describe and define poetry for his students. He devoted a great deal of attention to stylistic problems, following closely the teachings set forth in Hugh Blair's *Lectures* and George Campbell's *Philosophy of Rhetoric* and referring frequently to Kames's *Elements*. Supplementing the copious illustrations which Blair and Campbell provided as concrete examples of various forms of versification, diction, and imagery, Tucker added extensive quotations from his favorite poets, so that his students heard selections from almost all of the late seventeenth- and the eighteenth-century poets, as well as from Shakespeare, Moore, Rogers, Scott, and Byron.

In an effort to define poetry, Tucker distinguished it from other forms of expression, conveniently summarizing what he believed were its "outward characteristics." It differs from prose in having "greater melody of diction," inversion of word order, greater brevity or greater amplification, "greater dignity of language," "more varied & more abundant imagery," and, most importantly, "a more elevated tone of feeling & *wilder enthusiasm.*" Prose, he admitted, possesses "more or less" these same traits but lacks "perfect regularity" of structure, never exhibits all six attributes concurrently as does poetry,

61. Lecture XXVI.

and uses each only as an "auxiliary" to address "the will or the under-standing." In the same fashion, eloquence differs not only in wanting "regularity of diction" but in its intent: oratory, like poetry, "addresses itself to the feelings," but it does so "with a view to persuasion, whilst poetry addresses them only for the purpose of producing pleasure and kindling the same enthusiasm as that which excited it."[62]

Tucker thought so highly of the emotional aspect of poetry that, though he carefully covered the material in Blair and Campbell, he labeled the rhetorical aspects of poetry as superficial ornaments of the art.[63] His major interest was to explain how the poet utilizes the raw materials of experience to write verse which sympathetically arouses in his audience the same emotions and feelings which oc-casioned him to write. Before examining those of Tucker's lectures which deal in detail with poetic inspiration and communication, how-ever, a brief review of the philosophical and critical writings which influenced his theory is in order.

One of the most important contributions which the Scottish moral philosophers made to aesthetic and literary criticism, says Walter Jackson Bate, was the rationale which they provided for the subjective emotionalism which characterized much of the literature of the eight-eenth century. What had been "advocated or implied by the *je ne sais quoi* 'School of Taste' and by Shaftesbury and his ardent follow-ing" received support from the Scottish critics who explained on psychological grounds how the imagination and sensibility were inti-mately connected.[64] In his *Theory of Moral Sentiments* (1759), Adam Smith, elaborating upon a suggestion of David Hume, substituted for Shaftesbury's "moral sense" as man's internal monitor the emotion of sympathy, arguing that, though the moral judgment is in part in-stinctive, it is also greatly influenced by the operation of habit and custom, by the associations which are the product of the imaginative faculty. As a result of Smith's teaching, Scottish critics of the "moral sense" tradition formulated the aesthetic doctrines of "sympathetic imagination" on the part of the artist and "sympathetic participation" on the part of his audience, both of which became thought of as necessary for the creation and understanding of art.[65]

Extreme sensibility, and a consequent "enthusiasm" on the part of the poet, whether they were psychologically a part of imaginative action itself or

62. Lecture XXXIX.
63. Lecture XLII.
64. *From Classic to Romantic*, pp. 130-131.
65. *Ibid.*, pp. 133-135.

whether they were externally complementary in their working with it, were especially necessary for the complete self-absorption of the poet in the object of his contemplative concern, and for the sympathetic under-standing which he achieves by means of this absorption.[66]

Tucker was familiar with *The Theory of Moral Sentiments* and may have got this idea directly from Smith; yet he probably absorbed it as well from the works of Dugald Stewart, Archibald Alison, and Thomas Brown, all of whom extended Smith's doctrine from the moral to the aesthetic field. Although Tucker disagreed with some of the opinions of these critics, labeling part of Alison's theory of associationism, for example, as an "ingenious" but unwarranted de-duction of a "sound philosophy," he clearly supported their belief that the imaginative faculty works in harmony with the "moral sense." Thus, in speaking of the eye as the most delicate of all senses, Tucker said that sight is always

apt to excite those connected chains of thought which the mind has the faculty of linking together, and which must ever be chiefly employed about those chief objects of sensibility, the happiness of ourselves and our species. Hence it is that visible objects so often awaken agreeable recollections, raise up cheering anticipations, and in so many ways touch the cords of our sympathy or self-love.[67]

In this statement Tucker adumbrated much of what he was to insist on as making up the "essence" of poetry—its ability to impart pleasure by means of melodic, agreeable language so that the senses, the imagi-nations, and the "moral feelings" of the poet's audience would be sympathetically aroused.

Basic to Tucker's theory is the tenet that great poetry, which serves as a vehicle for the emotions, cannot be didactic. His belief that the end of poetry is pure pleasure, unalloyed with any attempt to persuade or instruct, rests upon the philosophic premise "that the strength & beauty of all metaphysical experience have their foundation in our pleasures & pains—those having the greatest effect which refer to our liveliest emotions."[68] Because Tucker assumed all emotional excite-ment to be enjoyable, he said that it is the duty of the poet "to awaken our sympathy by giving touching & natural exhibitions of human pas-sions & sentiments" and to "exhibit to our imaginations lively & faithful delineations of the most interesting forms of nature."[69]

66. *Ibid.*, pp. 135-136.
67. "On Beauty," *Essays* (1860), pp. 144-145.
68. "Lectures on Rhetoric and Belles Lettres," Lecture IX.
69. Lecture XXXIX.

That portion of the lectures which may have dealt in detail with the poet's description of human passions is missing.[70] What remains on that subject is Tucker's assertion that the "emotions of the heart" are manifested by "sentiments of love and pity and horror and disgust."[71] Tucker's definition of the "essence" or "soul" of poetry, however, suggests the nature of human passions and their relationship in poetry to the operations of the fancy:

This consists either in the elevation of the thought, or a fervid glow of feeling by which the poet seems to be hurried away by his subject—and which never fails to impart to the hearer or reader somewhat of the same animating warmth, which inspired it. Of all the qualities of poetry there is none to which it so much owes its success as this, or which so truly marks the genius of the poet. The rapturous feelings to which he gives utterance find a sympathetic tho' fainter response in every bosom to whom [*sic*] they are addressed, for his language is a faithful echo to his feelings. It is emotion, then, warm, generous, lofty emotion, such as the perception of the beautiful and the grand may inspire!—such as seems to raise him who feels it above the sordidness & petty concerns of ordinary life,—which seems to be the essence of poetry. . . . It is emotion which calls forth the electric spark of the mind, & the past & the future stand before him with the freshness & distinctness of a present picture or landscape & reendows every object of the scene with life & thot [*sic*] & passion—and objects of his lively sympathy.[72]

The balance of Tucker's discussion of poetic theory is found in his elaboration on the importance of the beautiful and sublime "in composition." He treated both concepts somewhat confusingly, first, in terms of physical objects or emotional states which inspire the poet and, second, as effects to be created by him. In so doing Tucker followed the Scottish critics in holding that the imagination and the "sensibility" work together to bring about the effect of "warm emotion," and in delineating the manner in which the poet evokes the sympathetic participation of his audience.

When Tucker discussed "beauty, as applied to composition," he insisted that the poet should not be limited to the "function of representing beautiful objects,"[73] a practice which, he said, gives so much charm to descriptive poetry that some poets, such as Erasmus Darwin, "by considering all poetry whatever to be merely a 'speaking

70. Lecture XXXVIII. Part of Lecture IX is also missing.
71. Lecture XLIV.
72. Lecture XL.
73. Lecture LXVI.

picture' have precluded themselves from excelling in its higher species, the pathetic and sublime."[74]

In *A Voyage to the Moon* (1827), Tucker satirized Darwin's theory of poetry, focusing his attention upon a passage in Darwin's *The Loves of the Plants* (1789). In an interlude between cantos, Darwin causes his Poet to say to his Bookseller that "as our ideas derived from visible objects are more distinct than those derived from the objects of our other senses, the words expressive of these ideas belonging to vision make up the principal part of poetic language. That is, the Poet writes principally to the eye. . . ."[75] As James Logan notes, Darwin's poetic theory, influenced by his physiological speculations, though it would not deny the qualities of sublimity or beauty, did emphasize that the chief art of the poet is to bring images before the eye.[76] Tucker satirized this mechanical theory of poetic invention, along with other of Darwin's ideas.[77] Joseph Atterley, the narrator of *A Voyage,* visits the home of Dr. Vindar [Darwin] and is shown a "poetry box," modeled upon an apothecary's medicine chest, in which are all the important materials for poetry. "Now," says Vindar,

as the excellence of poetry consists in bringing before the mind's eye what can be brought before the corporeal eye, I have here collected every object that is either beautiful or pleasing in nature, . . . as well as those that are strikingly disagreeable. When I wish to exhibit those pictures which constitute poetry, I consult the appropriate cabinet, and I take my choice of those various subjects which can best call up the image I wish to present to my reader. . . . It is astonishing what labour this box has saved me, and how much it has added to the beauty and melody of my verse.[78]

Tucker's denigration of Darwin's poetical theory did not result from a denial that beautiful physical objects are subject matter for poetry. On the contrary, Tucker felt that "the most copious sources of materials to the poet" are to be found in the "two species of beauty in the physical world." Poets address themselves forcibly and agree-

74. "On Beauty," *Essays* (1860), p. 189.
75. Pp. 48-49, as cited by James Venable Logan, *The Poetry and Aesthetics of Erasmus Darwin* (Princeton, 1936), pp. 78-79.
76. Logan, *Darwin,* pp. 78, 85.
77. In *A Voyage to the Moon: With Some Account of the Manners and Customs, Science and Philosophy, of the People of Morosofia and Other Lunarians* (New York, 1827), Tucker lampooned Darwin's theory of blood transfusion (p. 121) and his projected method of raising water by a mechanical contraption (pp. 123-124). For Darwin's practices and theories, see Logan, *Darwin,* pp. 13, 47 and n.
78. *A Voyage,* pp. 126-127.

ably to the imagination by representing, first, "soft & agreeable colours, melodious & symphonious sounds, gentle & graceful motions, symmetrical proportions and the numerous items which constitute personal beauty, and which make a world of itself," and, second, "the agreeable associations to which all these objects give rise."[79]   But, as Tucker explained in exalting the role of the poet in arousing the emotion of the beautiful, there could be a great heightening of the effect of beauty.   When the poet merely describes beautiful objects, said Tucker, there is in the poem a weakening of the force of beauty, since "the immediate perception or sensation more powerfully excites the mind than the mere conception." But, he pointed out, in the best poetry there are more than adequate compensations for this loss. Poems, more than any other composition or "any physical object whatever," "directly & forcibly" create in the mind that "moral beauty" which consists of those "softer & more amiable virtues" which are "so similar to the mixt feelings of love & admiration we experience for physical beauty." This is so, said Tucker, because "words are more perfect signs of thoughts & feelings than any mere combinations of form & colour": melody, rhythm, and rhyme, which "impart the character of music to articulate language," provide a desirable and gratifying sensual impact upon the ears, thus compensating for that loss of the direct sensual pleasure which occurs in the translation of a beautiful object from the physical through the mental realm into poetry; and the attributes of language also simultaneously excite "our minds" so as to stimulate the associating activity. In much the same fashion of musical verse, figures of speech—the products of the fancy—are inherently pleasurable and also contribute to the over-all effect of the poem. Indeed, said Tucker, when the poet contemplates the "beautiful or grand," he is moved to a state of "high wrought feeling," and when his mind is agitated, he sees and is able to utilize in language "analogies & resemblances which are not perceived by a mind in a state of quiescence." And, said Tucker, explaining how "sensibility" unites with the imagination in the creation of poetry, "according to the mechanism of the mind, the fancy & feelings mutually act upon one another, & whatever excites the one, has a tendency to lend new strength & activity to the other." The poet is inspired by a sort of Longinian frenzy and, because of the power of figurative and musical language, transfers by a kind of emotional chemistry his feelings to his audience.

79. This quotation and the balance of the discussion on beauty "in composition" are taken from Lecture LXVI, "Lectures on Rhetoric and Belles Lettres."

Before concluding his lecture on beauty and poetry, Tucker emphasized that a poem not only is "the vehicle of transmitting conceptions of beauty & the various emotions which accompany these conceptions" but in and of itself is "capable of having beauty—and that of the same two kinds," both of which are independent of its subject matter. It has, first of all, a "direct sensitive beauty" of ordered, melodious language which produces "the same sort of pleasure as the sound of a musical instrument," and, more importantly, there is awakened a feeling of beauty which is aroused by the "excellence of style" as well as a recognition that the poet, by the handling of language, meter, and plan, has succeeded in exciting the emotions of his readers.

Like many critics of his age, Tucker thought highly of poetry which evoked the emotion of sublimity.[80] He pointed out that this feeling always "arises from a reference to ourselves & our species" of such physical attributes as power and magnitude or such moral qualities as virtue and evil. Citing Shakespeare, Milton, and Byron as writers who reached the heights of sublimity, Tucker said that the poet could arouse the emotion in two ways. On the one hand, he could represent such sights as storm-tossed oceans or thunder storms, or, on the other, he could delineate such human beings as Robespierre, Medea, Timon of Athens, or Coriolanus, who, indifferent or invulnerable to those frailties and calamities common to humanity, are either utterly vicious or virtuous.

Although Tucker expressed the view that any excitement of emotion tended to be gratifying, he recognized, he said, that in real life the experience of observing such phenomena as inspired the sublime might become "unmingled pain." But, he said, emphasizing that successful artists create "as lively & impressive representations" as possible, when "sublime objects are represented to us through the imagination" they are always agreeable, and the sublime when but "a copy" may become "an object of beauty & admiration." Because of this softening effect of art, the writer who seeks to win the greatest admiration should portray the "most terrible and odious" phenomena and even "such horrible crimes as would produce abhorrence & disgust" in real life. Rather than attempting to diminish the effect of their material, then, "poets & those writers who would address themselves to the imagination" should do all possible to heighten the intensity of their works, only taking care not to over-exaggerate so as to pass beyond the sublime to the ridiculous, the distinction between

80. The following discussion of sublimity is taken from Lecture LXV, "Lectures on Rhetoric and Belles Lettres."

which is "a very nice one." For the sublime, obscurity is an asset, said Tucker, "whenever it favors the operation of the sense of danger & gives more play to our fears." Lastly and most importantly, the composition "should have a certain degree of singleness, since a variety of objects by exciting many ideas & emotions would prevent any one from having that force which concentration would give."

Tucker's poetic theory, as well as his discussions of prose, suggests the interesting possibility that he influenced the early Poe, indeed, helped to form some of Poe's most characteristic aesthetic doctrines and practices. Poe's theory of the unity of effect, generally thought to have its origins in the writings of A. W. von Schlegel,[81] but also recently traced by Robert Jacobs to Archibald "Alison's demand for a unity of emotion,"[82] seems to have been adumbrated by Tucker's postulate that each composition "have a certain degree of singleness." Other of Tucker's lectures which discuss the technical skills needed by a writer suggest Poe's stress upon a necessary unity of tone in a work of art and his theory of causal arrangement. In Lectures XXIV to XXVI, it will be recalled, Tucker said that all prose writings could be classified into three groups, according to their primary appeals to the understanding, the imagination, and the feelings. In addressing successfully any of these faculties, it was the writer's task, said Tucker in Lecture XXVII, to advance in logical steps, though carefully concealing his method from his readers. He should "begin in the tone with which he means to proceed," and should arrange his materials "so that one part may seem to rise naturally out of another," as in a "chain of cause & effect," thus skillfully leading the reader "by easy gradations to the conclusion."

Poe's famous attack upon didacticism has been traced to his reading of Coleridge's *Biographia Literaria,*[83] but perhaps it was first suggested by Tucker. Tucker emphasized in a number of ways that poetry's aim is pure pleasure, free from any taint of instruction or persuasion. Related to this hedonistic view of poetry is Tucker's tenet that music is an intrinsic element of poetry. Taken together, these statements

81. The influence of Schlegel has been documented by many Poe scholars. A recent work which stresses the influence of Schlegel and other German Romantics on Poe is Albert J. Lubell, "Poe and A. W. Schlegel," *JEGP,* LII (1953), 1-12. See also George Kelly, "Poe's Theory of Beauty," *AL,* XXVII (1956), 521-536.

82. See "Poe's Heritage from Jefferson's Virginia" (Johns Hopkins University diss., 1953), pp. 133-134 and *passim.*

83. See Floyd Stovall, "Poe's Debt to Coleridge," *University of Texas Studies in English,* X (1930), 85.

might well culminate in Poe's famous definition of poetry as "the rhythmical creation of beauty." In his review of Joseph Rodman Drake's *The Culprit Fay*,[84] Poe distinguished between two aspects of poetry.[85] First, "poesy" or "the Poetic Sentiment" he associated with the inspiration which evokes the poet's love of the beautiful and his sense of the sublime. For Poe this mood is "one in which the poet is impassioned and excited and has expansion of mind," corresponding "to . . . excitement or elevation of soul."[86] Second, Poe was concerned with the merits of the poem itself, that is, with the *"means"* by which the poet affects the minds and emotions of his audience. In Tucker's lectures is set forth a similar distinction. There Tucker defined the "essence" or "soul" of poetry as that which is called forth by "the perception of the beautiful and the grand"—that "fervent glow of feeling" which lifts the artist "above the sordidness & petty concerns of ordinary life." At the same time, however, Tucker, too, was concerned with the poem itself, as a means by which the poet conveys a sense of the beautiful and sublime to his readers, using carefully ordered, musical language, which, through the sensual pleasure it provides, more than compensates for that loss of pleasure that takes place when a beautiful object or experience undergoes a translation from the physical world into the world of art. Like Poe,[87] Tucker felt that the mere recording of "poetic" materials, though capable of providing a degree of pleasure, does not result in great poetry, which needs to be inspired and to be carefully arranged. It was for this reason that he emphasized the importance of approximating music in poetry by means of melody, rhythm, rhyme, and onomatopoeia.

Several examples of onomatopoeia provided by Tucker to illustrate the naturalness and universality of imitation suggest the possible use of his ideas by Poe in two famous poems.[88] The title of Poe's "Ulalume" seems to mean "wailing" or "light of or in sorrow" and comes

84. Review of Drake's *The Culprit Fay* in *The Complete Works of Edgar Allan Poe*, ed. James A. Harrison (New York, 1902), VIII, 282.

85. *Edgar Allan Poe*, eds. Margaret Alterton and Hardin Craig (New York, 1935), pp. xxix-xxx.

86. Stovall, "Poe's Debt to Coleridge," p. 97. Stovall's point was to distinguish "between the softened emotion succeeding an outburst of passion and the outburst itself," to show that, for Poe, the poetic mood "grows out of passion frequently, but composition never begins until the passion is tranquilized or transmuted into a spiritual exaltation" (*op. cit.*).

87. See Poe's review of Longfellow's *Ballads and Other Poems* in *Works*, XI, 71-72.

88. "Lectures on Rhetoric and Belles Lettres," Lecture XIII. Tucker apparently took his illustrations from an encyclopaedia, which he did not identify.

from the Latin word *ululare*.[89] In Tucker's lecture appears an illustration of how words, by their sounds, designate actions: "ὀλολύξω, *ululare, heulen, hurler,* to howl." The reason for Poe's puzzling spelling of "Yaanek" in the same poem as a name for Mount Erebus, down which "restlessly roll" the "scoriac rivers," is made clearer by another entry in the same Tucker lecture, in which he explained how vowel sounds, requiring "nothing but the simple opening of the mouth," offer "no obstacle to the emission of sound" and approximate the nature of the idea to be expressed. "Now," said Tucker, "we . . . see the probable origin of the Danish word *aa,* which signifies *river.* This generic term has in use become the name of three rivers in the Low Countries, of three in Switzerland, and of five in Westphalia—the vowels running without obstacle like the river." A third example, cited to show the close relationship between sounds and ideas, suggests a source for Poe's use of "tintinnabulation" in "The Bells," a problem which has concerned many critics.[90] "Ringing (tintinement), tinnitus, tintinnabulum, are words," said Tucker, "whose common radical *tin,* exactly imitates the clear, sharp & continued sound which is heard to diminish gradually when a metallic vessel is struck."

In Tucker's lectures, furthermore, Poe could have found the germ and justification for his belief that the beautiful could include the horrible; his utilization of the obscure in stories to heighten the effect of terror; and his assumption that "sensation" (horror) stories are legitimate forms of artistic expression, that, as Poe said, "even out of deformities" the imagination "fabricates . . . *Beauty.*"[91] Margaret Alterton[92] has plausibly suggested that in his review of Hawthorne's *Twice-Told Tales* Poe's defense of the horror story rests on the grounds that "it satisfied a human craving for excitement." Similarly, Tucker defended the portrayal of the "most terrible and odious," such "crimes as would produce abhorrence & disgust" in real life, by arguing, first of all, that emotional excitement is as basic to man as physical exercise and, second, that what is horrible in life is tempered by the artist to satisfy aesthetically this fundamental drive of man.[93]

89. Thomas O. Mabbott, *Explicator,* I (Feb., 1943), Item 25. See also *Selected Writings of Edgar Allan Poe,* ed. Edward H. Davidson (Boston, 1956), p. 497 n.

90. See, for examples, Fred A. Dudley, "Tintinnabulation: And a Source of Poe's 'The Bells,'" *AL,* IV (1933), 296-300; Killis Campbell, *Poems of Edgar Allan Poe* (Boston, 1917), pp. 281-282.

91. Quoted by Jay B. Hubbell, *The South in American Literature, 1607-1900* (Durham, N.C., 1954), p. 532.

92. *Edgar Allan Poe,* p. xix n.

93. "Lectures on Rhetoric and Belles Lettres," Lecture LXV.

Other possible influences on Poe's aesthetic theory, less specific, if not less important, may be traced in Tucker's work. Tucker perhaps provided Poe with a rationale for the treatment of purely "poetic" subjects for poetry—beautiful and sublime sentiments and objects. And, in a more general way, Tucker's philosophical theory may have stimulated Poe's interest in abnormal psychology. It is admittedly a long step from Tucker's delineation of Julia Moncrief's irrational father to Poe's treatment of Roderick Usher; but Tucker's belief, stated as early as 1804, that "delirium and madness, though remotely caused by corporeal disease, are the *immediate* effects of an imagination stimulated to preternatural vigour"[94] may well have interested Poe.

Although it has long been felt that Poe's thinking was strongly affected by his year at the University of Virginia in 1826,[95] no convincing case has ever been made for his literary theory having been formed there. Poe studied modern and classical languages and is not known to have attended Tucker's lectures, though it is possible that he audited Tucker's classes, looked at the notes of Tucker's students, or, perhaps, talked to Tucker about literature and aesthetics, since the two shared many tastes, especially that for Byron's poetry.[96]   Estab-

94. Tucker's statement appears in *The Rainbow*, p. 53.

95. See, for examples, Arthur Hobson Quinn, *Edgar Allan Poe: A Critical Biography* (New York, 1941), pp. 97-117; Hervey Allen, *Israfel: The Life and Times of Edgar Allan Poe*, 2nd ed. (New York, 1927), I, 147-180; Alterton, *Edgar Allan Poe*, pp. xx-xxiv.

96. Allen, *Israfel*, I, 179, speculates that William Wertenbaker and Poe passed part of Poe's last night at Charlottesville as guests of Tucker or Professor Blaetterman. Quinn, *Edgar Allan Poe*, p. 102, believes that Poe "would probably have gained most from intercourse with Tucker," of all the faculty members.
Several scholars have suggested that Poe knew and was influenced by Tucker. J. O. Bailey in "Sources for Poe's *Arthur Gordon Pym,* 'Hans Pfaal,' and Other Pieces," *PMLA*, LVII (1942), 513-535, thinks that Poe probably knew Tucker well; that for "Hans Pfaal," as well as for *Eureka*, Poe read Tucker's *A Voyage to the Moon*, either in manuscript or in printed form; and that Meredith Niel Posey ("Notes on *Hans Pfaal*," *MLN*, XLV [1930], 501-507) is wrong in thinking that Dr. Robley Dunglison's review of Tucker's book (*American Quarterly Review*, III [1828], 61-88) provided enough information for Poe's story of a voyage to the moon. Second, Alterton asserts that Poe's political theories were very similar to Tucker's. It should be pointed out that Alterton misinterprets Tucker's political and social ideas and could have made a much stronger case for Tucker's possible influence had she known that Tucker, like the Poe she describes, held more in common with the early Federalists than with the Jeffersonians. It seems certain that Poe knew Tucker's views, since he joined the *Southern Literary Messenger* only three months after Tucker published in it an article outlining some of his extremely conservative political and social theories ("A Discourse on the Progress of Philosophy and Its Influence on the Intellectual and Moral Character of Man," I [1835], 405-421). Like Poe, Tucker opposed perfectibilian reforms, especially those based upon *a priori* reasoning; distrusted the "ignorant rabble" of democracies; preferred the life of cities to the joys of rural life; and defended

lishment of a direct relationship between Poe and Tucker must await more concrete evidence, yet it seems not improbable that Tucker's interpretation of Scottish aesthetics aroused Poe's literary interests and provided him with several basic critical ideas which he developed and changed as he read further in the writings of German and English romantics.

CONTEMPORARY POETRY

In Tucker's analysis of the development of poetry, there exists an attempt to account for nineteenth-century taste in terms of essentially eighteenth-century thought. Tucker's working thesis of the evolution of English poetry—as reconstructed from somewhat fragmentary lecture notes and from statements in his essays—was that poetry had already reached its peak of excellence and that contemporary poets, because of the age in which they "chanced to live," were necessarily inferior to their predecessors. But, as in his discussion of prose, Tucker could not carry a theory of degeneration to its logical conclusion. His deep admiration for some of the romantic poets, whose achievements and popularity he had to admit, and his willingness to test greatness by public applause caused him to modify his thesis in order to account for the success of Byron and his contemporaries. Because of this conflict between theory and taste, Tucker's criticism contains contradictions which are not easily reconciled. He never ceased to believe that the refined, modern age was less favorable to poetry than was an earlier stage of society; yet he praised the romantics so highly that he comes dangerously close to concluding that the romantics were not so much inferior to, as different from, their predecessors.

While science and civilization are continually advancing, Tucker told his classes in belles lettres, "the beautiful & noble art of poetry, the most admired achievement of the human intellect, seems to be at a stand. It has perhaps even passed the meridian of its glory, and . . . emits a dimmer ray as well as a less genial warmth than at a former period."[97] The various reasons which Tucker provided for this state of affairs seem to have been drawn chiefly from eighteenth-century Scottish critics, who argued that modern, refined society,

---

slavery. For Alterton's discussion of Poe and Tucker, see *Edgar Allan Poe,* pp. lxxii-lxxiii, lxviii. Tucker's social and economic theories are discussed in this study in Chap. XII below.

97. "Lectures on Rhetoric and Belles Lettres," Lecture XLIV.

however beneficial to social happiness, was not conducive to the creation of great poetry.[98]

Tucker's explanations for the failure of poetry to advance with society may be divided into two categories. The first deals with the materials with which the modern poet must work and results in part from Tucker's agreement with the eighteenth-century belief in the uniformity of human nature.[99] Preceding poets, he said, had thoroughly canvassed the "great volume" of unchanging nature and had appropriated the "most impressive" poetical themes, images, and descriptions. Since there exists a "natural propensity of the human mind to follow the same train of thought into which it has once been led," modern writers cannot be original. At the same time, Tucker pointed out, modern poets were handicapped by the language they had to use, for modern English, while excellent for conveying "delicate touches of sympathy" and for expressing "discriminations of understanding," was a less vigorous, less figurative, and therefore inferior medium for poetry than was a "ruder" tongue.[100]

Tucker's second general category of causes for the inferiority of nineteenth-century poetry has to do with the influence of social conditions upon the writer. A short summary of the contrast which

98. See Roy Harvey Pearce, "The Eighteenth-Century Scottish Primitivists: Some Reconsiderations," *ELH*, XII (1945), 203-220. This same notion that poetry best flourished in an earlier age was promulgated well into the nineteenth century, for example, by Jeffrey and Macaulay in contributions to the *Edinburgh Review*. See Jeffrey's 1809 review of Cromek's *Reliques of Robert Burns* in Jeffrey, *Contributions to the Edinburgh Review*, 2nd ed. (London, 1846), II, 144-146; and Macaulay's 1825 essay on Milton in *Essays, Critical and Miscellaneous*, rev. ed. (New York, 1878), pp. 1-19. Ernest Lee Tuveson, *Millennium and Utopia: A Study in the Background of the Idea of Progress* (Berkeley and Los Angeles, 1949), pp. 207-219, relates this idea of the decay of poetry to the Scottish concept of progress.

99. See Arthur O. Lovejoy, "The Parallel of Deism and Classicism," *MP*, XXIX (1932), 281-299.

100. "Lectures on Rhetoric and Belles Lettres," Lecture LXIV. Tucker's point was that the "period of society most favorable to excellence in poetry is that in which the language retains much of its primitive form & figurativeness" but yet is "sufficiently copious"—"that middle point between refinement & originality . . . the happiest union of genius & taste" (Lecture XLIV). Tucker does not date this period in English literary history, but he said that poetry flowered before prose, the peak of which he placed (in 1814 and 1822) as beginning in the eighteenth and continuing into the nineteenth century. (See the analysis of "On Style," above, pp. 125-129.) Wellek, *The Rise of Literary History*, pp. 62-63, notes that in mid-eighteenth-century British criticism, the conflict between the beliefs in the progress and the decay of poetry was often resolved in a compromise. Thus Richard Hurd in *Letters on Chivalry and Romance* (1762) argued that the most favorable time for poetry "lies somewhere between the rude essays and uncorrected fancy, on the one hand, and the refinements of reason and science on the other. And such appears to have been the condition of our language in the Age of Elizabeth" (cited by Wellek, *op. cit.*).

Tucker presented between the situations of the ancient "Bard" and the modern poet suggests clearly his indebtedness to Blair and other primitivists.[101] In a "rude" and simple age, said Tucker, the Bard was a central figure in society. As he recited his verses, his audiences became enraptured, and their sympathetic responses to his already frenzied outpourings so heightened his enthusiasm that he composed yet more emotional—and therefore greater—poetry. But in the nineteenth century, complained Tucker, there was "less sensibility to poetical rapture." The "diversity of objects which the present improved & enlarged state of human knowledge presents" necessarily occupies almost all of the attention of the public, especially of the "higher classes," and the poet is thus deprived of that "sympathetic response" which is essential for the creation of great poetry.[102]

In expanding this argument of the lack of rapport between a poet and his audience, Tucker combined it with the Humean suggestion that past literary excellence discouraged the poet in his quest for fame.[103] In this portion of his lecture, however, Tucker allowed for the emergence of a Byron who admittedly had captured a wide and appreciative audience, including Tucker himself. In the "rude" age of Elizabeth, Tucker said, a writer such as Shakespeare could experiment until he "finally acquired the strength of wing which enabled him to reach those elevated regions in which he delights to soar." But "the modern votary of the Muses" had no such opportunity:

Early accustomed to the most finished and elegant specimens of poetry, his taste is likely to be in advance of his genius. He therefore does not find it very easy to please himself. If he surmounts this obstacle he is sure to encounter everywhere those individuals, who tho' incapable of producing anything themselves, are easily able to discover the comparative inferiority of his imperfect compositions, and if he should be so far fortunate to escape censure, he may be nevertheless sure of being received with the most chilling indifference. His bosom is filled with . . . the immeasurable thirst of fame, but he must necessarily undergo a long & labourious probation before he can obtain the commendation of them whose commendation alone he would value—and he is seldom found equal to this course of patient labour, unless he is animated & supported by that very praise, or should chance to be goaded by some violent truculent unappeasable resentment as was Byron, . . . whom the *Edinburgh Review* . . . stung . . .

101. See Robert Morell Schmitz, *Hugh Blair* (New York, 1948), pp. 51-60; Lois Whitney, "English Primitivistic Theories of Epic Origins," *MP*, XXI (1924), 337-378.
102. "Lectures on Rhetoric and Belles Lettres," Lecture XLIV.
103. For Hume's statement, see "Of the Rise and Progress of the Arts and Sciences" in *Essays*, I, 195-196.

into the madness which made him the first poet of his day. When such powerful stimulants are wanting, the modern candidate for poetical fame commonly contents himself with holding a place among those ephemeral rhymers that flit . . . away their little hour and are forgotten.[104]

Tucker's acceptance of the theory of poetic degeneration is thus clearly modified to account for the existence of such a favorite as Byron in an age which discouraged great productions. Presumably other modern writers whose emotions were sufficiently aroused could overcome the obstacles of living in an advanced society and achieve poetic success. Certainly Tucker highly praised other of the romantics, though he never explained their emotional stimulation. As early as 1815 in the Philadelphia *Port Folio* he commented on the growing fame of Scotland and named Scott and Campbell as the greatest contemporary poets; and in 1822, when he reprinted his essay, he added that "the star of Lord Byron had just begun to appear above the horizon."[105] In his lectures he asserted that the fame and excellence of Scott's *Lady of the Lake* and *Marmion* and, especially, Byron's *Childe Harold* rendered absurd Dr. Blair's contention that blank and not rhymed verse was the best medium for poems of "dignity and force."[106] In the same lecture in which he said that English poetry could no longer progress, he also stated that Byron, Scott, Moore, Rogers, Wordsworth, Southey, and Coleridge could "compare with the proudest names in the annals of English poetry"; and he classified as estimable Shelley, Keats, Hunt, Montgomery, Wilson, and Hogg.[107]

A fuller, if not clearer, picture of Tucker's attitude toward Byron and his contemporaries appeared in 1835, when he lectured to the Virginia Historical and Philosophical Society on the evidences of philosophy in the modern age. In all the arts and sciences, including poetry, the philosophical spirit of the age, he said, is present:

Her favourite occupation of late has been to delineate the dispositions and characters of men; to reveal the secret workings of the passions and the sources of human sympathy; to exhibit the human mind, in short, under its most impressive phases. The present taste of the age is for metaphysical poetry, poetry which lays bare the anatomy of the human heart, and discloses all the springs and machinery by which it is put into play. Those who are gifted with this beautiful talent, have conformed to the ruling taste, and their success has been proportionate.[108]

104. "Lectures on Rhetoric and Belles Lettres," Lecture XLIV.
105. "On American Literature," *Essays* (1822), p. 55.
106. "Lectures on Rhetoric and Belles Lettres," Lecture XLIII.
107. Lecture XLIV.
108. "A Discourse on the Progress of Philosophy," p. 408.

Thus, though Byron lacks the ability of earlier poets to embellish his verse with "smooth & felicitous diction" and "agreeable and varied rhythm" and even fails in "the higher attributes of lively imagery and lofty conception," still, said Tucker, "he is superior to any of his predecessors" in "exhibiting the most subtle processes of human passion." A poet, Tucker explained, does not create his milieu; he is, instead, like other men, governed by it. Byron was popular, Tucker said, not so much because he tried to conform to public taste "as because he himself partook of the character of his age; . . . he wrote metaphysically and philosophically because he spoke and thought this way, and he so spoke and thought from the very same causes as his contemporaries." To prove this, he said, we have only to observe the "same tincture of philosophy" in Wordsworth, Southey, Campbell, and Coleridge.[109]

Yet in a concluding passage to the lecture, Tucker demonstrated that this "tincture of philosophy" did not always enhance poetry. Qualifying his earlier estimation of Coleridge, he wrote:

Sometimes we see the spirit of philosophy controlling the poetic spirit, as was the case with Shelley, Coleridge and some others, in whose poetry the precepts of philosophy were more obscured by the restraints of verse than aided by its ornaments. It is an unnatural alliance, and both the poetry and the philosophy are the worse for the union.[110]

In treating American poetry, Tucker always thought in terms of progress and accomplishment, not decay; and though his theory of poetic degeneration made his predictions and evaluations of American verse more temperate than those dealing with other areas of American letters, his nationalism nevertheless is strong. In 1835 in his "Discourse on the Progress of Philosophy," he said that poetry was not "destined again to receive honors, or even the same profound homage" of an earlier age, for the "highest province of intellect" in America would be needed "to aid us in the arduous duties of life." Yet, he added, the combined pleasures of "rhythm, imagery, and fervid sentiment" were immutable, and poetry would always occupy "a high place in the world of letters."[111] In his 1837 "Discourse on American

109. *Idem.* In a footnote Tucker pointed out that "the recent poetry of continental Europe exhibits the same psychological character, as for instance, that of Alfieri and Monte in Italy, of Goethe and Tieck in Germany, and of Beranger in France."

110. *Idem.* Tucker's evaluation of Coleridge and Shelley is about the same as that held by many American critics in the 1830's, who often found ideality and intellectuality in poetry to be distasteful when they made for obscurity. See Charvat, *Origins,* p. 82.

111. "A Discourse on the Progress of Philosophy," p. 418.

Literature," a more forceful optimism prevails. America, said Tucker, had not yet produced "stars of the first magnitude, such as are equally objects of the admiring gaze of common and of learned observers"; yet the "beautiful art," he argued, had "not been stationary while the other departments of letters were progressive," and American poets were "equal to any living poets" in Europe. In addition to Bryant, he cited in general the work of the minor Knickerbockers, Fitz-Greene Halleck, Joseph Rodman Drake, and N. P. Willis. Of the New England literati, he praised the versatile James Gates Percival and Grenville Mellen, both Byron's imitators, and Lydia Huntley Sigourney, the American counterpart of Felicia Hemans. Singled out as especially worthy of commendation by Tucker were Miss Davidson[112] of New York, "whose gentle, delicate, plaintive muse has met with honor on both sides of the Atlantic," and Drake, an ethereal spirit now "ascended to . . . congenial skies" whose *Culprit Fay,* despite some weaknesses in versification and plan, shows such "fertility and originality, and manageable wildness of fancy" that, were it finished, it "must have placed him on the summit of Parnassus."[113]

THE DEVELOPMENT OF AMERICAN LITERATURE

A constantly recurring theme in Tucker's writings is that of the "future destiny of the United States." Although he was in many respects a regionalist, concerned with bettering the economic condition of Virginia and with defending the Southern way of life, Tucker was basically a nationalist with a Whiggish desire to promote national prosperity. He believed that once America became, as it must, the world's great political and economic power, with a population density equal to that of the Old World, the United States would also achieve a great culture. In papers on American letters he sought to explain America's present inferiority in the arts and, more importantly, predict its eventual triumphs in literature.

The most important of Tucker's discussions of the state of American literature came in two different periods of his life—early, from 1814 to 1816, when he first thought seriously of becoming a professional author, and again in 1837, when he was Professor of Moral

112. Tucker was probably referring to one of two Davidson sisters of Plattsburg, New York, whose verses were reviewed favorably in America and England. Lucretia Maria died in 1825 at the age of seventeen, and Margaret Miller in 1838 at the age of fifteen.

113. "Discourse on American Literature: Delivered Before the Charlottesville Lyceum, December 19, 1837," *Southern Literary Messenger,* IV (1838), 85.

Philosophy.[114]   One of the early essays, here attributed to him, dealt with the low state of polite letters in Virginia and appeared in the satire, *Letters from Virginia* (1816). Although this work was published two years after Tucker's essay "On American Literature," it will for convenience be discussed first. It is Tucker's sole extended discussion of regional literature and is related only indirectly to his primary concern—the development of a national literature.[115]

In keeping with the attitude of many of the essays in *Letters from Virginia,* purportedly written by a French traveler, Tucker, the probable author of the volume, in his discussion of Virginia's literary backwardness, showed as much interest in attacking the self-satisfaction of some Virginians as in explaining the causes for the cultural lag in the Old Dominion.[116]   Tucker recounted that the first settlers of Virginia were fortune hunters and, like their successors, were too busy to devote time to the cultivation of the arts.[117]   The rich, made indolent by their slaves, spent their time in "eating, drinking, gambling, horse-racing," and indulging "the whole herd of vulgar passions,"[118] and the clergymen, "the standing army of literature in modern times," were of inferior intellects and, moreover, had to apply all their leisure to earning a living.[119]   Schools were deficient: William and Mary College, because of "some vice either in its constitution or in its management, has done but little for the cause of letters in this state."[120] Colonists, most of whom were of the merchant class, found more profit in their ledgers than in polite letters.[121]   The Revolutionary War, he said, stimulated Virginians only to strive more than ever for power

114. Tucker repeated the main points of his essay "On American Literature," *Port Folio*, 3rd ser., IV (1814), 44-59, in the concluding chapter of his *History of the United States from Their Colonization to the End of the Twenty-Sixth Congress, in 1841* (Philadelphia, 1856-58), IV, 410-418.

115. Hubbell, *The South in American Literature*, p. 216, states that Tucker wrote "Thoughts on the Choice of a Profession in Virginia," *Virginia Literary Museum*, No. 21 (Nov. 4, 1829), 321-324, in which the author wrote that "the minds of our youth should expand to a nobler emulation than the mere scuffle after a law-suit or a case of bilious fever." The article is signed "A Subscriber," and I have found no reason for attributing it to Tucker, who edited the magazine and used other pseudonyms for his contributions. See Pt. II, pp. 95-99, for a discussion of authorship in the *Literary Museum*.

116. The authorship of *Letters from Virginia* is discussed in Pt. II, pp. 65-70.

117. *Letters from Virginia, Translated from the French* (Baltimore, 1816), Letter XVI, pp. 133-134.

118. *Ibid.,* p. 135.

119. *Ibid.,* pp. 135-137.

120. *Ibid.,* pp. 137-138.

121. *Ibid.,* pp. 138-139.

and wealth in the fields of politics and money speculation and did not help them to create literature.[122]

In that portion of his essay which is devoted to the present state of letters and the future hopes for literature in Virginia, Tucker's opinions differ little from those expressed in his essay "On American Literature" (1814), in which he analyzed the progress of literature in the United States in general.[123] "On American Literature" was an attempt to prove that America's literary backwardness was caused not, as had been alleged by foreign critics, by inferiority of "our natural genius," but by temporary "moral causes."[124]   First of all, Tucker explained, education, "the most favourable" training for an author, was poorly provided for in the United States, where relatively few students enrolled in colleges, and then for short periods to study under inferior professors, many of whom were either Europeans who could not find professorships in their native lands or Americans of second-rate talent.[125]   Men of "cultivated intellect" practiced law, divinity, medicine, or statecraft, professions in which they earned more money than in teaching or writing; since it was only "from the *redundancy* of educated men" that professors and, especially, professional writers came, college posts were held by incompetents, and literature, when produced at all, was composed in leisure moments by very active men.[126]   Since public speaking was the chief road to fame and fortune in America, most writers were also orators, or at least were affected by public speaking, and American authors found it difficult to keep out of their writing the "false splendour," the "rant and declamation" of oratory.[127]   Poetry especially suffered, explained Tucker, because of the particular circumstances of the age.   Because preceding writers had long ago used up "the whole stock of natural images," contemporaries could build a reputation only by "elegant correctness," which required long and patient study, the time for which was difficult to find in America where all energies were directed to earning a living.   The most powerful stimulus for creating professional writers, poverty, would not exist in the United States for years to come.[128]   Moreover,

122. *Ibid.*, p. 140.

123. He complains that "there are . . . no large cities, no learned clergy, no liberally endowed colleges, no well-furnished libraries; tho' I see . . . some faint glimpses of improvement in all these particulars" (pp. 140-141).   He also speaks of the competition of the "ready and redundant supply of books" from England (p. 141).

124. *Essays* (1822), pp. 41, 43.

125. "On American Literature," *Essays* (1822), pp. 44-45.

126. *Ibid.*, pp. 45-46.

127. "On Style," *Essays* (1822), pp. 161-162.

128. "On American Literature," *Essays* (1822), pp. 46-47.

there were in America no large cities providing an audience to "cheer the author in his labours and to encourage him to bolder and more felicitous exertions."[129]   Another great general cause for America's cultural backwardness lay in the domination which the British exerted on American taste, opinion, and literature, the effect of which was to limit the praise and reduce the income of native writers, whose works, without the stamp of British approval and with the competition from English books, had little chance of success.[130]

To prove his point that American intellect was not inherently deficient, Tucker cited America's accomplishments. In literature, he stated, in epigrams and sonnets—works "elicited at the single heat of the mind"—and in portions of such histories as Marshall's *Life of Washington,* except for the slight differences resulting from the "inferior taste" of less disciplined minds, Americans' works approached the quality of comparable British productions.   Tucker listed in painting the achievements of John Singleton Copley, Benjamin West, John Trumbull, Gilbert Stuart, all of whom received in Europe "the instruction and the patronage . . . to mature their natural endowments."[131]   In oratory, he said, in that field which tended to debase American writing but which was a sure indication of natural genius, Americans were superior to the British, especially in political and legal debates, and, he added in a footnote to the 1822 edition of the *Essays,* America furnished as great a pulpit oratory as any in the world. Finally, by citing the inventive genius of Dr. Franklin, the "comprehension of mind, foresight, judgment, and invention" which went into the making of the Constitution, the "cogent reasoning" of Hamilton in the Federalist Papers, the diplomatic skills of Jefferson, King, Monroe, and Madison, and the excellence of American medical teachers, Tucker proved that "genius is not the exclusive gift of any country," but he warned that without a "cherishing culture" it could not mature.[132]

After noting the decline of the cultures of Greece and Rome and the rise of English and French cultures, Tucker concluded his essay by stating that "the literature of each nation has kept an equal pace with its civilization and general prosperity," and he implied that next it would be America's turn to be the literary center of the world.[133]

129. *Ibid.,* pp. 53-54.
130. *Ibid.,* pp. 51-53.
131. *Ibid.,* pp. 65-67. In 1822 Tucker added the names of Washington Allston and John Vanderlyn to his list.
132. *Ibid.,* pp. 56, 58-63, 65-66.
133. *Ibid.,* p. 64.

He was more specific about the future of art in the United States in two other essays. In one—"On the Density of Population"—he considered the effect which a thick population would have upon the fine arts in America. When people were scattered over a large area, literature was practiced only as an avocation. "The literary character" of the country would improve once there existed an excess supply of educated men with ample leisure who would write for the prospects of gain and of being read—"the two chief incentives to authorship." As Tucker himself said, "almost all the circumstances which have been mentioned to explain the inferiority of American to European literature, are inseparably connected with our dispersed population."[134]

The development of a great national, even international, literature was in Tucker's mind inextricably bound up with economic progress. To him America was unique. The history of the world, he said in his essay "On the Future Destiny of the United States," indicated that the progress of civilization, as manifested by a nation's ability to provide for an "increase of population," had always been slow and gradual. But Americans, Tucker exulted, were "in possession of an immense continent, capable of supporting twenty or perhaps fifty times their present number."[135]

[English] will be the mother tongue, in less than two centuries, of more than half the number of people probably now living in the whole world! How glorious a prize does it offer to the candidate for literary fame, both in this country and in England, that his writings, if they reach posterity, will be read and understood by the hundreds of millions with which this continent will one day teem! The plaudits of any single nation now existing, sink into insignificance compared with those which hereafter await the successful cultivator of English literature.[136]

In the last portion of his "Discourse on American Literature," presented before the Charlottesville Lyceum twenty-three years later, Tucker elaborated his theme of the advance of American literature. The future, he said, was bright. Because of the "civil liberty and the federative charter of our government," and because America would soon have an excess of professional men driven to literature by *ennui,* need, or love of glory, who were apt to be "less trammelled by the tyranny of customs—to be more bold, fearless, and adventurous—more pliant and accommodating to uncontrollable circumstances," America

---

134. *Essays* (1822), pp. 72-73.
135. "On the Future Destiny of the United States," *Essays* (1822), p. 2.
136. *Ibid.,* p. 20.

would have a great literature. Competition among men in teeming cities and between states and sectional areas, as exemplified in the rivalries between North and South, and between East and West, "the ardent, generous west," would make the literature even greater. And this literature would "afford to individuals the best security against vicious and immoral habits" by providing a means of rational rather than purely sensuous pleasure and would reach an audience of a hundred million spread out from the Atlantic to the Pacific oceans and from Hudson Bay to the Mexican Gulf.[137] Repeating his theme of the westward movement of civilization, Tucker explained that progress was cyclical within nations but continual for all mankind:

. . . and the sun of civilization, which has been traveling to the west, as far back as history records, will, when it has completed its circle round the earth, by traversing the American continent, be found to have still increased in splendour, in its course; and as it shone more brightly in Greece and Rome, than it had done in Asia; and in England and France, than in Rome or Greece, so, if the auguries do not prove deceitful, its progressive brightness will continue with us, and when it shall be setting to Europe, it will here in its meridian, beam with an effulgence that the world has never yet witnessed.[138]

137. "Discourse on American Literature," pp. 86-87.
138. *Ibid.,* p. 88. See Chap. XII below for Tucker's acceptance of the idea of progress.

CHAPTER X

PHILOSOPHICAL THEORY[1]

TUCKER ATTACHED great importance to his investigations in "the science of metaphysics," a field of inquiry which he defined as that "mental science" which deals with the faculties and workings of the human mind.[2] His lectures and essays on metaphysical subjects reveal a good deal about the mode of his thought and the quality of his mind, and an analysis of them contributes to an understanding of his work in other fields.

Further, Tucker's professional eminence suggests that his works

1. This chapter does not deal with Tucker's ethical theory, which he seems to have been content to express in his fiction and in his work in economics. The standard textbook for his classes in ethics was Dugald Stewart's *Philosophy of the Active and Moral Powers,* which was used continuously from 1832 to 1845, except from 1834-35 to 1837-38, when Paley's text was used. (See the catalogues from 1825 to 1845 in *A Catalogue of the Officers and Students of the University of Virginia* [Charlottesville, Va., 1880], and Tucker, "Education in Virginia," *Quarterly Journal of Education,* IV [1832], 49-71.) No record exists for the textbooks used from 1825 to 1832.

In the "Notes on the Lectures of Moral Philosophy by George Tucker, Esq.," "Metaphysics," title page signed Merit M. Robinson, Cabell Deposit, University of Virginia Library, pp. 3-4, Tucker defined ethics as dealing with "man's various duties as a rational & accountable being; & as a member of civil society." The nature of Tucker's teaching in ethics may possibly be gauged by an essay written for Tucker by a Richard B. Gooch, in which the student, after insisting that "whatever the propensities of man, we must maintain that which is right," stresses the commonplace virtues of early rising and the profitable use of time. In Tucker's hand is the comment "Much good sense well expressed." (Gooch Family Papers, University of Virginia Library.)

2. See "Notebook of Merit Robinson," pp. 3-4, and "Metaphysics," *Virginia Literary Museum,* No. 46 (April 28, 1830), 721. The latter work is unsigned, but it is almost a word-for-word summary of part of Tucker's lectures as recorded in the "Notebook of Merit Robinson." In a second article, "The Metaphysics of Language," *Literary Museum,* No. 48 (May 12, 1830), 753-757, which is signed "Q," the author referred to "Metaphysics" as an earlier work of his. Such evidence helps to prove that all articles signed "Q" are Tucker's. See above, Pt. II, pp. 95-99, for attributing other pseudonymous articles in the *Literary Museum* to Tucker.

are worth examining for their historical value. He was professor of philosophy in the South's leading University for twenty years, and recently he has been classified "one of the most significant figures in American philosophy in the South prior to the Civil War."[3]   An analysis of his philosophic works, as Herbert W. Schneider remarks, helps clarify the status of philosophical speculation in the Old South, which, because of the concentration of attention on the literature of the slavery problem, has never been adequately explored by cultural historians.[4]

EARLY WORK IN METAPHYSICS

Until he was appointed by Jefferson to the chair of moral philosophy at the University of Virginia in 1825, Tucker was interested in philosophy chiefly because of its importance to the study of literature and aesthetics.   By the mid-eighteenth century, as Ronald S. Crane points out, "the philosopher (in the current sense of an inquirer into the operations of the mind)" was exalted "over the artist or the mere critic as the expert best qualified to determine the rules of art,"[5] and in Scotland, "from which the bulk of contemporary criticism emanated," the relationship between philosophy and criticism "was very close."[6]   A brief examination of two of Tucker's early aesthetic essays sufficiently demonstrates that he followed the mainstream of eighteenth-century criticism in associating philosophy and aesthetics and that his opinions were derived mainly from the common sense philosopher-critics of Scotland.

Tucker's first work to reflect an interest in philosophy is his essay "On the Illusions of Fancy" (1804).   After stressing the need for the "metaphysician of taste" to understand the workings of the human mind in order to form the rules of literature, Tucker explained the operation of the associating faculty. The fancy (or imagination), he said, though seemingly discursive and irregular in its movements, in

3. Richard H. Popkin, "George Tucker, An Early American Critic of Hume," *JHI*, XIII (1952), 375.

4. *A History of American Philosophy* (New York, 1946), p. 217.   Wilson Smith, *Professors & Public Ethics: Studies of Northern Moral Philosophers before the Civil War* (Ithaca, N.Y., 1956), p. 5, lists Tucker as one of forty-eight important moral philosophers, but does not discuss Tucker's works.   Smith believes that a separate study is required for Southern moral philosophers, who tended, after the 1830's, to "use moral philosophy as a rationale for proslavery arguments" (*op. cit.,* p. 5 n.).

5. "Neo-Classical Criticism," in *Dictionary of World Literature,* rev. ed., ed. Joseph Shipley (New York, 1953), p. 123.

6. Walter Jackson Bate, *From Classic to Romantic: Premises of Taste in Eighteenth-Century England* (Cambridge, Mass., 1946), p. 97.

reality acted upon a few "regular, simple" principles which the mind could control—the universal laws of association—*"proximity of time or place, resemblance or contrast."*[7]

Although Tucker cited no authorities for the beliefs expressed in this early work on associational psychology, his general philosophical affiliation seems clear. One scholar has pointed out that between Locke and the end of the eighteenth century, British associationism developed in two directions. One group of thinkers, including David Hartley, Joseph Priestley, and Erasmus Darwin, regarded the mind as totally controlled by associations, whose actions they explained by physiological and biological theories. The second, made up of a "large body of writers who comprised the Scottish 'Common-Sense School' of Criticism," admitted that the association of ideas influenced thinking but assumed that the mind was endowed with the capacity to receive and control associations.[8] Tucker's position on simple and limited association expressed in his first published essay on philosophy makes it clear that from the start he allied himself with the conservative "common sense" school of contemporary philosophy.

Further and more definite evidence for Tucker's early indebtedness to the Scottish philosophers is provided in a work published in 1815 in the *Port Folio,* eleven years after "On the Illusions of Fancy." This essay "On Beauty" has already been discussed in connection with Tucker's aesthetic beliefs, but a review of its probable history is necessary here to suggest the nature and degree of his use of the Scottish common-sense philosophy. The immediate motivation for "On Beauty" was Francis Jeffrey's commentary on the Reverend Archibald Alison's *Essays on the Nature and Principles of Taste* (1790). In 1811 in the *Edinburgh Review,* a magazine which Tucker read assiduously, Jeffrey reviewed Alison's work and popularized the theory that beauty was a completely subjective impression, an idea which Tucker found "repugnant to the common sense of mankind."

A close examination of texts suggests that Tucker owes much to Dugald Stewart, for whom he had the greatest esteem. In his *Elements of the Philosophy of the Human Mind* (1792) and later in more detail in as essay "On the Beautiful," which first appeared in *Philosophical Essays* (1810), Stewart discussed the Alisonian theory, giving qualified acceptance to the influence which associated ideas have upon the concept of beauty. In his *Philosophical Essays,* Stewart planned to

7. *The Rainbow; First Series* (Richmond, Va., 1804), pp. 49-50.
8. Bate, *From Classic to Romantic,* pp. 100-102.

write on "the more simple and general principles on which depend the pleasures that we experience in the case of actual perception" and later to deal with the charm which the imagination (association of ideas) adds.[9] Pleasures to the eye, he concluded, were derived primarily from colors, "certain modifications of form," and motion; though he was in agreement with the general tenor of Alison's remarks, he was "disposed to ascribe more to the mere organic impression . . . independently of any association . . . whatsoever."[10] When Tucker set out to refute the "speculators" who excluded "the visible properties of matter from all *direct* agency in creating the sensation of beauty,"[11] he, too, was willing to admit that the association of ideas affected the emotion. The physical beauty of objects, he said, consisted primarily in certain colors,[12] in particular forms and shapes,[13] in their power of reflecting light,[14] and, lastly, in varieties of the preceding properties.[15] All, however, were "sometimes heightened, sometimes diminished, and sometimes entirely effaced by the association of ideas raised by visible objects."[16]

Tucker's position on the importance of associated ideas in calling up the beautiful is, then, very similar to Stewart's. What is important, however, is not that Tucker may have derived his ideas specifically from Stewart, but that his early philosophical and aesthetic judgments were formed by a reading of the psychological criticism which was coming from the Scottish universities and appearing in the influential Scottish periodicals. Nor did Tucker ever change his philosophical allegiance. He used the essay "On Beauty" as the basis for three lectures in metaphysics[17] and for two in rhetoric and belles lettres,[18] and he reprinted the piece in his 1822 *Essays* and again in 1860—almost half a century after "On Beauty" first appeared.

9. In *The Collected Works of Dugald Stewart, Esq., F.R.S.S.,* ed. Sir William Hamilton, Bart. (Edinburgh, 1854), V, 189-190.

10. *Ibid.,* V, 205-208.

11. "On Beauty," *Essays on Various Subjects of Taste, Morals, and National Policy* (Georgetown, D.C., 1822), p. 170.

12. *Ibid.,* p. 176.

13. *Ibid.,* p. 182.

14. *Ibid.,* p. 172.

15. *Ibid.,* p. 185.

16. *Ibid.,* pp. 170-171.

17. "Notebook of Merit Robinson," pp. 164-172.

18. Tucker, "Lectures on Rhetoric and Belles Lettres . . . at the Seventh Session, 1830-31," Tucker-Harrison-Smith Papers, University of Virginia Library, Lectures LXV, LXVI.

ACADEMIC RELATIONS WITH THE SCOTTISH
PHILOSOPHY

Tucker's appointment to teach metaphysics and ethics at the University of Virginia came in 1825, about a decade after his essay "On Beauty" first appeared. Jefferson, the leading organizer of the University, by the time of its opening seems to have formed definite views not only about the philosophy he wanted taught, but also about the kind of man he wanted to teach it. As Professor of Philosophy, he desired at first to hire "a young man, formerly a student at William and Mary, who had been later educated at Edinburgh, and was considered one of the most distinguished students ever there."[19] Certainly he did not want a clergyman who would teach authoritarian dogma, but rather a well-educated layman, for mental philosophy, after all, was "a branch of science of little difficulty to any ingenious man. Locke, Stewart, Brown, Tracy, for the general science of mind furnish materials abundant, and that of Ethics is still more trite. I should think any person with a general education rendering them [*sic*] otherwise worthy of a place among his scientific brethren might soon qualify himself."[20]

The significance of Jefferson's first trying to obtain an Edinburgh-trained man and spelling out the realm of philosophy is that "he put his faith in the Scottish school of common-sense empiricist philosophy in preference to the more metaphysical variety of philosophy then fashionable at Oxford and Cambridge."[21] As a man of good education with scientific interests whose early publications indicated a close acquaintance with the Scottish writers, Tucker must have been acceptable to Jefferson when he was suggested for the professorship of moral philosophy.

It is evident, I think, that during his twenty years at the University of Virginia, Tucker taught orthodox Scottish common sense philosophy. There is no account of the textbooks he used from the opening of the University in 1825 until 1832, but after that time, the college catalogues and his own statement in the *Quarterly Journal of Education* provide a full record. During the year 1832-33, and probably during the years before, seniors studying metaphysics were assigned

19. Jefferson to Madison, Nov. 15, 1817; and Madison to Jefferson, Nov. 29, 1817, Madison Papers, Library of Congress, quoted by Adrienne Koch, *Jefferson and Madison: The Great Collaboration* (New York, 1950), p. 265.

20. Jefferson to Madison, Oct. 30, 1824, Madison Papers, Library of Congress, quoted by Koch, *Jefferson and Madison,* p. 274.

21. Koch, *Jefferson and Madison,* p. 274.

Stewart's *Elements of the Philosophy of the Human Mind*, Thomas Brown's *Lectures on the Philosophy of the Human Mind*, and Locke's *Essay on Human Understanding.* From 1834-35 until 1845, however, the only text assigned was Brown's *Lectures*.[22] An analysis and comparison of student notebooks, one for 1831 and one for 1835,[23] with Tucker's essays published during his professorship and after his retirement lead one to the conviction that Tucker was a close follower of the empirical branch of the Scottish philosophy. For his lectures he depended heavily upon Brown's *Lectures,* and when he did not draw his theory and examples directly from Brown, "the profoundest writer" on mental philosophy since Locke, he took the position of some other Scottish philosopher, sometimes Thomas Reid, or, most frequently, Dugald Stewart.

APPROACH TO PHILOSOPHY

Before analyzing Tucker's position on what he believed were basic philosophical problems on which he had contributed original ideas, it is perhaps important to review his over-all opinion of the "philosophy of the mind" and to see how closely he followed the methodology and intentions of the common sense philosophers. The Scots, as many students of philosophy have observed, looked to introspection and to the empirical analysis of the actions and conduct of men as sources of knowledge.[24] All claimed that their analyses were scientific extensions of the Baconian observational method of empirical evidence; all based their methods of philosophical inquiry on the Newtonian principle of analysis-synthesis;[25] and, lastly, most would have followed Stewart in

22. See catalogues from 1825 to 1845 in *A Catalogue of the University of Virginia;* and Tucker, "Education in Virginia," pp. 49-71.

23. "Notebook of Merit Robinson"; "Notes on Mental Philosophy," signed William W. Harris, University of Virginia, October 7th, 1835, Tucker-Harrison-Smith Papers, University of Virginia Library.

24. See, for examples, I. Woodbridge Riley, *American Thought from Puritanism to Pragmatism and Beyond* (New York, 1915), p. 119, who states of the Scottish realism that (1) its method is "observation and induction"; (2) its "doctrine is that of self-consciousness as the instrument of observation"; and (3) its "spirit is that of common sense"; and Torgny T. Segerstedt, *The Problem of Knowledge in Scottish Philosophy* in Lunds Universtets Arsskrift, N.F. Avd. Bd. 31, Nt. 6 (Lund, 1935), pp. 47-48.

25. See Stewart, *Outlines of Moral Philosophy* in *Works,* II, 7. Stewart describes in detail the inductive method of analysis-synthesis in *Elements* in *Works,* III, 258 ff. See George Campbell, *The Philosophy of Rhetoric* (Edinburgh and London, 1808), I, 4-5, who says that in the study of rhetoric "we rise from the individual to the species, from the species to the genus, and thence to the most extensive orders and classes" eventually to arrive "at the knowledge of general truths." See also Helen Whitcomb Randall, *The Critical Theory of Lord Kames,* Smith College Studies in Modern Languages, Nos. 1-4, XXII (1940-41), 24-26.

approving William Robertson's tract on "the glory of the *present* age" and in agreeing with Robertson's sentiment that the literary taste of the eighteenth century "has everywhere turned the spirit of philosophical inquiry from frivolous or abstruse speculations, into the business and affairs of men."[26]

Tucker, too, concurred in all these beliefs and expounded them in his introductory lectures to his classes in metaphysics and repeated them in more polished form in the pages of the *Literary Museum* (1829-1830). In an essay entitled "Metaphysics," Tucker defended the "progress" made in mental philosophy against the attacks on its scientific methodology by Francis Jeffrey in the *Edinburgh Review*. In discussing Stewart's *Account of the Life and Writings of Reid,* Jeffrey claimed, somewhat to the consternation of the Scottish empiricists, that mental philosophy was destroying itself because it was too much concerned with examining the human consciousness and too little interested in experimental science. Tucker aligned himself solidly with the *Quarterly Review* against Jeffrey. Few writers, he said, have contributed as much as has Dugald Stewart to philosophy "partly, because neither his modesty nor his judgment would suffer him to lose sight of the sobriety of nature, and the common sense of mankind; and partly from the charms of his style, which at once easy, lively and perspicuous, reflects the thoughts of the amiable writer with the distinctness and brightness of a mirror."[27]

Stewart, Tucker continued, like Reid, Locke, Hume, and Condillac, utilized "the same process of inductive reasoning which had proved so efficacious in the investigation of the laws of nature."[28] Tucker lamented that Stewart had twice been called upon to defend himself and "his favourite science" against the Edinburgh reviewers "who, if not the most metaphysical writers of the most metaphysical country in Europe, at least owed mainly to the science they thus thought to undervalue, their most successful disputations in morals, politics and literature."[29]

26. *Dissertation: Exhibiting the Progress of Metaphysical, Ethical, and Political Philosophy, Since the Revival of Letters in Europe* in *Works,* I, 26-27 and n.

27. "Metaphysics," p. 721.

28. *Idem.*

29. *Idem.* See "Notebook of Merit Robinson." The attack on Stewart first appeared in the *Edinburgh Review,* III (1804), 269-287, in Jeffrey's review of Stewart's *Account of the Life and Writings of Reid* (1803). Stewart answered his former student in the "preliminary dissertation" to his *Philosophical Essays* (*Works,* V, 24-25), and Jeffrey replied again in the *Edinburgh Review,* XVII (1810), 167-211. According to Sir William Hamilton, Stewart's editor, Jeffrey later admitted that Stewart had convinced him of his error, but Jeffrey's attack must have angered many of the

Tucker, like all the Scottish metaphysicians, first pointed out the scientific validity of the methodology of the common sense philosophy and, second, stressed the philosophy's great utilitarian value. Metaphysics, as Tucker told his students, was concerned with tracing the faculties, principles, and operations of the mind with the view of improving them and studying their "uses in the pursuits of life."[30] The opening paragraph of the essay "Metaphysics" in the *Literary Museum* contains additional sentiments—also expressed in his lectures to students—which might have been written by almost any common sense philosopher, most of whom were given to contrasting the darkness of the past with the light of the present:

The superiority of modern science is in few things more conspicuous than in Mental Philosophy. This is now regarded by its Votaries as a branch of the knowledge of nature; as it is studied, like the physical sciences, by observation of its natural phenomena. No principle is considered established which every person of reflexion cannot find *verified* by attending to the operations of his own consciousness; or *probable* by observing the apparent operations of the minds of others. The deductions of the science are thus made to rest on a solid basis; its pursuits and objects are limited to what is attainable, and they who cultivate it, tied down to such things as can be seen, felt, and understood, are no longer suffered to "shoot madly from their spheres," into regions of conjecture, mysticism and absurdity.[31]

To prove that this knowledge of the human mind was a basic requirement for orators, poets, legislators, writers, and educators—for all, indeed, whose business it was to operate upon the understanding, taste, feelings, or passions of men, Tucker, like Stewart, remarked that Hume, Burke, Turgot, and Smith had all done work in mental philosophy before entering other fields. Thus, both deduced, had Smith not written *The Theory of Moral Sentiments,* he would never have been able to compose *The Wealth of Nations.*[32] Eventually, Tucker asserted, philosophers will discover the laws by which the mind

---

common sense philosophers and may have led to Tucker's caricaturing him in *A Voyage to the Moon* as the arrogant coxcomb "Reffei." A concise account of the quarrel is given in Stewart, *Works,* X, lxv and n.

30. "Notebook of Merit Robinson," pp. 3-4.

31. "Metaphysics," p. 721. That Tucker had in mind the same procedure of investigation advocated by Brown and Stewart is clarified in a later statement in the same essay that the Baconian method, which had led to many creations and achievements in physical science, could properly be applied to mental philosophy (p. 727). See also "Notebook of Merit Robinson," p. 12.

32. "Metaphysics," pp. 722-727. See Stewart, *Outline of Moral Philosophy* in *Works,* I, 475.

is pleased by perception, those which reveal the influence which opinions and emotions exert upon each other, those which control the formation of tastes and causes and kinds of intellectual variety, those which will allow man to regulate his passions and desires without destroying them, and, lastly, those which will teach man how to eliminate bad habits.[33]

How these basic laws were to be discovered by means of the introspective process was set forth by Tucker most clearly, perhaps, in an address in 1835 before the Virginia Historical and Philosophical Society, in which he said that mental philosophy, by using the techniques followed in physics, by analyzing compound states of the mind, could trace many seemingly devious operations to one simple principle. To be convinced of the validity of the Scottish method, he said, "we have only to regard the theory of the associations as it now is, compared with the slight and vague notice of it by Locke."[34]

ACADEMIC ORTHODOXY

Tucker's academic orthodoxy is manifested both in his practice of acquiring knowledge by means he considered empirical and in his adherence to the basic tenets of the common sense school. By gathering data from what he deemed to be scientific observation of the actions and conduct of men, Tucker tried to establish probable truths about the human mind.

His first and most famous application of this method approved by the Scots came in 1830. It was in the hope of "throwing light on, perhaps settling, some controverted questions in mental philosophy" that he sought to interview Chang and Eng, the Siamese twins, who were touring Virginia in 1830. Since both had the same environment and the same pleasures and pains, Tucker reasoned that, if an examination discovered them to have different powers and propensities, those, like Helvétius, who denied that men were born with different characters would be refuted. If he could entice the twins to visit Charlottesville, he said, he would, for example, test their memories and their associations "as to their *liveliness, variety,* and peculiar *kind*" and perhaps "overturn the ingenious fabric" of the "real or pretended" science of phrenology.[35] Tucker thought so well of his "scientific"

33. "Metaphysics," p. 725.
34. "A Discourse on the Progress of Philosophy and Its Influence on the Intellectual and Moral Character of Man," *Southern Literary Messenger,* I (1835), 409.
35. "Q," "The Siamese Twins," *Literary Museum,* No. 34 (Feb. 3, 1830), 529-530. See Tucker to Cabell, March 18, 1832, Cabell Deposit, University of Virginia Library.

scheme that, though he failed to lure the twins to Charlottesville, six years later he traveled all the way to New York to interview them in the Clinton Hotel. He conducted the tests, though he had misplaced part of his prepared questions, whispering questions to one twin while Mr. Hale, the twins' conductor, quizzed the second. In the results of the interview, presented before the American Philosophical Society, Tucker said that there was "a difference in their original cerebral organizations" and that both liked yellow as their favorite color, a preference which Tucker "ascribed to associations growing out of the customs of their country, especially as *red* seems to be the colour which is preferred by all civilized nations, whatever may be their natural complexion."[36] Although Tucker had to admit that the experiment did not provide conclusive answers to the questions he set out to solve, he believed that Chang, the stronger and older brother, was more willful than his twin, but he also thought that Eng may have been more reflective and intelligent. If this were so, he said, Helvétius' claim that environment alone determines mental character was erroneous.[37]

Most frequently, however, Tucker tried to establish knowledge not by observing the conduct of other men, but by introspection. By searching his own consciousness and by citing what he believed to be the most authoritative sources, he sought to propagate undeniable truths arrived at by all thinking, reasonable men. Throughout his work, Tucker, following the Scottish writers, tried to refute skeptical and materialistic philosophers whose speculations were in conflict with the common sense of mankind. However modest his achievements in technical philosophy may have been, one must, as Richard H. Popkin points out, give him credit for dealing with basic and purely metaphysical problems in an age in which most of America's philosophers dealt almost exclusively with moral and religious issues.[38] Tucker concerned himself with (1) supporting the belief in man's instinctive knowledge, (2) examining the problems in perception, (3) proving the existence of the real world, (4) investigating the

36. American Philosophical Society *Proceedings,* II (1841-42), 22-28; and "On the Siamese Twins," *Essays, Moral and Metaphysical* (Philadelphia, 1860), pp. 246-256.

37. *Proceedings,* II, 27. Tucker did not measure the phrenological bumps of the twins, not only because he thought the examination would be premature, but also because he was not in sympathy with the theories of phrenology.

For a modern sociologist's evaluation of Tucker's experiment, see Jessie Bernard, "George Tucker: Liberal Southern Social Scientist," *Social Forces,* XXV (1946-' 131-145, 406-416.

38. "Critic of Hume," p. 375.

nature of the relationship between cause and effect, and (5) describing the influence which the association of ideas has in the acquisition of knowledge.

Tucker, following the example of Dugald Stewart in *The Elements of the Philosophy of the Human Mind,* attacked materialistic philosophers who insisted that natural language was not the ultimate source of artificial language nor an intuitive power, and who instead accounted for the development of natural language by experience or by physiology. Against Erasmus Darwin, Joseph Priestley, and other "speculatists," Tucker, writing in the *Literary Museum,* said that "reading the natural language of the passions" was a purely instinctive faculty:

We entirely concur with Mr. Stewart on this subject; and really can see no more difficulty in believing that certain expressions of the countenance are naturally agreeable or disagreeable to the observer, independently of experience or associations, notwithstanding all that Priestley and Darwin have written to the contrary, than that some sounds are naturally pleasing and others offensive to the ear, or what is still less likely to be questioned that some tastes and smells are grateful and others disagreeable.[39]

Rather than believe, then, the "philosophical trifling" of Darwin, who claimed that children read the passion in another's expression "according to a physiological connexion between . . . passion and its natural signs," Tucker held that "we must believe that they are taught to read this language by the same inscrutable power which formed their characters."[40]

In the same fashion and again closely following Stewart's statements in the third volume of his *Elements,* Tucker added to what he called "ultimate facts in our constitution" both the propensity to imitate and the power of imitating at will. Experience could develop the power of mimicry but could not explain it.[41]

The issue of perception was of critical importance in the Scottish philosophy since Berkeley and Reid were at opposite poles in their criticism of Locke, the former denying the existence of a material world independent of spirit or mind and the latter denying the true

---

39. "K," "Natural Language," *Literary Museum,* No. 49 (May 19, 1830), 769. Both Stewart and Tucker were objecting to the materialism in Darwin's *Zoonomia* (Vol. I, Sect. 16, 6) and Priestley's *Examination of Reid* (pp. 91 ff.). See Stewart, *Elements* in *Works,* IV, 8, 139, 257-277.

40. "Natural Language," pp. 769-770.

41. "K," "The Principle of Imitation," *Literary Museum,* No. 51 (June 2, 1830), 803-806. In effect, Tucker, who admits his debt to Stewart, is merely summarizing Stewart's discussion of "Sympathetic Imitation." See *Elements* in *Works,* IV, 116-184.

existence of ideas between the perceiver and the perceived. Tucker's classroom approach to the problem illustrates how closely he adhered to what is perhaps the most basic tenet of common sense realism and how faithfully he derived his discussions directly from the writings of the Scottish philosophers. In his class lecture, Tucker summarized Lectures XXV to XXVIII of Brown's *Lectures,* in which Brown, though in sympathy with Reid's intention to refute Berkeley's idealism and Hume's skepticism, took the founder of the Scottish school to task for what he believed to be his ineffectiveness. Brown argued that the mind can perceive nothing but sensations, but that each sensation, unlike certain mental states which have causes within the mind itself, must have a cause outside the mind, in matter. Brown's position depends, says James McCosh, on an intuitive conviction of causation, and, though not a form of idealism as Sir William Hamilton, Reid's editor, thought, had more in common with the work of Destutt de Tracy, the sense-philosopher and friend of Condillac, and the French ideologists, than with Reid and Stewart.[42] As a teacher, Tucker was more interested in stressing the essential conflict between idealism and natural realism than in clarifying the differences among the members of the Scottish school. He told his class to remember that Reid, Stewart, and Brown were in essential agreement about the mind and that the difference between Reid and Brown, for example, "is much confined to nice words." And though he taught from Brown's *Lectures,* Tucker followed Reid closely for his point that perception involves (1) the mind which perceives, (2) the operation of that mind, and (3) the object perceived. The false theory of ideas, Tucker taught, had been thoroughly refuted by Reid and Stewart: man has "an irresistible conviction," which is intuitive and not the result of reasoning, of the existence of the perceived object.[43]

Thus Tucker, like all natural realists, insisted that the world is real independently of mind. By logical analysis, he proved to his own satisfaction that skeptical and idealistic philosophers erred in doubting or denying the existence of the material world. In his essay "On Our

42. *The Scottish Philosophy, Biographical, Expository, Critical from Hutcheson to Hamilton* (New York, 1875), pp. 334-335.

43. "Notebook of Merit Robinson," pp. 47-59. For the importance of the issue in Scottish philosophy, see Gladys Bryson, *Man and Society: The Scottish Inquiry of the Eighteenth Century* (Princeton, 1945), pp. 54-55; and I. Woodbridge Riley, *American Philosophy, The Early Schools* (New York, 1907), p. 18. For Reid's statement in *Essays on the Intellectual Powers of Man,* see *The Works of Thomas Reid, D.D., with Notes and Supplementary Dissertations,* ed. Sir William Hamilton, Bart., 8th ed. (Edinburgh, 1895), I, 293.

Belief of an External World" (1860), Tucker wrote that "the most unlettered clown, no less than the philosopher distinguishes between the object he sees and that which he remembers," and even Berkeley, Tucker insisted, had a thorough conviction of the existence of matter. It is, then, this inconsistency between "practical belief" that the world exists and "speculative theory" which claims that matter is nothing but perceptions, which leads men to inquire into the source of conviction. Some, he said, say "the belief is instinctive," but this is a stratagem to which men resort when "all rational explanation fails." It was in Brown's theory that Tucker found the germ for his proof of matter. As Tucker told his classes, Brown, like many others before him, attributed his belief in the real world to the sense of touch, but Brown went further than his predecessors, indeed went "against the general impression of mankind" when he borrowed from the Count de Tracy the belief that resistance to muscular motion was a special sense.[44] Tucker reasoned that the sense of touch explained an infant's awareness of the distinction between the material world and the mind: by touching himself, the child received the double sensation of feeling and of being felt, which made it easy for him to distinguish himself from all else. Moreover, by seeing the resemblances of his body to all other bodies, in having extension and resistance, and also in recognizing the one difference that existed—in his having feelings and consciousness—the infant was able to satisfy himself about the duality of mind and matter.[45]

Probably no part of Hume's philosophy concerned Tucker more than did the skeptic's theory of causation. In his *Treatise of Human Nature,* Hume claimed that, although an object or an event may be contiguous and prior to another, there could be no proof that the former produced or caused the latter, and that only the repetitive pattern of associated ideas or custom led men to believe in necessary causation. As early as 1829 Tucker examined Hume's doctrine and found that the best answer to skepticism was to affirm that the idea of

44. "Notebook of William T. Harris," pp. 13-16. Compare "Notebook of Merit Robinson," p. 35. See "C.C.," "Premises and Causes—Cause and Effect," *Literary Museum,* No. 22 (Nov. 11, 1829), 349, in which Tucker ridiculed Brown's belief that "outwardness" or the knowledge of the external world is "first obtained by a failure of sequence." Brown, said Tucker, claimed that a child learned of the outside world when he tried to move his arm but met resistance. "Were this true," objected Tucker, "the failure of a spark to light a mass of gun-powder, of a horse, as yet unmatched, to win a race, of a belle to excite attention, or of a mint sauce to improve the taste of lamb should all excite the idea of outwardness." Brown's theory is set forth in his *Lectures on the Philosophy of the Human Mind* (Boston, 1826), I, 227-246.

45. "On Our Belief of an External World," *Essays* (1860), pp. 7-15.

necessary causation is a primary law of nature. In the *Literary Museum* Tucker, signing himself "C.C.,"[46] attacked not only Hume's theory but also Brown's attempt to reconcile Hume's theory with religion. In a small pamphlet called *Inquiry into the Relation of Cause and Effect,* a work greatly enlarged in its third edition of 1818, Brown accepted, says James McCosh, Hume's point that the relation of cause and effect consisted "merely in invariable antecedence and consequence." Yet, instead of claiming that the mental principle which induced men to believe in the relation was custom, as Hume did, Brown allied himself with the school of Reid by holding the relation of cause and effect to be an "irresistible intuitive belief."[47] Tucker, who read Brown's statements either in the *Inquiry* or in Brown's summary in his *Lectures* (1826),[48] thought that only Reid had effectively answered Hume.[49] *The Treatise of Human Nature,* said Tucker, beneficially led philosophers to an empirical study of the mind, but Hume's intolerable skepticism, which makes man "nothing more than a bubble of ideas which chance . . . arranged in sequence,"[50] was reinforced, not refuted, by Brown. Brown's assumption that "we know of no other relations of things but their position in time and space"[51] and his argument that the invariable continuance of ideas explained necessary connection has led to chaos: "In Hume's system

46. I have treated in more detail in Pt. II, pp. 95-99, the causes for assigning to Tucker essays in the *Literary Museum* signed "C.C.," "K," "Q," and "V." Several objections may be made about attributing this refutation of Hume to Tucker. In the preface to his 1850 edition of *An Essay on Cause and Effect; Being an Examination of Hume's Doctrine, that We Can Perceive no Necessary Connexion Between Them* (Philadelphia, 1850), Tucker wrote that "for several years" he taught Hume's and Brown's theories to his classes; and Samuel Allibone, *Critical Dictionary of English Literature and British and American Authors* (Philadelphia, 1876), III, 2464, says Tucker refuted Hume as early as 1842. Neither statement, of course, offers firm proof that Tucker did not in 1829 attempt to refute Hume. Because of his interest in mental philosophy, Tucker, among all the known contributors to the *Literary Museum,* was the most likely writer to discuss the theories of Reid, Hume, and Brown. It may be pointed out that many passages in the essay are almost exactly like Tucker's statements either as recorded in student notebooks or in his acknowledged work. For example, "C.C." ("Premises and Causes," p. 349) ridicules, as Tucker did in his classes and in "On Our Belief of an External World (*Essays,* [1860], pp. 7-15), Brown's claim that a belief in an external world "is first obtained by a failure in sequence." See above, p. 166, n. 44.

47. See McCosh, *The Scottish Philosophy,* p. 321.

48. See *Lectures,* I, 65-75.

49. Reid's position is given in his *Essays on the Intellectual Powers of Man* in *Works,* I, 457-460.

50. "Premises and Causes," p. 344, in which Tucker cites end of appendix and Pts. IV, VI, VII.

51. *Ibid.,* p. 345.

events pass as the phantoms before Macbeth. Brown has added the ghost of Banquo who points to the phantoms, and holding up the mirror of belief shews many that are yet to come."[52]   A belief in causation as a "fundamental principle of the mind"—as Reid long ago set out—is "undoubtedly the true solution of the enigma," and Reid's strictures against Hume applied equally to Brown.[53]

In 1858, in his autobiography, Tucker told of presenting before the American Philosophical Society in Philadelphia a more mature refutation of Hume's doctrine of cause and effect. To his surprise, a committee appointed to read it gave him a complimentary notice for his work but refused to recommend it for publication in the transactions, because, Tucker said he later learned from one of the three committee members, two members had planned an attack on Hume and were unwilling to admit that Tucker "had discovered what had escaped their discernment."[54]   Certainly the committee sympathized with the purpose of Tucker's work, for it praised his attempt "to protest against that cheerless skepticism which calls in question all knowledge which would consign to the reproach of folly or superstition all faith in the supernatural."[55]   Tucker's pamphlet was, he said, a rational defense to prove that "philosophy is not really in conflict with the common sense of mankind on the subject of cause and effect, but finds in that hackneyed theme . . . another occasion to admire the truth, as well as wise purpose of our intuitive judgments and instinctive beliefs."[56] Since Hume's "ingenious essay," said Tucker, most philosophers, including Stewart and Brown, have held that "we have no proof of a necessary connection between effect and its seeming cause," but rather only the "invariable antecedence of the cause, and the invariable consequence of the effect."[57]   Tucker tried to show that Hume's theory was

---

52. *Ibid.*, p. 346.

53. *Ibid.*, pp. 347-348. Tucker summarized his fundamental differences with Hume and Brown in the following statements: (1) "that the idea of continuance and the idea of cause are not fundamentally the same"; (2) "that the idea of cause remains as distinct, after Brown has explained that it does not exist, as it was before"; (3) "that invariable sequence is never known to us except in a peculiar sense, and used in that sense we may ask—is it at the first, or the second recurrence that belief commences, and does it fail with the failure in the sequence"; (4) "that a belief in causation may *just* as well be a primary law of the mind as a belief in continuance, and explains the whole matter, which the latter does not" ("Premises and Causes," pp. 348-349).

54. "Autobiography," manuscript copy, Tucker-Harrison-Smith Papers, University of Virginia Library, p. 51.

55. American Philosophical Society Committee MS Report.

56. "On Cause and Effect," *Essays* (1860), p. 69. The first complete printing of the essay appeared as *An Essay on Cause and Effect* (1850).

57. *Ibid.*, p. 23.

based upon peculiar illustrations in which material changes in magnitude, form, arrangement of parts, and motion and rest were too minute for observation. In the changes of matter in which there were, for example, processes cognizable by the senses—such as the change from ice to water—the relationship from cause to effect was necessary and knowable.[58] It followed, then, since modern science tended to show that small portions undergo the same changes as great portions, that only man's senses were at fault, and that, consequently, in all cases of successive events the causal connection was almost as certain as a mathematical conclusion.[59]

Richard H. Popkin, who recently examined Tucker's essay, rightfully praises him for criticizing Hume on intellectual rather than on religious grounds.[60] It must be pointed out, however, that Tucker, like Stewart and Brown before him, took refuge in intuitive beliefs when necessary and recommended such procedure as a guide for common people. He explained, for example, that mankind "expects that like causes will produce like effects," not because of habit, as Hume and Brown explained, but because of an "instinctive belief in the verity of . . . sensations, and consequently in the identity of objects."[61] And when no causal connection can be observed, Tucker explained that the belief in the relationship in causal effect is "an original feeling of the mind, resulting from its constitution"—it is "instinctive, complete, and resistless."[62] Thus, Tucker's frequent flight to an "internal sense" links him closely to the common sense tradition that began with Reid, who also utilized the empirical analysis of consciousness but held, when convenient, that experience gives a direct, intuitively believable knowledge of things.

Tucker's indebtedness to the Scottish common sense philosophers is perhaps nowhere more apparent than in his essay "Association of Ideas," which he presented before the American Philosophical Society in 1843 and which he published in pamphlet form,[63] in Judge Stryker's *American Quarterly Register and Magazine,*[64] and in the volume *Essays, Moral and Metaphysical* (1860). Tucker rejected Brown's proposal to use "suggestion" to replace "association" on the principle that "one mental act never did, and never can, suggest another, unless

58. *Ibid.,* pp. 29-35.
59. *Ibid.,* pp. 42-43.
60. "Critic of Hume," p. 373.
61. "On Cause and Effect," *Essays* (1860), pp. 44-49.
62. *Ibid.,* pp. 60-63.
63. "Association of Ideas," *Virginia University Faculty Publication* [1843].
64. III (1849), 466-477.

the two have been previously associated, either directly themselves, or indirectly by their signs."[65]   Thus Tucker opposed Brown's somewhat revolutionary extension of the theory of association to the act of perception, by which Brown tried to show that the "supposition of *prior co-existence*" did not account for those connections of ideas which were not associated until "the moment of actual suggestion."[66]   Tucker, however, seems to have agreed with Brown's three-fold classification of "primary laws of suggestion"—resemblance, contrast, and nearness in time and space, although he divided the last relationship into "Contiguity or Proximity of Place" and "Proximity or Contiguity of Time."[67]   In addition, those six conditions which Tucker listed as controlling the intensity of the association of ideas are, though numbered differently, essentially Brown's "secondary laws of suggestion."[68] Like Brown, Stewart, and all the Scottish philosophers, Tucker refused to discuss the vibrations and vibratiuncles which Hartley said take place in the brain during the thinking process, for "the *modus operandi* of these material agencies on the sentient principle we are utterly ignorant of, and must remain so."[69]

Tucker's explanation of the association of ideas, however, is predicated on "a more general or elementary law" than the principles of contrast, proximity and so forth, which are mere corollaries.   To arrive at such an all-encompassing explanation of mental phenomena, it seems, was the aim of the common sense philosophers as they first analyzed the actions of the mind and then synthesized their findings into one general principle.   Thus Brown concluded that all the laws of association could be comprehended under a form of proximity.[70] Tucker's all-embracing principle "is a law both of the material and

65. *Essays* (1860), p. 97.

66. *Lectures*, I, 404-405.

67. "On Association of Ideas," *Essays* (1860), pp. 112-113.

68. *Ibid.*, pp. 108-111.   For example, Tucker (p. 108) says that the copy is stronger when the original impression is stronger.   Brown (*Lectures*, I, 372) says "the parts of a train appear to be more closely and firmly associated, as the original feelings have been *more lively.*"

In 1831-32 Tucker said that Brown's secondary laws were reducible to (1) the vividness of the suggesting idea or sensation, and (2) "individual differences" ("Notebook of Merit Robinson," p. 95).

69. "On Association of Ideas," *Essays* (1860), p. 107.   Stewart in *Essays* in *Works*, V, 6, says Hartley's speculations are "unphilosophical" and "altogether hypothetical and visionary."   Elsewhere (*Elements* in *Works*, II, 266) he says "the train of our ideas depends on courses which operate in a manner inexplicable by us."   Brown (*Lectures*, I, 438-441) says Hartley's theories, popular "chiefly in the southern part of the island," have "seduced philosophers from the proper province of intellectual analysis."

70. *Lectures*, I, 402.

sentient parts of our nature, that whatever body or mind has once done, they find it easier to do again, and have a propensity to repeat." As examples of this "propensity" he cited, in the physical world, the regularity of sleeping, the tendency of men to use given amounts of sugar to sweeten their food, and, in the mental world, the fact that whatever is presented to the senses so as to produce sensation, "that same mental act the mind immediately copies or repeats" when the object is gone.[71] The degrees of intensity of the trains of thought, of course, were modified by those conditions which Tucker borrowed, for explanation, from Brown's secondary laws of association. By this "force of habit," "this repeating tendency," then, Tucker said, were explained all conceptions, memory, and imagination.[72] Moreover, the faculty of association provided all the materials of profound and simple reasoning.[73]

For his basic point, however—that the principles of connection were all referable to the "propensity to repeat" and not to ultimate facts—Tucker seems to have based his discussion not on the work of Brown, who provided him with much of his technical terminology, but on the writings of Thomas Reid, who, like Tucker, restricted the role which the association of ideas played in the functioning of the mind. In his *Essays on the Intellectual Powers of Man* Reid wrote:

I believe the original principles of the mind, of which we can give no account but that such is our constitution, are more in number than is commonly thought. But we ought not to multiply them without necessity.

That trains of thinking, which, by frequent repetition, have become familiar, should spontaneously offer themselves to our fancy, seems to require no other original quality but the power of habit.[74]

REVALUATION

Although an early historian, perhaps overly anxious to prove that the South's contributions to philosophy were not "a blank and barren

---

71. "On Association of Ideas," *Essays* (1860), pp. 103-107.

72. *Ibid.*, p. 112.

73. *Ibid.*, p. 125.

74. *Works*, I, 387. Tucker certainly read Reid before composing his essay. He cites Hamilton's notes in Hamilton's edition of Reid (*Essays*, p. 101), and he seems to have made use of Hamilton's survey of past theories of associational psychology, given in *The Works of Thomas Reid*, II, 910-917. Tucker himself notes that his own discussion of resemblance as a principle of connection is exactly that given by Hamilton in his notes to *The Works of Reid* (II, 913). "It is proper to add," wrote Tucker, "that it was used in my lectures many years before Hamilton's work was published" (*Essays* [1860], pp. 114-115).

page," placed Tucker among those men "whose works are worthy to rank as original and valuable contributions to the technical literature of philosophy,"[75] it is clear that, as a philosopher, Tucker contributed nothing original to American thought. All of his ideas were derived from the Scottish common sense philosophers, whose thinking determined the scope and depth of his. When he did not paraphrase the *Lectures* of Dr. Thomas Brown, he turned to the writings of Dugald Stewart or Thomas Reid for his opinions. Indeed, Tucker showed no sympathy at all for philosophy which was "ingenious" or highly speculative. The only American philosophers he ever mentioned were Thomas C. Upham, professor of mental and moral philosophy at Bowdoin College, and Francis P. Wayland, president of Brown University, both adherents of the Scottish philosophy,[76] and both, as Tucker said in 1837, "of great respectability."[77] Tucker's only notice of German idealistic philosophy came in 1841 in his unpublished novel, "A Century Hence," in which, in discussing the lethargy of the British in the complicated world of 1941, he said that the English in their degeneration had lost their "spirit of enterprise, either civil or military," and were content to manifest their genius in the philosophical treatises of men who were more transcendental "than Kant, Sommerfaden, and Dunkildunst[*sic*]."[78]

As a "natural realist," Tucker followed closely what Woodbridge Riley has designated as the school's chief traits: the belief in the reality of the world, the method of observation and induction, the doctrine of "self-consciousness as the instrument of observation and not the mere observation of the brain or nerves," the spirit of common sense which reaches "natural, original, and necessary" principles.[79]

Tucker's philosophical position was eminently typical of his age. As one historian of ideas has summarized the conclusions of investigators of nineteenth-century philosophy, "the most striking influence

75. Henry C. White, "The South's Contributions to Philosophy," *History of the Literary and Intellectual Life of the Southern States,* ed. John Bell Henneman, Vol. VII in *The South in the Building of the Nation* (Richmond, Va., 1909), p. 263.

76. For Upham's philosophical beliefs, see Schneider, *History of American Philosophy,* pp. 240-241; for Wayland's see Schneider, pp. 242-243, and Joseph Blau, *Men and Movements in American Philosophy* (New York, 1953), pp. 82-92.

77. "Discourse on American Literature: Delivered Before the Charlottesville Lyceum, December 19, 1837," *Southern Literary Messenger,* IV (1838), 85.

78. Manuscript copy, Tucker-Harrison-Smith Papers, University of Virginia Library, p. 110.

79. *American Thought,* pp. 118-119.

upon American metaphysics in general is that of the Scottish 'Common-sense' school, the doctrines of which . . . may be considered the official academic belief of the period."[80]   Most scholars believe that about 1820, when the Scottish philosophy began to dominate American colleges, philosophy became academically orthodox.   Interest shifted from "speculative inquiry to systematic instruction" by men whose aim "was to be orthodox . . . to instruct their students in correct doctrine by relying on the best authors, by using systematic texts, and by inventing precise terminologies."[81]

No thorough study has yet been made of the entrance of Scottish philosophy into the Southern states.[82] Riley argues that its vogue in the South came late because the area "had too much of the Anglican indifference, too much of the Gallic skepticism, to accept as final the dogmatism of a small group of Northern British philosophers."[83] The reception of "natural realism," he says, was aided by the growth of denominational colleges along the eastern seaboard, and, in the South particularly, by the movement of a large body of Scotch-Irish who "carried along with their Presbyterian conventions their philosophy of common sense."

To trace this movement into the Allegheny Mountains and down the valleys of Virginia and of the Cumberland, is to trace a kind of intellectual glacier . . . which moved slowly southwards and ground out all opposition. . . .   Because of it deism disappeared, save in the tide-water counties where planters of English blood still remained, and materialism

---

80. Howard Mumford Jones, "The Influence of European Ideas in Nineteenth-Century America," *AL*, VII (1935), 251.   See, for example, Riley, *American Thought*, p. 119, and L. van Becelaere, "L'Influence écossaise" in *La Philosophie en Amérique depuis les origines jusqu'à nos jours* (New York, 1904), p. 54.   On the other hand, Merle Curti, "The Great Mr. Locke, America's Philosopher, 1783-1861," *Huntington Library Bulletin*, XI (1937), 107-151, denies that Locke's influence waned.   He admits that the texts of Stewart, Campbell, and Brown had replaced Locke's *Essay* in the colleges, but he claims that many of the American texts embodied Locke's ideas and paid high tribute to Locke (pp. 117-118).   The Scots themselves, of course, praised Locke and discussed him, usually to find that, though he was a pioneer in mental philosophy, he did not have enough data upon which to draw his conclusions.   See Tucker's typical attitude, above, p. 162.   Smith, *Professors & Public Ethics*, p. 29 n., 38 n., suggests that the influence of the Scottish philosophers has been overemphasized.

81. Schneider, *History of American Philosophy*, pp. 225-226, 238.

82. William Charvat, *The Origins of American Critical Thought, 1810-1835* (Philadelphia, 1936), p. 35, states that the philosophy was popular in the South in the nineteenth century, but his conclusion is based solely on examinations of the Baltimore *Portico* from 1816 to 1818 and the Charleston *Southern Review* from 1828 to 1832.

83. *American Philosophy*, p. 18.

was wiped out, save in the Gallicised portions of the country, such as the Carolinas, and the Bourbon sections of Kentucky.[84]

The fortuitous union of church and college in America undoubtedly contributed to the domination which the common sense philosophy exerted over American thought, as Riley and other scholars have noted,[85] but in Virginia the philosophy was popular for additional reasons. Tucker, for example, a moderate Episcopalian of English origin rather than a Scotch-Irish Presbyterian, a man whose intellectual, economic, and social ties were with the Tidewater aristocrats, was an early reader of the common sense philosophy, in which he became interested because of its close relationship with literature and aesthetics, as expressed in the Scottish rhetorics and in the *Edinburgh* and the *Quarterly* reviews,[86] both popular and influential in the South. When he became professor of moral philosophy at the non-sectarian University of Virginia, he selected as textbooks the safe, teachable, and popular works of the Scottish philosophers, which he already knew and favored. It seems, then, an exaggeration to state, as does Merle Curti, that the appointment of William A. McGuffey, a Scotch-Irish Presbyterian minister, to replace Tucker as professor at the University reflected the victory of the "middle-class doctrine of morality, piety, and orthodox faith" over the "older rationalism of the plantation aristocracy."[87] McGuffey may have given more theological emphasis to his teaching than Tucker, but he assigned essentially the same readings that Tucker had assigned in mental philosophy, ethics, rhetoric, and political economy; and the appointment reflects, instead of a sharp break, a continuing tradition in the teaching of philosophy at the University of Virginia.

84. *Ibid.*, p. 478. Cf. George P. Schmidt, *The Old Time College President* (New York, 1930), p. 122. Donald Robert Come, "The Influence of Princeton on Higher Education in the South Before 1825," *WMQ*, 3rd ser., II (1945), 359-396, traces in detail the manner in which Princeton graduates carried Scottish realism to Southern colleges.

85. Riley, *American Philosophy*, pp. 478-479. See Sydney E. Ahlstrom, "The Scottish Philosophy and American Theology," *Church History*, XXIV (1955), 257-272, for an excellent explanation for the philosophy's popularity among Protestant clerics.

86. The relationship between Scottish common sense philosophy and Scottish criticism in the quarterlies and in the popular rhetorics of Blair, Kames, and Campbell never has been adequately studied. See Charvat, *Origins*, p. 52.

87. *The Growth of American Thought*, 2nd ed. (New York, 1951), p. 440.

CHAPTER XI

DOMESTIC SLAVERY

MORE THAN ANY other single issue, domestic slavery exerted a strong and lasting influence on Tucker's development as a writer interested in Southern problems. A pamphlet on slavery published in 1801 won him his first public applause and the title of "man of letters" among the Richmond literati. Tucker's concern with the South's most complicated social and economic institution continued for the rest of his life, and in most of his writings from the beginning of the nineteenth century to the eve of the Civil War there are lengthy discussions of slavery.

Although a large portion of Tucker's opinions are to be found in essays and volumes on sociological, economic, and political topics, slavery also appears as an important ingredient in his imaginative writings. *The Valley* (1824), for example, Tucker's most important literary work, contains a full account of slavery in relation to Southern plantation life. This delineation, remarkable both for its historical accuracy and for its value as Southern propaganda, illustrates more clearly than any of Tucker's non-fictional works how he viewed the moral and social problems connected with slavery. In "A Century Hence," written almost twenty years later than *The Valley* and having as its setting not the ante-bellum South but the cosmopolitan world of the future, Tucker also felt compelled to say something about slavery, predicting its continued existence in America to vex the descendants of those who a hundred years before were faced with the problems to which it gave rise.

No comprehensive study of Tucker's attitudes toward slavery exists, but because his early anti-slavery statements have been held to be representative, or because his later writings have been misinterpreted, Tucker is often erroneously thought of as opposing slavery for all of his life.   Leonard C. Helderman, for example, contends that Tucker always believed that slavery was a "positive evil" whose death was both desirable and certain.   To support his contention, Helderman claims that Tucker, once an ardent opponent of Malthusian population doctrine, became an expounder of it and, moreover, dissented from Ricardian economics, which supposes that wages cannot fall below the level of minimum subsistence, because he found in the modification of these theories "some hope for the eventual death" of slavery "by the operation of economic laws."[1]

A careful study of Tucker's many and frequently contradictory statements on slavery, however, indicates that, for most of his life, he was not interested in abolishing slavery and that his predictions of the end of the institution stemmed as much from attempts to take slavery out of the realm of political controversy and to apologize for its continued existence as from a conviction that it was doomed to destruction in the immediate future.   His attitudes toward slavery were determined primarily by his desires to enhance the economic welfare of

1. "A Social Scientist of the Old South," *Journal of Southern History*, II (1936), 159, 160-161.   See also Jay B. Hubbell, *The South in American Literature, 1607-1900* (Durham, N.C., 1954), pp. 247-248; Jessie Bernard, "George Tucker: Liberal Southern Social Scientist," *Social Forces*, XXV (1946-47), 140-144.

A perceptive but brief analysis of Tucker's writings on slavery is in Joseph Dorfman, *The Economic Mind in American Civilization, 1606-1865* (New York, 1946), II, 543-550.   Dorfman centers most of his attention on statements made from 1816 to 1825 but is aware of Tucker's claims in 1837, 1843, and 1859 that slavery would die in a hundred years.   Dorfman's conclusion is that Tucker was never truly interested in freeing the slaves or in solving the many problems to which the institution gave rise. Joseph J. Spengler, "Population Theory in the Ante-Bellum South," *Journal of Southern History*, II (1936), 360-389, provides an excellent discussion of Tucker's early rejection and later acceptance of Malthusian population doctrines.   Although Spengler assumes that Malthusian population theory provided "the most important, though not always explicitly recognized, basis of the proslavery argument" (p. 360), he declines to assert whether Tucker was attacking slavery or, as I believe, apologizing for it.

For brief treatments of the place of slavery in Tucker's economic theory, see the following works: Joseph J. Spengler, "Population Doctrines in the United States," *Journal of Political Economy*, XLI (1933), 433-467, 639-672; John Roscoe Turner, *The Ricardian Rent Theory in Early American Economics* (New York, 1921), pp. 83-109, who discusses Tucker's understanding of Ricardo and praises him as an acute thinker.   For a less favorable view of Tucker's comprehension of classical economics, see George Johnson Cady, "The Early American Reaction to the Theory of Malthus," *Journal of Political Economy*, XXXIX (1931), 601-632.

Historians who mention briefly Tucker's attitudes on slavery are: Merle Curti, *The Growth of American Thought*, 2nd ed. (New York, 1951), pp. 441-442; and Clement Eaton, *Freedom of Thought in the Old South* (Durham, N.C., 1940), pp. 200-201, who notes that Tucker, after predicting the death of slavery in 1837, became an apologist for the institution in the 1850's.

the South, to protect property, and to retain for the wealthy classes the political control of Virginia. At the same time, Tucker's views were influenced by an understandable fear of racial conflict and by a strong and honest wish to preserve the Union.

EARLY OPPOSITION TO SLAVERY

THE BACKGROUND OF ANTI-SLAVERY SENTIMENT

When Tucker emigrated to the United States in 1795, he probably carried with him from Bermuda the conviction that slavery was an undesirable institution. An attempted slave rebellion in 1761 lingered in the minds of the islanders, and, as one governor of that British colony complained in 1779, slavery sapped the foundations of respect and obedience to government and lowered economic production because the "poor white inferior people" gained an exalted opinion of their status and disdained manual labor as fit only for blacks.[2]

Anti-slavery sentiment which Tucker found in Virginia was, if anything, stronger than in Bermuda because slaves, for some years generally thought to provide an unprofitable form of labor, were causing serious social problems as well. Questions concerning emancipation and insurrection were much discussed by many Virginians from 1790 to 1802, a period during which, for several reasons, discontent among the slaves was more widespread and intense than in any previous period in Southern history. The South was suffering from an economic depression which, particularly in Virginia and North Carolina, resulted in an exodus of whites from the states and a consequent increase in the proportion of blacks to whites. Certain religious sects, especially the Quakers and the Methodists, preached the idea of equality to the blacks, whose restlessness in their bondage increased as they became more educated. Negro unrest was stimulated further by "the revolutionary philosophy then prevalent abroad and at home" and more immediately by bloody slave rebellions in the near-by French Indies. The uneasy situation was complicated by the Federalist claim that the Republican party's support of the French Revolution,

2. Governor Bruire, cited by Wilfred Brenton Kerr, *Bermuda and the American Revolution, 1760-1783* (Princeton, 1936), p. 141. Kerr points out that slaves made up about fifty percent of the islands' population.

For treatment of the slave revolt in Bermuda, see Henry C. Wilkinson, *Bermuda in the Old Empire: A History of the Island from the Dissolution of the Somers Island Company Until the End of the American Revolutionary War: 1684-1784* (Oxford, 1950), p. 242.

which encouraged Negro efforts to achieve freedom, undermined America's social structure.[3]

Among the Southern leaders who gave attention to the slavery issue were two of Tucker's American relatives, both of whom undoubtedly influenced his thinking. Tucker studied law under St. George Tucker at William and Mary College and was in constant communication with him until the judge's death. His affection for Thomas Tudor Tucker began even before he came to America, when he met the Edinburgh-trained doctor and Federalist legislator during Thomas Tudor's visits to Bermuda. And during Tucker's three terms in Congress, from 1819 to 1825, he lived with or near Thomas Tudor, who during that time was serving as Treasurer of the United States. Thomas Tudor anticipated one of the positions later taken by George Tucker when, as a representative to Congress from South Carolina, he resisted the claim that Congress had the power to pass legislation to satisfy anti-slavery groups, then made up mainly of religious zealots. Speaking before the House of Representatives on February 12, 1790, Thomas Tudor warned that Congressional attempts to emancipate slaves would lead to civil war.[4]

On the other hand, St. George Tucker composed one of the more famous expressions of anti-slavery sentiment in the South. "Greatly influenced by the natural rights thinking of Blackstone" and sympathetic with Jefferson's early schemes to release slaves, he published *A Dissertation on Slavery* (1796) in which he advocated a plan of gradual emancipation, supporting it with the doctrine of natural rights contained in the Virginia Bill of Rights. Slaves should be emancipated, he argued, because "all men are by nature *equally* free and independent" and have the inalienable rights of "life and *liberty,* with the means of *acquiring* and *possessing* property." He argued further in private correspondence that Americans who fought for their own freedom surely could not "disapprove an attempt to carry so incontestable a moral truth into practical effect."[5] But even St. George's wish to free the slaves resulted almost as much from a fear of an uprising of the blacks as from a belief in the philosophic principles of

3. Herbert Aptheker, *American Negro Slave Revolts* (New York, 1943), pp. 44 and n., 100-105, 150-153 and nn., 209-210.

4. William Sumner Jenkins, *Pro-Slavery Thought in the Old South* (Chapel Hill, N.C., 1935), p. 51.

5. Quoted by Henry W. Farnam, *Chapters in the History of Social Legislation in the United States to 1860,* ed. Clive Day (Washington, D.C., 1938), pp. 170-171.

natural rights. On June 29, 1795, before his plan of emancipation was prepared, he wrote to a Dr. Belknap that "the calamities which have lately spread like a contagion through the West India Islands afford a solemn warning to us of the dangerous predicament in which we stand."[6]

ATTACKS ON SLAVERY

In this climate of opinion Tucker composed his first work dealing with slavery, a pamphlet which he was motivated to write by an uprising of slaves near Richmond. On September 1, 1800, Tucker wrote to St. George of a contemplated slave revolt which he ridiculed as the laughable attempt of "one or two villains, of address enough to enlist some followers, and not a general or even an extensive conspiracy."[7] In little more than a month, however, Tucker realized the seriousness as well as the significance of the intended uprising and decided to write a pamphlet in which he would concern himself less with the "existing evils" of slavery than with "the still greater evils it threatens."[8]

Tucker had excellent cause to be alarmed by the implications of the revolt. The uprising was not a slight one, raised by the "hewers of wood" on the spur of the moment, as he had first imagined. Instead, the rebellion, which was to take place on August 30, two days before Tucker's first letter to St. George, was carefully planned as early as the spring of 1800 and involved Negroes from all over Virginia in numbers estimated at from one thousand to fifty thousand. Led by an intelligent slave, Gabriel, the rebels intended to join with a number of poor whites to sack the city of Richmond, sparing the lives only of Quakers, Methodists, and Frenchmen, all of whom they believed to be friendly to their cause. On the morning of the revolt, some one thousand slaves, armed with guns, bayonets, clubs, and knives, rendezvoused six miles from Richmond, only to be kept from sacking the capital by a torrential rainstorm which washed out the bridge into the city. Some time later Gabriel was captured in Norfolk

6. Jenkins, *Pro-Slavery Thought*, p. 63 and n. St. George expressed similar sentiments in 1800 in the notes to his well-known edition of Blackstone's *Commentaries* (Jenkins, *op. cit.*).

7. Tucker to St. George Tucker, Sept. 1, 1800, Tucker-Coleman Collection, Colonial Williamsburg.

8. Tucker to St. George Tucker, Oct. 10, 1800, Tucker-Coleman Collection, Colonial Williamsburg.

and returned to Richmond for trial and execution along with at least thirty-four of his followers.[9]

Tucker's *Letter . . . on . . . the Late Conspiracy of the Slaves* (1801) contains the only concrete proposals he ever advanced to solve the slave problem, which, of course, grew more and more complicated as the century wore on. This early treatise, though it is not based upon a theory of natural rights, reflects the influence of egalitarian eighteenth-century liberalism. For example, Tucker wrote that he would not discuss the baneful effects of slavery upon moral character nor its inconsistency with the "truest principles of republicanism." Rather Tucker's recommendations are predicated on two assumptions. As a result of "a progress in human affairs which . . . may be retarded" but never averted, the slaves will become more educated, and like the slaves in all other periods of history, will, when they have the force, revolt.[10] Second, Tucker assumed that, because of the fecundity of the Negro and the exodus of whites from Virginia to the south and west, the proportion of blacks to whites would increase at an alarming rate.[11] Neither palliation of the slaves' grievances nor the passage of stringent laws, he argued, would solve Virginia's problems.[12] The "ingenious" remedy of emancipation appealed more to the heart than to the head because, unfortunately, slaves, unlike European peasantry, would not be content with freedom without political and social equality.[13] Tucker suggested, therefore, that only colonization afforded a practicable solution. He pointed out that it would be too expensive to transport slaves to Africa, and to carry them to the West Indies would be a cruel and unsatisfactory arrangement, because the islanders might not welcome them and especially because sympathetic and humane slaveholders could never suffer their blacks "to be torn from those tender attachments which now soften the miseries of

9. Aptheker, *Slave Revolts*, pp. 219-225, has the fullest account of this famous revolt. He claims that its magnitude has never been fully appreciated, largely because contemporary newspapers, fearful of inciting other slaves to revolt, played down its importance, as did Virginia Republicans, like Jefferson and Monroe, who did not want the Federalists to make capital of the truth that the doctrines and principles of the French Revolution inspired the uprising.

10. *Letter to a Member of the General Assembly of Virginia, on the Subject of the Late Conspiracy of the Slaves with a Proposal for Their Colonization* (Baltimore, 1801), pp. 5-7.

11. *Ibid.*, pp. 12-13, 16-17.

12. Aptheker, *Slave Revolts*, pp. 235-236, discusses the reactions of many Southerners, who determined to restrict severely the liberty of the slaves and to punish infractions of codes with harsh penalties.

13. *Letter . . . on . . . the Late Conspiracy of the Slaves*, pp. 14-16.

servitude." He advocated that the United States, with funds financed by a tax levied upon each Negro and mulatto, buy from Spain a section of land west of the Mississippi upon which Negroes could be settled. Because the Negroes' birth rate would drop severely once their subsistence was not guaranteed, they would offer no serious military threat to the United States, which would serve, on the other hand, to protect them from foreign domination.[14]

Although fear of Negro rebellion provided the immediate motivation for Tucker's first attack on slavery, a second impelling motive was also at work. Tucker was convinced that slavery was detrimental to the South's economic welfare, causing both whites and blacks to be non-productive: no country, he said, "can attain a great height in manufactures, in commerce, or in agriculture, where one half of the community labours unwillingly, and the other half does not labour at all."[15] When Tucker condemned slavery as unprofitable, he was not merely repeating the opinions of many slaveowners in the Tidewater whose eroded lands could no longer be gainfully farmed by slave labor. Instead, he was looking at slavery with the eyes of a philosopher-economist who adhered to a theory of progress and civilization, one axiom of which was that a nation could reach a coveted state of economic opulence and cultural refinement only by accumulating a dense and industrious population. Since Tucker held the belief, later reversed, that slaves could not be made to work hard because their subsistence was guaranteed, and since he felt that the rapidly multiplying Negroes only served to drive a much-desired white laboring class to the West, he was thoroughly opposed to slavery.

Ten years following his proposal for the colonization of Negroes, Tucker repeated his assertions about the economic drawbacks of a slave economy. *A Letter . . . on the Navigation of the Roanoke and Its Branches* (1811), written to induce Virginia and North Carolina legislators to strengthen their states' commercial positions, joins with the attack on slavery a denunciation of Jefferson's Republican policies and lends weight to the belief that Tucker's early anti-slavery sentiment stemmed in great part from his theory of economic progress. Tucker complained that "the deadening influence of slavery, which consigns one half of the community to idleness, and the other to reluctant labour," caused Virginia to lag behind Pennsylvania and the

14. *Ibid.*, pp. 16-18.
15. *Ibid.*, p. 21.

New England states in wealth and political prominence.[16] A nation's welfare and strength, he explained, are in direct proportion to its population, whose growth is in turn dependent upon the available means of subsistence. Since slavery prohibited the accumulation of a hardworking white labor class needed to support the growth of manufactures, commerce, and agriculture, it should be abolished.[17]

In addition to the blighting effects of slavery, Virginia's climb to opulence, Tucker argued, was also hindered by the ill-advised policies of the Republican administration, whose legislation not only limited the number of immigrants entering Virginia, but whose purchase of the Louisiana Territory provided a shelter for those discontented whites who had no desire to help swell the population of the existing states, to increase the means of subsistence, and to contribute to the luxury of the rich. "For my part," Tucker said, "unless our citizens would be restrained from crossing the Mississippi, I cannot but consider the acquisition of the western part of Louisiana as a national misfortune."[18]

Tucker's early attacks on slavery, thus inextricably tied to his hostility toward Jefferson's agrarian and expansionist politics, help explain the manner in which he used an attack on slavery to belittle Jefferson in *Letters from Virginia* (1816), a satire which was published pseudonymously but probably written by Tucker. The anti-slavery sentiments contained in this volume, already discussed for their pro-Federalist political implications,[19] however, can be thoroughly understood only by also taking into account certain of Tucker's intellectual and emotional attitudes toward slavery. The ethnological opinion expressed in Letter XI—that the inferiority of the black is a result solely of "time and circumstance" and not of natural causes—though used to attack Jefferson, also reflects Tucker's honest conviction. Only late in life did he modify this belief, which, he said, resulted in great part from the fact that in Bermuda, before he attended school, a Negro boy companion taught him the multiplication tables.[20]

16. *A Letter to a Member of the General Assembly of North Carolina on the Navigation of the Roanoke and Its Branches* (Richmond, Va., 1811), p. 18.

17. *Ibid.*, p. 8.

18. *Ibid.*, pp. 19-21.

19. See above, Pt. II, pp. 65-70, for reasons for attributing the work to Tucker.

20. "Autobiography," manuscript copy, Tucker-Harrison-Smith Papers, University of Virginia Library, p. 3. Tucker wrote in 1858 that his companionship with this Negro boy and "other similar experiences" created "doubt about the inferiority of intellect with the colored, tho' I admit that the arguments in favor of that hypothesis are very strong" (*op. cit.*).

The attack on slave trading in Letter V of the same volume apparently is related to Tucker's economic and political philosophy only insofar as it is included in a volume which contains a good deal of political propaganda. It describes in very sentimental fashion a band of manacled Negroes being led by an indifferent slave trader for sale to a North Carolina plantation. "Traveller," Tucker's spokesman, points out that for the blacks the forced exile from the Old Dominion —"their home, the scene of their childhood with all its native innocent pleasures"—is painful; they dislike to be parted from their friends, their families, and especially, their masters.[21]

Tucker's attack on slave trading was not unusual. Many Southern slaveholders who implicitly sanctioned slave trading as an unpleasant but necessary accompaniment of plantation economics, publicly condemned the practice as "barbarous."[22] Eight years later, when he was an apologist for slavery, Tucker treated essentially the same issue in *The Valley,* but with a different emphasis. In the later work, though he again made the point that the greatest evil involved in selling slaves is the dissolution of the affectionate ties between master and slave,[23] he stressed the grief of the sellers, not the sold. In all likelihood, Tucker shared the Virginia gentleman's distaste for slave trading, and since, at the time the *Letters* was written, he probably still held the opinion that slavery impaired the South's economic development, he was willing to criticize the institution by sentimentalizing its attendant social evils. In any event, the volume contains Tucker's last attack on slavery, which, in the future, he was to utilize his talents to defend.

APOLOGY FOR SLAVERY IN THE MISSOURI DEBATE

Tucker's only speech in the House of Representatives came in the midst of the debate on the Missouri Compromise, a landmark in the growth of sectionalism in the United States. Although the South was still divided on many questions in 1820, Southern statesmen and politicians, jealous of the ever-growing political power of the North, joined in urging that Missouri be allowed to enter the Union without a restriction on slavery. In his maiden address before Congress, Tucker staunchly defended the spread of slavery into the western

21. *Letters from Virginia, Translated from the French* (Baltimore, 1816), Letter V, p. 33.

22. See Kenneth Stampp, *The Peculiar Institution: Slavery in the Ante-Bellum South* (New York, 1956), pp. 237-278.

23. See below, p. 191.

territories, into the very area which he at one time wanted as a sanctuary for colonized Negroes and, a bit later, which he heartily condemned Jefferson for purchasing from France. Tucker no longer asserted that slavery was detrimental to the South's economic welfare, nor did he recommend any plan of gradual emancipation. In his new role as apologist for slavery, however, he did not hesitate to make new use of the old theme of racial conflict. His opinions on slavery in 1820 were those of a man with a considerable amount of money tied up in slave property, a nationalist who feared a division of the Union, and a Southerner who desired to live in an area which had both a controllable number of blacks and a political influence equal to that of the North.

Tucker's personal investments in slaves undoubtedly helped change his attitude toward slavery, but the degree to which this is so is difficult to determine. In 1809, shortly after he moved to "Woodbridge," he traded some Richmond property for "a parcel of negroes," to add to a number he already owned. Although two of his new acquisitions ran away before the passage of two months, somewhat dampening his enthusiasm for the trade he had made, Tucker remained generally pleased with his deal and, after some trouble, at last found "an excellent overseer" to manage his blacks.[24] In 1813, when he was deeply in debt, he followed the common practice of selling the labor of his slaves. He wrote to St. George that, because he found farming to yield but a small return from the capital invested in it, he planned to "rent out the plantation & hire . . . [his] negroes, except three or four." Since in the same letter he also spoke of two house servants dying, Abraham from dropsy and Jenny from breast cancer, it seems not unreasonable to conjecture that Tucker was among the relatively few Southerners who held more than twenty slaves.[25] And by 1820, with improved agricultural techniques in Virginia itself and with the demand for slaves growing with the rise in the price of cotton in the South and the expanding markets of the western territories, slaves were valuable property.[26]

24. See Tucker to St. George Tucker, Feb. 23 and April 14, 1809, Tucker-Coleman Collection, Colonial Williamsburg.

25. Tucker to St. George Tucker, May 28, 1813, Tucker-Coleman Collection, Colonial Williamsburg. Stampp, *Peculiar Institution,* p. 30, notes that in 1860 eighty-eight percent of the slaveowners had less than twenty slaves, and seventy-two percent less than ten.

26. Charles Henry Ambler, *Sectionalism in Virginia from 1776 to 1861* (Chicago, 1910), states that from 1817 to 1828 eastern Virginia's chief economic resource was surplus slaves (p. 112). From 1810 to 1820 the number of slaves in the valley

The position in which his father-in-law, Charles Carter, found himself may also have helped change Tucker's attitudes toward slavery. In 1821 he wrote to Carter, urging him not to move west and presenting as reason for staying in Virginia the fact that a sale of Mississippi Negroes would provide for him and his family a comfortable means of existence for the rest of their lives.[27] And Tucker and Carter's brother-in-law bought a dozen of Carter's field hands that Tucker held in trust for Carter on one of his own plantations, which Carter managed for their joint profit.[28]

In addition to having personal economic reasons for wishing to extend the life of slavery, Tucker was impelled by two other motives. He felt, first, that Northern tampering with the rights of Southern states would lead to the dissolution of the Union, that, indeed, the slavery issue was the "great question which now shakes the union to its center." Moreover, Tucker was still seriously concerned about the imbalance between the black and white populations in the South. Just before his speech in the House of Representatives, he wrote to St. George that:

If we should succeed in getting Missouri admitted without restriction, it seems quite certain that slavery will be prohibited in the Territories; and this exclusion must necessarily have the effect of increasing the ratio of black to white population in the slave holding states & what may be the extent of this progressive change or its effects an hundred years hence, no man can accurately see, but many men may perceive they are dangerous and alarming.[29]

In his speech before Congress, Tucker insisted that abstract moral speculation was out of order when discussing slavery. To distinguish between the rights of the original thirteen states and the rights of Missouri, he told his colleagues, was an "invidious discrimination," one "repugnant to the common sense of mankind." He pleaded that his fellow legislators forgo "too much subtlety and refinements . . . in reasonings," and he stated that he himself was going to make his appeal by "simple, direct and manly reasoning, conforming to the

---

increased as tobacco raising became more profitable and slaveowners hired out their blacks to salt-makers for cash wages (p. 107).

27. Tucker to Charles Carter, Aug. 26, 1821, Tucker-Harrison-Smith Papers, University of Virginia Library. It is not clear from the letter whether Tucker was referring to a sale of slaves from Virginia to Mississippi or whether the Negroes already were in the deep South.

28. "Autobiography," pp. 20, 32-33.

29. Tucker to St. George Tucker, Feb. 12, 1820, Tucker-Coleman Collection, Colonial Williamsburg.

common sense of mankind." To those who held that Missouri's rights were not impaired by the restriction of slavery because it was impossible to take away the right to do a "moral wrong," Tucker said that they confused "political with moral restraints; power with right; the possession of the power with the virtuous exercise of it."[30]

Much of his analysis of the future evils of restricting slavery to its present boundaries Tucker based on the belief that, as Sir James Steuart, Franklin, and, especially, Malthus predicted, population would increase until means of subsistence was reduced. "From these undeniable principles," he explained, "if the blacks be confined to the present slaveholding states, while the whites are left free to emigrate to the more tempting regions of the west, the ratio of blacks to whites must be continually increasing, until our population has reached the Pacific."[31] Though he thought that race relations presented a "subject of peculiar delicacy" which should not be publicly debated, he felt it necessary to emphasize what the future might hold for the nation. Since the "wildest political visionary does not think it practicable" for blacks and whites to live in economic and political equality, either the South must be surrendered to the Negroes or the races must wage a "war of extermination."[32]

On the other hand, Tucker pointed out, should slavery be allowed to expand into the western territories, in due time, as waste lands were brought into cultivation, the value of labor would drop, and the self-interest of masters would cause them to emancipate their slaves. Consequently, since the blacks would be spread over the country evenly with the whites, there would be, he claimed, no racial conflicts.[33]

Tucker's essential position was not unique. Many pro-slavery advocates advanced the same "spread theory," not because they had any objections to slavery as such, but because they insisted that the society in which they lived be one in which whites were free from fear of blacks:

In order to understand the full significance of this theory . . . it is pertinent to hold in mind a factor almost constant in the history of pro-slavery thought. To the Southern mind, the institution of domestic slavery af-

30. "Missouri Question, Speech of Mr. Tucker (of Virginia), in the House of Representatives," *Niles' Weekly Register*, XVIII [VI, n.s.], (March to September, 1820), 453-454.
31. *Ibid.*, p. 454.
32. *Ibid.*, p. 456.
33. *Ibid.*, pp. 456-457.

forded the best relationship under which a superior and inferior race could live together provided that a proper ratio of those races was maintained. The slave trade theory of the Colonial period was predicated upon this idea. It appeared again in the compromise of the Constitutional Convention on the importation provision. . . . It appears, therefore, that the spread argument, instead of being evidence of a deprecation of slavery, was a way of defending it.[34]

What Tucker added to the conventional "spread theory" was the Malthusian explanation of how slavery, if it were allowed to flourish, would eventually die by the hand of unalterable economic laws. In order to utilize Malthusian population theory thus to defend the expansion of slavery as advantageous to the nation's well-being, Tucker in 1820 had to reverse himself on the attacks which he made upon Malthus' theory in 1814 and 1815 in the *Port Folio* and again in 1822 in his *Essays,* two years after his speech on the Missouri question. In these papers Tucker did not deal with slavery, but he did issue an early and effective, if confused, attack on the theories of Malthus, from whose writings, nevertheless, he derived his chief justification for the continuation of slavery.[35]

Admittedly wishing to argue from expediency and seemingly aware that the Missouri debate was a trial of strength between the North and the South, Tucker was too shrewd a politician to rest his case for the expansion of slavery solely upon the Southern point of view. He attempted to win Northern approbation for his position by appealing to the mutual interests of both sections. A state, he told his fellow congressmen, possesses "more wealth, and strength, and weight in the legislature, when inhabited by freemen than by slaves." In the future, when America completes its expansion to the west, all the Atlantic seaboard—North and South—will hold business and economic interests in common against the increasingly powerful West. The eastern commercial states, "natural allies," must work together—here by voting against restriction—to limit the "political influence" of the West by reducing the number of its free white voters.[36]

34. Jenkins, *Pro-Slavery Thought,* p. 70.

35. See, for examples, Spengler, "Population Doctrines," pp. 436-437; and Cady, "Reaction to Malthus," pp. 616-617. Neither Spengler nor Cady is aware of Tucker's 1820 speech utilizing Malthusian theory to predict the end of slavery. Dorfman, *Economic Mind,* II, 544-545, notes the conflict between Tucker's early attacks on Malthus and his use of Malthusian theory in the Missouri debates but does not recognize the important fact that Tucker's third essay attacking Malthus was first published in 1822.

36. "Missouri Question," pp. 456-457.

As early as 1820, then, Tucker, though he professed to oppose slavery on "moral and political grounds,"[37] expressed political, economic, and social justifications for it, justifications which he was to repeat, with some interesting modifications, until the eve of the Civil War. Rejecting the scheme of colonization as "hopeless and impracticable," he found in the expansion of slavery a "common sense" solution which would benefit slaveholders, protect the Union, and keep the blacks in a state of governable inequality.

SLAVERY IN *THE VALLEY OF SHENANDOAH*

One of the most interesting features of *The Valley* is its treatment of slavery. The novel was written and published at a crucial point in Tucker's development as a Southern thinker. He was convinced by 1824 that slavery was to remain a fixture in the Southern economy and furthermore that the institution offered an economical source of labor as well as the best system under which a superior and an inferior race, each with different cultural values, could live together. In Tucker's only published novel we get a considerable amount of propaganda for the Southern attitude and an early contribution to the plantation theme in American literature, in which happy and irrational blacks work contentedly under the Southern sun for kind, aristocratic masters. Nevertheless, Tucker brought together reflections of twenty years of experience as a planter and slaveowner and discussed with coherent lucidity certain aspects of slavery which later Southern novelists, fearful of giving ammunition to abolitionists, shunned altogether.

Tucker's portrayal of Southern life contains many of the clichés of later pro-slavery novels.[38]   The slave, he said, is content on a plantation: "His simple wants are abundantly supplied, and whatever of coercion there is on his will, it is so moderate and reasonable in itself, and, above all, he has been so habituated to it, that it appears to be all right, or rather, he does not feel it to be wrong," for he sees himself as part of a happy family.[39]   Negro field workers are depicted by

37. *Ibid.*, p. 455. Tucker said that if he lived in Missouri, he would "probably" be "one of the number" who opposed slavery.

38. Francis Pendleton Gaines, *The Southern Plantation: A Study in the Development and the Accuracy of a Tradition* (New York, 1924), recognizes Tucker's contribution in *The Valley* to the plantation theme in literature, but erroneously asserts that Tucker, though he admitted the benefits of slavery to the blacks, saw slavery as detrimental to whites. In reality, Tucker did not commit himself, but implied that slavery was beneficial to the whites. See below, p. 192.

39. *The Valley of Shenandoah; or, Memoirs of the Graysons* (New York, 1824), II, 206.

Tucker as reveling in their bondage. Happy harvest hands, "plentifully supplied with good whisky," wave at "Master Edward" as they race with one another to do their work.[40] The only slave who expresses any discontent is an ex-houseboy who has been relegated to the fields for illicitly fathering the child of a fourteen-year-old girl, the favorite housemaid of Mrs. Grayson. When, however, Edward indicates his forgiveness, the slave, whose suffering is due to the remorse he feels for having aroused the displeasure of "my master," clasps Edward's hand in speechless gratitude.[41] In the Tidewater area, as in the Shenandoah Valley, the slaves are contented and the masters benevolent. As Gildon, the New York visitor, watches the blacks gather fodder, singing as they work, Planter Jones points out that there exists a mutual harmony between slaves and masters. The blacks' poetry and music, especially in their "corn songs," reflect "praise of their master, gratitude for his kindness, thanks for his goodness, praise of one another, and, now and then, a little humorous satire." The joys of Virginia slavocracy are thus apparent:

These expressions of joy . . . are peculiarly gratifying from the slave, because it pleases us to see them happy under that privation, which we have been taught to believe is greater than any other; besides, the exercise of our sympathies is always more or less agreeable, and it is doubly so, when we sympathize with feelings of joy.[42]

In the novel are several stock Negro characters, all of whom are content with their condition. At "Beechwood," the plantation home of the hero, Edward Grayson, Granny Moll, a garrulous old family nurse, lives quietly and comfortably in a clean little hut, where, upon visits from the whites, who are most solicitous for her comfort, she dwells nostalgically upon the glorious days of the past.[43] Other house servants, however, betray an inherent shiftlessness in spite of their loyalty and servility. The Grayson's old Uncle Phill ingeniously praises the "quality" of his masters but has the usual Negro traits of dishonesty and irresponsibility.[44] Old Jeffrey, a one-time valet but now hostler at the home of the Fawkners, is described as "a shrewd, artful, ready-witted knave, who having long assumed the privilege of

40. *Ibid.*, I, 65.
41. *Ibid.*, I, 66-67.
42. *Ibid.*, II, 116-117.
43. *Ibid.*, I, 81-87, 298-300; II, 180-182.
44. *Ibid.*, I, 315; II, 6-7.

great familiarity with his superiors, was at length suffered quietly to enjoy it. . . ."[45]

Perhaps because Tucker's intention in 1824—to present a true picture of the South as he knew it—was not obstructed by the need to refute abolitionist propaganda, which was not especially strong until the 1830's, in *The Valley* he treated without apology three of slavery's controversial aspects, later portrayed by anti-slavery writers as vicious social evils. First of all, Tucker criticized the system of absentee management through the use of overseers, a surprising attitude since he as a master employed managers to run his estates and also followed the practice, much attacked even in the South, of "hiring out" his Negroes to other white men. Thus, at "Easton," the Grayson's second plantation, the overseer, Cutchins, obviously mistreats and mismanages the slaves, all of whom long to be under the control of the good Edward Grayson. Many of the blacks, badly housed and nursed and subsisting on poor food, are sick with ague.[46] Edward commends the thrift of the overseer in treating, himself, the slaves' illnesses with liberal doses of "salts and tartar and ipecac," but advises him in the future to call a doctor if the blacks' sicknesses appear violent or rare.[47]

Tucker also takes for granted as a natural accompaniment of plantation life slave breeding, which was widely carried on in the South, especially in Virginia and other border slave states, though most Southerners denied the practice, claiming it was a libel invented by Northern abolitionists.[48] It is not the genteel Graysons, however, who benefit from slave breeding, but the Fawkner family, the descendants of "Dutch graziers." Granny Moll, always bitter at the financial decline of the Graysons and the rise to affluence of the Fawkners, regrets that old Colonel Grayson traded "Chloe's mother and another girl named Patty" to the Fawkners for two horses, both of which were "good for nothing." From the young blacks, the old Negress complains, Major Fawkner bred more than thirty Negroes.[49]

45. *Ibid.,* I, 32-33.
46. *Ibid.,* II, 44-45.
47. *Ibid.,* II, 40. Tucker's picture of the slaves' condition and of the remedies offered is realistic. Stampp in his study of domestic slavery writes that most slaves in the South suffered from malnutrition and the lack of proper medical care, especially since many whites, including many of the South's most competent physicians, assumed that the blacks thrived on special remedies and diets (*Peculiar Institution,* pp. 295-314). Tucker, of course, was criticizing more the economic advantage which Cutchins takes of Edward than his treatment of the blacks.
48. Stampp, *Peculiar Institution,* pp. 245-251.
49. *The Valley,* I, 298-299.

A third feature of slavery which Tucker discussed in his novel was that of slave trading, a practice which many Southern defenders and apologists for slavery publicly condemned but privately sanctioned as a natural right of property holders and even resorted to as a necessary, if unpleasant, reality of economics.[50] In *The Valley,* most of the Grayson family's slaves must be sold at auction to pay the debts accumulated by the dead Colonel Grayson, one of whose faults as a manager, incidentally, was that he did not force the slaves to work hard enough. At first the slaves are terrified at the prospect of leaving Virginia, believing that they will be forced to work "up to their necks in water" on an indigo plantation. But they have "implicit confidence" in the goodness of their owner, who quickly quiets their fears by assuring them that their new master will be chosen on the basis of his reputation for kindness and liberality.[51] Although Tucker commented that those who are not accustomed to slave sales are shocked by seeing humans sold like "horses or cattle," he made it clear that most of the evils of slave trading are palliated by the benevolence and watchfulness of Virginia gentlemen. When a libertine buyer tries to purchase a "likely" eighteen-year-old mulatto girl to carry her to prostitution in New Orleans, he is sent packing by the kind Lawyer Trueheart.[52] Since the whites thus do all in their power to see that the blacks find good homes, and also strive to keep families together, most painful for the slaves, Tucker said, is the necessity of leaving their masters, "for their simple hearts are very susceptible of warm attachment." When the blacks leave "Beechwood," they cry as they give their goodbyes to Mrs. Grayson: "Heaven bless my kind mistress wherever she goes, and send her good luck!"[53] Nevertheless, except for a few "unamiable characters," even those Grayson slaves who are about to be sold to pick cotton in Georgia, admittedly to a kind owner, are placated by Mrs. Grayson's gifts of a few pieces of second-hand clothing or, later, portions of sugar and molasses. All in all, Tucker described the scene of the slave auction as a "moral picture of genuine benevolence," more trying to the whites than to the blacks.[54]

50. Stampp, *Peculiar Institution,* pp. 237-278, provides a full account of slave managing. He relates that between 1830 and 1860, Virginia planters profited greatly from the sale of 300,000 slaves, almost the whole of the state's natural increase, to the new territories (p. 238).
51. *The Valley,* II, 196, 198-199.
52. *Ibid.,* II, 207-210.
53. *Ibid.,* II, 212-213.
54. *Ibid.,* II, 196-201.

Tucker's attitude toward the moral problems involved in keeping slaves is most clearly seen in a discussion held between slaveholders and James Gildon. Gildon, who is at first awed at the power which he believes Edward Grayson possesses as a master, defines "liberty" as consisting in acting as one pleases and questions whether the slave master does not enjoy controlling others, like a feudal baron. Grayson, however, tells Gildon that any social system is imperfect insofar as it does not approach the ideal state in which all have liberty. But Tucker had the slaveowner justify the expediency and necessity of slavery by explaining that colonization is impractical, that emancipation would lead to a Santo Domingo massacre, that, in short, wise men must realize that there is no remedy except "what time may bring some centuries hence." Since to give slaves rights, he said, would mean the loss of "still higher and dearer rights," all those schemes which advocate colonization or emancipation for the Negro are the result of "well meaning but shortsighted enthusiasm . . . sheer folly or the hypocritical pretense of the lovers of mischief." Too many white men, he said, forget that the slaves are like animals, or, less harshly, like children; "there is as much difference between their feelings respecting their condition, and those of a white man, as is the privation of sight to one who is born blind, and one who has become so."[55] Nor was Tucker in 1824 still convinced, as he once was, that slavery was detrimental to the habits of whites. Perhaps, Edward Grayson admits to Gildon, slavery may cause some whites to believe labor degrading or unnecessary and lead them to the vices of gambling or drinking, but he concludes without elaboration that its "moral effects . . . present a wide field for speculation, and are not unmingled with good."[56]

To complete his *volte-face,* Tucker reversed himself on the economics of slaveholding. Unlike many apologists, he did not claim that slaves were unprofitable and kept in bondage by the whites only for the good of society. Rather he set forth the theory that slaves, if carefully managed, were valuable assets on a plantation and almost as profitable as free labor. Fear of punishment, habit, emulation, and competition with other plantations and with one another overcame the slaves' self-interest to produce as little and consume as much as possible.[57]

55. *Ibid.,* I, 62-64.
56. *Ibid.,* I, 69-70.
57. *Idem.* Stampp, *Peculiar Institution,* pp. 383-388, analyzes the standard Southern claim that slavery was an unprofitable burden assumed by humane Southern whites for the good of society and finds it to be untrue.

PROFESSORIAL DEFENSES

In his capacity as Professor of Moral Philosophy and Political Economy at the University of Virginia from 1825 to 1845, Tucker continued to justify the existence of slavery. Utilizing every opportunity that came his way, he skillfully argued his thesis that slavery would disappear by itself.

In 1827 in a review of Thomas Cooper's *Outlines of Political Economy* (1825),[58] Tucker set forth in clear terms the basis for much of his later theorizing on the place of slavery in a modern economy. He asserted that, since Adam Smith had already settled most of the questions of economics which concerned the welfare of society, especially that luxury supported by industry is beneficial and not socially dangerous, the modern economist was concerned with the "refinements" of the science—with such a problem as the source of value. In the first stages of civilized society, Tucker said, when population was sparse, there was little division of labor and no rent. Although value then, as always, was determined by supply and demand and, especially, by the cost of production, landowners were not as well off as they are in advanced societies because land was too abundant. With a great increase in population, however, the number of landless men would increase, and these men, in their desire for the landowner's surplus food, would sell their labor cheaply. Competition would continually act to lower the value of labor until, after the worker's aliment was changed from a more expensive to a cheaper kind, the limit of population would, for all intents and purposes, be fixed. At this point in the nation's development, Tucker said, the peaceful end of slavery would come about, for owners would discover that the cost of feeding a slave was more than his value as a laborer. Cooper's assertion, therefore, that slavery was the dearest kind of labor, profitable only in the rich lands of Georgia and South Carolina, states in which the climate made it impossible for whites to work efficiently, was, said Tucker, all wrong. There were "other and better arguments" to prove that slavery, if left unbothered, would die peacefully. That day would arrive when the free laboring class must live on a "bare subsistence."

In a number of pseudonymous articles published in the *Literary*

58. "Political Economy," *American Quarterly Review*, I (1827), 309-331. The analysis of Tucker's economic theory is drawn from that of Joseph Dorfman (*Economic Mind*, II, 549-550), who also discusses Cooper's *Outlines* (II, 538).

Museum, Tucker argued for the rights of slaveholders to control the political destiny of Virginia. In the Virginia Constitutional Convention of 1829, the state was split between two forces. The majority of representatives from western Virginia wished to broaden the franchise and destroy the economic power of the slaveholders, most of whom were from eastern Virginia. Those from the Tidewater and Richmond areas, on the other hand, wished to preserve slavery and to retain their political control of the state, first, by limiting the suffrage basis and, second, by allowing slaveholders extra weight in the ballot by giving to them the votes of their slaves.[59] Tucker sided with the "slavocracy" in advocating that representation be based on the sum of white property holders and three-fifths of the slave population. Explaining urbanely that slaves were human—like children—and deserved to have their rights protected through the votes of their masters, Tucker also suggested that the South's representation in Congress, figured on a three-fifths ratio, would come under attack by Northern politicians if Virginia disregarded slaves in apportioning state representation. More significantly, he argued that those who held property had a right to protect it, that masters had to keep control of the legislative machinery to be assured that their slaves would not be taxed too highly.[60]

Tucker's pro-slavery opinions and conservative political affiliations, thus influenced by his desire to protect property, were reinforced by his hostility to Jacksonian democracy and, therefore, his opposition to the rise of the common man to a position of power in Southern politics. Because he was an ardent supporter of Henry Clay and a friend of Clay's campaign manager, Senator Josiah S. Johnston of Louisiana, Tucker probably was aware that Andrew Jackson was elected to the presidency in 1828 largely, as Clement Eaton points out,

59. Jenkins, *Pro-Slavery Thought,* p. 82; Eaton, *Freedom of Thought,* pp. 27-28.

60. "V," "Constitution of Virginia, Letter II," No. 8 (Aug. 5, 1829), 121-124. Tucker's support seems to have been divided between those whom Ambler distinguished as the "older" conservatives, led by Madison and Monroe, who were "devoted to the teachings of 1776" and who argued for representation for the slaves on the ground that they were human beings, and the more reactionary "newer" conservatives led by B. W. Leigh and Abel P. Upshur, who followed the principles of Calhoun, opposed contractural government, and argued that property was more important than "metaphysical subtleties" in deciding the franchise (*Sectionalism in Virginia,* pp. 150-154). Tucker in 1833, when attacking Jackson's administration, highly praised Leigh, whom Dorfman calls "the most reactionary of Virginia leaders" (*Economic Mind,* II, 883). For Tucker's statements, see "The President's Late Manifesto, No. 3," *National Intelligencer,* Oct. 16, 1833. Tucker's use of the letter "V" to sign his articles in the *Literary Museum* is discussed in Pt. II, pp. 97-98.

on the strength of votes from poor whites in the West and South.[61] And Tucker, who railed against Jackson for his attacks on Nicholas Biddle's second National Bank and who thought of Jackson as an unscrupulous demagogue who would destroy property in his struggle for power, was, by supporting slavery and slaveholders, working hard to keep Virginia in the conservative fold.

Tucker's early desire to build Virginia into an industrial and commercial center still existed. But he no longer believed as he did at the turn of the century that slavery was an obstacle to this goal. Although in a later acknowledged work on economics he admitted that the utilization of slaves in factories would prolong the life of slavery,[62] in 1829 in the pages of the *Literary Museum,* again under a pseudonym, Tucker was in favor of so employing them on the grounds that the wealth of the state would be augmented and that whites would be kept from migrating from Virginia. The South, he said, could well compete with the North as an industrial center because it had a ready and cheap supply of black laborers who were as easily controlled as the children who were profitably employed in the North.[63]

Tucker's statements on slavery from 1837 to 1845 are contained in his textbooks on economics, except for the brief but important comments in his unpublished novel, "A Century Hence." Although his position during this period underwent no basic alteration, nevertheless his works evidence his growing concern over the possibility of the dissolution of the Union. Extremists in North and South, he felt, were about to carry the problems of slavery from the field of economics, where they belonged, and settle them, if necessary, by force. His perception was acute, for after 1835, Southerners answered abolitionists' cries for immediate emancipation by acclaiming more than ever before the positive benefits of slavery.[64] In the Old Dominion, Virginians, who viewed the slave revolt of 1835 in Southampton County led by Nat Turner as a direct result of Northern propaganda, also became more insistent than ever before that only the South could

61. *Freedom of Thought*, p. 28. The conservative attack on broadening the franchise was part of a "protest against . . . Jacksonian Democracy" (Ambler, *Sectionalism in Virginia*, p. 162).

62. *Progress of the United States in Population and Wealth in Fifty Years, as Exhibited by the Decennial Census* (Boston, New York, Philadelphia, Washington, D.C., 1843), pp. 114-117.

63. "K," "The Policy of Encouraging Manufactures, No. 3," No. 4 (July 8, 1829), 59-61.

64. Jenkins, *Pro-Slavery Thought*, p. 89.

solve the Negro problem. And in the decade of the 1840's, Southern advocates of secession became vocal and numerous.[65]

In 1837 in his volume *Laws of Wages, Profits and Rent Investigated,* Tucker codified and restated his views on slavery. Reversing himself on his statements made in *The Valley,* he was bold enough to refute Southern fire-eaters who found slavery equally beneficial to whites and blacks. He said that the worst effects of slavery resulted from the debilitating influence which the institution had upon free men. It caused them to scorn labor as degrading and, in their idleness, to practice the "habits of waste and dissipation." In the present society, however, slave labor was economical and beneficial. Although fear, he admitted, was not so great a stimulus to productivity as self-interest, "yet it is more universal," as seen in the fact that "the number of utter idlers is less among slaves than it is among the poorer classes of free labourers."[66] In the future, within sixty to eighty years, Tucker said, once the cotton and sugar raising states were supplied with all the slaves they needed, the value of the Negro would drop. Moreover, Tucker said, repeating his early opinion, one used by many pro-slavery advocates,[67] once slave labor became "economically

65. Clement Eaton, *A History of the Old South* (New York, 1949), pp. 384-385.

66. *The Laws of Wages, Profits and Rent Investigated* (Philadelphia, 1837), pp. 46-47.

67. See Spengler, "Population Theory," p. 372 and n., who says: "A similar argument was implicitly or explicitly presented by various writers, among them Edward Brown who considered slavery essential to civilization and to evolution from a pastoral to an agricultural economy (*Notes on the Origin and Necessity of Slavery* [Charleston, 1826], 10, 31-32, 34); Edward B. Bryan (*The Rightful Remedy* [Charleston, 1850], 101); J. H. Hammond (in *Pro-Slavery Argument* [Charleston, 1852], 121-122); Samuel Seabury (*American Slavery Distinguished from the Slavery of English Theorists and Justified by the Law of Nature* [New York, 1861], 311-312); and in *De Bow's Review* (XXIX [1860], 551)."

Although Tucker never directly predicated his defense of slavery on a theory of "conjectural" history, which assumed that slavery was a necessary or inevitable institution in the progress of a nation from savagism and barbarism to refinement, it is interesting to speculate that this philosophical rationale for progress, which he otherwise strongly embraced, may have been in the back of his mind. Edward Brown, who, as noted above, predicted the death of slavery, like Tucker, by the operation of Malthusian population laws, openly defended the need for slavery thus in his *Notes on the Origins and Necessity of Slavery:* "Slavery has ever been the stepping ladder by which countries have passed from barbarism to civilization. History, both ancient and modern, fully confirms this position. It appears, indeed, to be the only state capable of bringing the love of independence and of ease, inherent in man, to the discipline and shelter necessary to his physical wants. . . ." (p. 6). "Hence the division of mankind into grades, and the mutual dependence and relations which result from them, constitutes the very soul of civilization; and the more numerous these grades are, in a country, the more highly civilized may we expect to find it" (p. 38). The

unsound," as it must in highly advanced societies in which great industry and economy would be required to support the masses with subsistence, masters would willingly free their slaves.[68]

When in 1841 Tucker composed his unpublished novel, "A Century Hence," he dealt only passingly with the issue of slavery, perhaps because of increasingly vigorous Southern attacks on any claims that slavery was not a permanent institution or because he was not really as certain as he professed to be about its extinction. In any event, in Tucker's novel, the scene of which is set in 1941, the "natural euthanasia" of slavery, which he insisted in his economic treatises of 1837 and 1843 must take place by the passage of sixty to eighty years, has not occurred. William Carlton, the father of the novel's hero, explains that the problem of slavery still exists. In Virginia, Kentucky, Tennessee, North Carolina, and "this state"—Missouri—no slaves remain, but in the deep South there are fourteen million blacks whose owners are reluctant to free them, claiming that only Negroes can work in the tropical climate and that the whites and blacks can live together only in a slave system. Agitation for the slaves' freedom, Tucker caused Carlton to state, was dormant until a group was formed to purchase the slaves. But the scheme was totally impractical, since, figured at the price of two hundred dollars per slave, emancipation would cost $2,800,000,000—four times the annual national revenue. Compromise legislation was proposed, therefore, whereby the rights of the whites would be preserved. Black children born after the passage of the act would be freed at the age of twenty-five years with money repaid partly by a tax collected from the free Negroes and partly from the savings from the salaries earned by slaves on their days off. Such a plan, Carlton explains, is admirable, for "those only will obtain their liberty who by their industry & good conduct have proved themselves worthy of it, and likely to make good use of it."[69]

Hard-headed realist that he was, Tucker obviously recognized that slavery was profitable and that, consequently, enlightened planters and industrialists, whose acts were controlled by self-interest, had no intention of losing an economical source of labor. Nor is there any good reason for believing that Tucker himself wished to see the

---

quotations are found in Jenkins, *Pro-Slavery Thought*, p. 73.

For a discussion of Tucker's use of the Scottish "conjectural" history, see below, Chap. XII.

68. *Laws of Wages*, pp. 48-49.

69. "A Century Hence: Or a Romance of 1941," manuscript copy, Tucker-Harrison-Smith Papers, University of Virginia Library. Tucker's comments on slavery are contained in five extra pages added to the end of the manuscript.

South's "peculiar institution" abolished. In 1842, at about the same time that he was publicly admitting that the utilization of slaves in industry would prolong the life of slavery,[70] he was advocating in his classes, just as he did in 1829 and 1830 in the *Literary Museum,* that slaves be used in place of free white labor in factories in the South, since slaves were cheaper and more easily managed than whites. As proof for his contention that slaves could be taught to perform tasks in a modern industry, Tucker cited to his students the excellent use made of them in the factories of western Virginia, Petersburg, and Richmond.[71] Like other Southern leaders who saw in slavery a way to avoid the labor problems of the North,[72] Tucker assumed that industrialization and slavery were mutually beneficial and could progress together.

In a volume first published in 1843 and again with revised statistics in 1850 as *Progress of the United States in Population and Wealth,* Tucker most openly revealed his fear that the constantly increasing abolitionist propaganda would lead the South to dissolve its ties with the North. As in 1837, Tucker stated that slavery would die a natural death in sixty to eighty years. At the same time, he insisted that the federal government's interference with slavery was "not only un- warranted by the constitution, but . . . inconsistent with a continuance of the union."[73] The evils of slavery, then, could best be remedied if the North would respect the "comity due to sister States, and . . . the solemn pledges of the federal compact." Abolitionist propaganda, he said, embittered the slaveholder, hurt the condition of the slave, and solidified Southern opposition:

Philosophy no longer ventures to teach that this institution is . . . injurious to the master . . . ; religion has ceased to refuse it her sanction, and even the love of liberty, which once pleaded for emancipation, is now enlisted against it. Statesmen and scholars have tasked their ingenuity to show that slavery is not only legitimate and moral, but expedient and wise.[74]

70. *Progress in Population* (1843), pp. 114-117.

71. "Notes on Political Economy" (1842), "Notebook of Robert Lewis Dabney," Dabney Papers, University of Virginia Library.

72. Stampp (*Peculiar Institution,* p. 65), notes that in 1842 the Tredegar Iron Com- pany in Richmond first began to use slave labor as a means to cut costs. Angered white workers finally struck against the company's practice in 1847, and as punishment for their "illegal combination" Tredegar, content to use all slave labor except for supervisory personnel, refused to re-hire any of the strikers.

73. *Progress in Population,* p. 110.

74. *Ibid.,* p. 108.

Even worse than the growing intolerance in the South, Tucker lamented, unscrupulous politicians seized upon the sectional ill will to promote their own ambitions, even daring to "look with evil eyes on the future strength and greatness of this republican confederacy, to indulge in hopes of its dissolution."[75]

A review of Tucker's utterances from 1827 to 1845 and an examination of the discrepancies between his statements in published and acknowledged works and those in his unpublished and pseudonymous writings indicate the extent to which he was willing to compromise his intellectual integrity. During this period he did not, for the most part, view slavery or its attending problems in the light of settled social and economic theories which he held with conviction. Rather, he treated the institution solely in terms of political and economic expediency, defending and justifying it with whatever methods he thought most effective. If he was not, as it seems he was, intentionally dishonest in publicly predicting in 1837 and again in 1843 that slavery would die in sixty to eighty years, he was, as the treatment of slavery in "A Century Hence" (1841) shows, at least quite uncertain of his claims. It seems clear that Tucker did not really believe that the end of slavery was to come before the lapse of a century. He may have subscribed to the notion he stated in *The Valley*—that the remedy for the problems of slavery was "centuries," not a century, hence.[76] But Tucker, who viewed slaves as property to be protected instead of humans to be freed, was far less interested in the problems of emancipation than in quieting Northern opponents of slavery. If, he may have reasoned, the North could be made content with a theory which justified the immediate necessity for slavery, they could tolerate its existence and, perhaps, in time come to realize that slavery was beneficial to all the nation. Self-interest, the great motivator of all except slaves, who were more governed by fear, would bring men to see to it that property consisting of slaves was protected and, more importantly, that the Union, with each individual state making its unique contribution to the welfare of all, would be preserved.

FINAL HYSTERIA

Although Tucker in his last years continued to justify slavery on the grounds of expediency, he became more outspoken and more irrational in his defenses. His urbanity failed him in his old age and was replaced by a moderate hysteria as he pondered the possibilities

75. *Idem.*
76. *The Valley,* I, 69.

that the South might not remain exclusively a white man's country
or that the North and South, which he in 1820 claimed were "natural
allies," might go to war. From Philadelphia in 1855 Tucker wrote to
his daughter Eliza, who still lived in Charlottesville, asking about an
incident at the University of Virginia. An article entitled "Virginia
Chivalry," he said, related how Harriet Beecher Stowe's sister had
been insulted with a mock serenade during which the novelist of
abolition was burned in effigy. Although he deplored the lack of
gentlemanly behavior in Virginia, in the same letter he revealed how
unsympathetically he viewed the actions of those who urged racial
equality. He related how the Episcopal convention in Philadelphia
was discussing "the propriety of permitting a black preacher to a seat
among them," a proposition which the bishop endorsed. "I wonder,"
Tucker said, "if the Bishop would be willing to let his daughter be
married to a 'black brother' however unexceptional in other respects."
It seems, concluded the defender of the *status quo,* that many in the
civilized world "are crazed on the subject of African slavery."[77]

In the analyses of slavery written near the end of his life in his
History of the United States (1856-1858) and in *Political Economy for
the People* (1859), Tucker discussed the effects of slavery upon masters
and found the good to outweigh the bad. The leisure which slavery
gave the master sometimes led him to indulge himself in the sports
of the turf, the cockpit, the chase, and the gaming table, and the inhabitants of the South were sometimes haughty and not punctual in
paying debts.[78] Yet these defects, common to any aristocratic society,
he concluded, were more than balanced by virtues that derived from
slavery. Observation shows, he said, that the relation between slave
and master formed for the master habits of "forbearance and self
restraint," traits evident in such typical Southerners as Madison, Jefferson, Monroe, and Calhoun. If the manners of General Jackson,
he said, seemed to contradict this rule, it must be remembered that

77. May 18, 1855, Tucker-Harrison-Smith Papers, University of Virginia Library.
In his autobiography, written in 1858, Tucker expressed a belief in the myth that one
motive of the Negroes in their revolt of 1801 was to rape white women. He wrote
that the aim of the blacks was "to seize the capital—amounting to many thousands—to
possess themselves of the money in the banks, to set fire to the town in different places,
and in the confusion thus created to massacre the whites, reserving however for
worse fate the ladies most distinguished for beauty" (p. 15). See Aptheker, *Slave
Revolts,* p. 224 and n., who says there is no evidence of "rape or attempted rape in the
history of American slave revolts."

78. *A History of the United States from Their Colonization to the End of the
Twenty-Sixth Congress, in 1841* (Philadelphia, 1856-1858), I, 97.

"his character was formed before he became a slaveholder."[79] Tucker explained that the Southern way of life, inducing the "habit of command," fitted men best for the "higher duties of civilized life." Jefferson believed, said Tucker, that slavery led to "overbearing manners," but empirical observation refuted the "fallacies of ingenious theory," because "the manners of the cultivated classes in slave holding states differ little or nothing from those of people of rank in Europe."[80]

Tucker also labeled as the fruits of "ingenious theory" by "mere speculators" all claims that slave labor was nonprofitable. When Negroes were freed, he said, as in the West Indies and Jamaica, they worked only for high wages for limited periods of time, but in the South skillful overseers made the slaves work hard, not by exacting punishment, but by exciting emulation among them and by holding out small indulgences and rewards. Under the plantation system the blacks instinctively became aware that they were part of the "same patriarchal family" for which they worked.[81]

In defending the social theory of slavery, Tucker followed the stock argument promulgated, for example, by William J. Grayson in *The Hireling and the Slave*—that the Negro was treated better than his white counterpart in the North. Even though the blacks were in bondage, they were as well cared for "and in fact as happy" as white Yankees, for in the North, he elaborated, workers "are not treated with the same easy familiarity and kindness as by Southern gentlemen"; there does not exist "the mutual affection and goodwill that reigns in the South."[82]

The nature of Tucker's late utterances on the problems raised by slavery reflects his desperation at the course which national events seemed to be taking and indicates that his recommendations, certainly at the present time and perhaps in the past as well, were intended not to solve the problems but to postpone and wish them away. In his *History of the United States,* Tucker, in a piece of sophistry that he himself had derided in *Laws of Wages, Profits and Rent* almost twenty years before, said that colonization would solve most of the nation's problems. The states and the federal government could easily afford to colonize eighty thousand slaves a year. And the troublesome free blacks, led by "political ambition," he said, would

79. *Ibid.*, I, 98-99.
80. *Political Economy for the People* (Philadelphia, 1859), pp. 86-87.
81. *Ibid.*, pp. 84-85.
82. *Ibid.*, p. 87.

probably voluntarily emigrate to Africa.[83]   Tucker in *Political Economy for the People* also continued to predict the death of slavery because of over-population but at the same time admitted that there would be no population pressures for centuries certainly, and perhaps never.   Even if slavery continued as a permanent institution, he said in his *History of the United States,* Northerners "who are most bigoted in favor of negro emancipation" may eventually see the injustice of their sentiment.   Just as the French were anxious to confer civil liberty on all in Europe but paled at the "frantic schemes of the Red Republicans in 1849," Americans would come to realize that indifference was the best attitude to take toward Negro slavery.   Liberty, explained Tucker, "must be qualified by justice, order, and obedience to the laws."   In its largest sense, liberty "is the desire to do what we please, and it is this desire which associates the tyrant, the criminal, and, in short, every violator of the law.   We must not," he irrationally concluded, "fall into the error of the miser, who values money for its own sake, and not for its uses."   Liberty, when it is properly restrained, is merely a means of achieving happiness.   All people are restricted in their liberty.   Since all slaves have the same liberty as all freemen, differing in its enjoyment only in "degree, and not of kind," it was best for all men to trust Negroes' well-being, "like that of children, to the common feelings and sympathies of our nature, and which experience tells us is . . . a sufficient reliance."   Surely the welfare and happiness of the whites were as important as those of blacks.   But even, concluded Tucker, if "the misapplied sympathy" of the North were not abated, self-interest would prevent the West from allowing any "treasonable project" of "Atlantic malcontents" to disturb their union or the South's privilege in continuing her peculiar institution.[84]

83. *History,* IV, 428.
84. *History,* IV, 428-430.   For a similar discussion of the concept of liberty, see, for example, that of Albert Taylor Bledsoe, professor of mathematics at the University of Virginia (Jenkins, *Pro-Slavery Thought,* p. 113).

CHAPTER XII

PROGRESS AND CIVILIZATION

THE CONCEPT OF PROGRESS

UNDERLYING ALL OF Tucker's writings is the presupposition of the progress of society, an optimistic view of the past and future which, in one form or another, captured the imaginations of many men in eighteenth- and nineteenth-century America.[1] In Tucker's fiction, his concern with the "progress of society" is clearly manifested in his sociological delineations of the "habits, manners and customs" of a people. Although *The Valley of Shenandoah* illustrates that Tucker could look with admiration upon the social virtues of an earlier age, this emotional nostalgia does not obscure the fact that he was a "progressivist" who accepted as natural and good a "law of progress" —that as population increases, society changes and becomes more competitive and complicated. In "A Century Hence," Tucker continued to write about the march of civilization, but instead of looking to the immediate past, he envisioned the distant future, depicting with satisfaction the United States enjoying all the benefits of material progress but at the same time facing the complicated political and social problems which accompany inevitable industrialization.

1. The importance of the idea of progress in American culture is outlined in Arthur A. Ekirch, Jr., *The Idea of Progress in America 1815-1860* (New York, 1944). See also Charles A. Beard's "The Idea of Progress" in *A Century of Progress,* ed. Beard (New York, 1932), and Beard's introductory essay to J. B. Bury's *The Idea of Progress: An Inquiry into Its Origin and Growth,* new ed. (New York, 1932).

For the backgrounds and currency of the related concept of civilization in America, see Charles A. and Mary Beard, *The Rise of American Civilization in the United States,* Vol. IV in *The American Spirit: A Study of the Idea of Civilization in the United States* (New York, 1942).

An interesting feature of Tucker's non-fictional writings which deal with the idea of progress is his utilization of the old concept—brought to the fore in the quarrel between the ancients and the moderns—of the waxing and waning of cultures by which the torch of learning and culture is passed from one people to another.[2] Despite its fatalistic implication that each nation contains within itself the seeds of its dissolution,[3] this general idea was endorsed by Americans as a kind of deterministic, historical proof for their future greatness. Henry Nash Smith, who traces the popularity of this cyclic theory to Berkeley's (1720) lament that "Westward the course of empire takes its way," says that a belief in a "fatal succession of world states" was widely discussed in eighteenth-century America and England.[4] In essays discussing the development of literature in the light of society's advancement, Tucker applied this doctrine of historical process, though considerably modifying the cyclic theory that the fine arts in each nation rise to a point of excellence from which they inevitably decline. Tucker believed that the literature of each nation keeps "an equal pace with its civilization and general prosperity." By arguing that the ever-westward movement of ruling civilizations assured the triumph of American prosperity, Tucker could explain the absence of a great American literature and yet predict its eventual emergence with the certainty of a prophet. Thus, in his "Discourse on American Literature," Tucker utilized a cyclic theory of history but converted it into a theory of progress by stating that the "sun of civilization" in its passage to the west had grown continually brighter and that in America "it would beam with an effulgence that the world has never yet witnessed."[5] Although he discussed the possibility of America's decay, Tucker concluded that the cultural cycle could be arrested at its peak in the Western Hemisphere—that America, if its progress

2. Bury, *The Idea of Progress*, p. 91. See also Richard Foster Jones, *Ancients and Moderns: A Study of the Background of the Battle of the Books,* Washington University Studies in Language and Literature, n.s., No. 6 (St. Louis, Mo., 1936). Ernest Lee Tuveson, *Millennium and Utopia: A Study in the Background of the Idea of Progress* (Berkeley and Los Angeles, 1949), pp. 153-167, suggests that the idea of the westward course of empire stems as much from seventeenth-century Christian "apocalyptic theorists" as from such Renaissance historiographers as Hakewill.

3. See Frederick J. Teggart, "A Problem in the History of Ideas," *JHI*, I (1940), 494-503.

4. *Virgin Land: The American West as Symbol and Myth* (Cambridge, Mass., 1950), pp. 8-9. See also Benjamin T. Spencer, *The Quest for Nationality: An American Literary Campaign* (Syracuse, N.Y., 1957), pp. 22, 70.

5. "Discourse on American Literature: Delivered Before the Charlottesville Lyceum, December 19, 1837," *Southern Literary Messenger*, IV (1838), 88.

were guided by wise men of property, would lead the world in a brighter future.

But despite the optimism inherent in Tucker's thought, it is apparent that his devotion to the idea of progress was qualified by his highly conservative political and social beliefs. Unlike many of his contemporaries, Tucker went out of his way to emphasize the moderation of his hopes for the future. He was, for example, familiar with Jefferson's liberal social and political doctrines, which were largely a result of Jefferson's attempt to promote the liberal ideas of the Enlightenment.[6] But, excluding the general belief that man's progress had been impeded by the superstitious veneration and absurd metaphysical speculation of the Dark Ages, Tucker had little in common with Jefferson, whose overly "buoyant and sanguine temper," as witnessed, for example, in his continued support of the French Revolution, Tucker characterized as that of the "infatuated gamester."[7] The nature of Tucker's interpretation of America's destiny can be best understood by examining those European social theories which were of the utmost significance in forming his opinions.

Although he was conversant with both French and British philosophies of progress, Tucker never countenanced the rash optimism and radicalism which characterized the thought of the Encyclopaedists and Godwin and Condorcet. First of all, the French rationalists and Godwin conceived of man as a purely rational creature, willing and able to be guided by "naked reason," while Tucker, like the Scottish philosophers, distrusted abstract reason and felt that man was a social animal whose reason was but an instrument of his passions and feelings, which controlled his actions and thoughts. Secondly, Tucker could not accept the assumption which J. B. Bury has explained as providing the basis for the thought of the French radicals and Godwin—that man was capable of perfection.[8] Lastly, and most importantly, Tucker was at odds with the motives and especially with the results of the philosophical speculations of Godwin and the eighteenth-century French thinkers. Although Tucker in his youth approved of the French Revolution, his Jacobinism soon faded, and from the early nineteenth century until the end of his life he was a political

6. See Edwin T. Martin, "Thomas Jefferson and the Idea of Progress" (University of Wisconsin diss., 1941).

7. *The Life of Thomas Jefferson, Third President of the United States, with Parts of His Correspondence Never Before Published, and Notices of His Opinions on Questions of Civil Government, National Policy, and Constitutional Law* (Philadelphia, 1837), II, 52-53.

8. *Idea of Progress*, p. 162.

conservative, distrustful of extreme democracy and hostile to those theories of progress which provided the rationale for the destruction of existing social and political institutions. Like Dugald Stewart,[9] Tucker believed that the pernicious writings of Godwin and Condorcet sparked all the radical and revolutionary movements in Europe from the time of the French Revolution to the middle nineteenth century. Godwin's anarchism and Condorcet's belief that institutions were contrivances for the enslavement of mankind were anathemas to Tucker. Insofar as the doctrine of progress rested upon the belief that there should be political and economic equality among a nation's citizens, then that doctrine, thought Tucker, was erroneous and baneful.

On the other hand, Tucker believed that progress lay in augmenting the wealth of the nation through increased industry and commerce and through the protection of property and established institutions. His interpretation of progress closely adhered to that advanced by a large group of economists, philosophers, and historians in Scotland whose leaders were Adam Smith, David Hume, Adam Ferguson, Dugald Stewart, and John Millar. These Scots, also products of the Enlightenment, held attitudes toward progress which, if less spectacular than the perfectibilians', were far-reaching and widely disseminated.[10] Insisting that the study of history and politics begins with psychology, these philosopher-historians, says Gladys Bryson, thought that the feelings, rather than reason, controlled human ac-

9. Speaking of the "progress of society," Stewart deplored Condorcet's "utopian picture of human affairs" as inflaming the passions of the mob; and he further attacked "the extravagant doctrine" of the "indefinite perfectibility of the race" as leading to such a cataclysm as the French Revolution. See *Elements of the Philosophy of the Human Mind* in *The Collected Works of Dugald Stewart, Esq., F.R.S.S.*, ed. Sir William Hamilton, Bart. (Edinburgh, 1854), III, 492, 497.

10. The fullest background study for the Scottish writers is found in Gladys Bryson, *Man and Society: The Scottish Inquiry of the Eighteenth Century* (Princeton, 1945). See also Tuveson, *Millennium and Utopia*, pp. 153-203. Bury, *Idea of Progress*, mentions the importance of Smith's "history of the gradual economic progress of human society" in the development of the idea of progress (pp. 220-221). A study which places Smith as the leader of the Scottish conjectural historians is Duncan Forbes, " 'Scientific' Whiggism: Adam Smith and John Millar," *Cambridge Journal*, VII (1954), 643-670. See also the opening chapter of Forbes's *The Liberal Anglican Idea of History* (Cambridge, 1952). Also pertinent are: Roy Pascal, "Property and Society: The Scottish Historical School of the Eighteenth Century," *Modern Quarterly*, I (1938), 169-179; and his "Herder and the Scottish Historical School," *English Goethe Society Publications*, n.s., XIV (1938-1939), 23-42. Ronald L. Meek, "The Scottish Contribution to Marxist Sociology," in *Democracy and the Labour Movement*, ed. John Saville (London, 1954), pp. 84-102, emphasizes that the Scots anticipated Marxist social theory, but his doctrinaire study is too much concerned with pointing out the obvious—that the Scots were not Marxists.

tivity.[11] Since they also emphasized that man is born in and for civil society, the Scots by deduction traced society's probable development from various stages of "rudeness" to "refinement," frequently stressing the progress of commerce and industry. In writing what Dugald Stewart first called "conjectural" or "theoretic" histories of men, the Scots, because of the dearth of information, substituted conjecture for fact by considering in what manner men "are likely to have proceeded, from the principles of their nature, and the circumstances of their external situation."[12] In so doing, the Scottish moralists focused their attention upon the social changes in history, the variations, as Hume put it, in "habits, customs and manners" among different societies in their progress.[13] Embracing a belief in what one cultural historian calls "the law of the heterogeneity of ends," they saw progress as an incontrovertible law of history, a process not controlled by the actions of men.[14] The Scots' view of progress, then, because it emphasizes not the actions of individual reformers but the social and economic factors in historical process, is essentially deterministic. But, unlike many other advocates of progress, the Scots never accepted the idea of perfectibility, and in their writings there exists what J. B. Bury believes to have been characteristic of British writers generally—the tendency to "see salvation in the stability of existing institutions, and to regard change with suspicion."[15] The most important British contribution to the theory of progress and a work which strongly influenced Tucker—Adam Smith's *Wealth of Nations,* "a history of the gradual progress of human society"—stresses the importance of opulence for the development of civilization and happiness, not the need to change the nature of institutions.[16] Moreover, almost all of the Scottish moralists, in the face of their firm belief in the necessary progress of humanity, invoked the fear of the possible decline or dissolution of individual societies—usually as a result of the enervating effects of luxury and the consequent extinction of the martial spirit. After carefully weighing the advantages and disadvantages of civilization and recognizing that progress benefits only

11. *Man and Society*, Chap. V, *passim*.

12. Stewart, "An Account of the Life and Writings of Adam Smith" in *Works*, X, 32-35.

13. For an excellent study of the place of "conjectural history" in Hume's thought, see Eugene Rotwein's introduction to *David Hume: Writings on Economics* (Madison, Wis., and London, 1955), especially pp. xci-civ.

14. Forbes, " 'Scientific' Whiggism," p. 651.

15. *Idea of Progress*, p. 218.

16. *Ibid.*, pp. 220-221.

the few and tends to brutalize the many, they remained essentially optimistic about the future, satisfied that the progress from simple savagism to complex civilization was desirable as well as natural.[17]

It was in general to this theory of gradual progress that Tucker adhered. It is not contended that his interpretation of progress derived exclusively from a reading of the Scots, some of whose ideas were common property in the cosmopolitan Enlightenment, nor that he always embraced Scottish-held opinions. But it is clear, I think, that Tucker followed the general tenets of the Scottish school, making use of its theory of "conjectural history" to acclaim American commercial and industrial society, borrowing its over-all view of social and economic progress, interesting himself in the movements of whole societies rather than in the actions of individuals, and holding that all parts of society are interdependent and progress together—that economics, literature, philosophy, and the fine arts influence the development of one another.

Though striking parallels in thinking between Tucker and the Scots will be noted in the following analysis of his statements and attitudes toward civilization and progress, no attempt will be made to find specific sources for his ideas. It may be pointed out, however, that Tucker had innumerable opportunities for digesting Scottish social theory and that, considering his great familiarity with Scottish works, it would have been difficult for him to have missed absorbing it. Tucker read the doctrine in Adam Smith, who exerted a great influence on his economic theories.[18] He found the same "conjectural" view of civilization in, for example, the works of Dugald Stewart, his favorite philosopher and prose stylist; in the writings of Lord Kames, who was influential in molding his aesthetic and literary theory; in the essays and histories of David Hume, whose social and economic views, much like those of Smith, he found more acceptable than

17. See Bryson, *Man and Society,* pp. 41-52, and Chap. IV, *passim;* Forbes, "'Scientific' Whiggism," p. 650. For the Scots' ability to blend ideas of primitivism and progress, see Lois Whitney, *Primitivism and the Idea of Progress in English Popular Literature of the Eighteenth Century* (Baltimore, 1934), pp. 277-291.

18. See Leonard C. Helderman, "A Social Scientist of the Old South," *Journal of Southern History,* II (1936), 166-167; Jessie Bernard, "George Tucker: Liberal Southern Social Scientist," *Social Forces,* XXV (1946-1947), 132. Tucker sometimes said that Smith's theories should be modified but always claimed to embrace Smith's basic economic doctrines. Tucker read with approval *The Wealth of Nations* (1776) and *The Theory of Moral Sentiments* (1759) as well as *Dissertation on the Origin of Languages* (1761), which, as Tucker knew, Stewart praised as a model of "conjectural history." See "Q," "The Metaphysics of Language," *Literary Museum,* No. 48 (May 12, 1830), 753-757.

Hume's philosophic skepticism; in the histories of William Robertson, whom Tucker praised for being "philosophical" and for taking "large views" of society;[19] in innumerable issues of the *Edinburgh Review;*[20] and, finally, perhaps less directly, in the writings of his favorite novelist, Sir Walter Scott.[21]

While admitting that Tucker's interpretation of civilization, essentially formed by a reading of Scottish history, philosophy, and aesthetics, was undoubtedly also affected by other forces, especially by the optimistic climate of opinion in America as reflected in essays and speeches, only one other major influence need be mentioned—the population doctrines of the Reverend Thomas R. Malthus. *An Essay on . . . Population as It Affects the Future Improvement of Society, with Remarks on the Speculations of Mr. Godwin, Mr. Condorcet, and Other Writers* (1798) was, as the title suggests, Malthus' attempt to refute the perfectibilian doctrines of Godwin and Condorcet, both of whom recommended that mankind's rate of progress be accelerated by substituting for private ownership and capitalism collective ownership and management of property. Malthus argued that if these plans were carried out, vice, misery, and the fear of misery—the only checks which kept population from exceeding subsistence—would be eliminated and the working classes would eventually be more wretched than ever. In his second edition (1803) and in later editions, Malthus concentrated his attention on illustrating how population tended to increase faster than the food supply, but he never ceased to deprecate the socialistic ideas of Godwin and Condorcet as destroying private capital, the very foundation upon which man's progress must be built.[22]

Since Malthus, like Tucker, drew heavily from the Scottish writers for materials for his economic theory, it was not at all difficult for Tucker to incorporate into his interpretation of civilization the iron

19. "Lectures on Rhetoric and Belles Lettres . . . at the Seventh Session, 1830-31," Tucker-Harrison-Smith Papers, University of Virginia Library, Lecture XXV.

20. John Clive, *Scotch Reviewers: The Edinburgh Review, 1802-1815* (Cambridge, Mass., 1957). Chap. 7, "Rude and Refined," traces the use by Francis Jeffrey, Francis Horner, and Lord Brougham of the Scottish theory of progress to advocate various reforms in which they were interested.

21. Duncan Forbes, "The Rationalism of Sir Walter Scott," *Cambridge Journal,* VII (1953), 20-35, stresses the influence on Scott of Stewart's "conjectural" interpretation of history.

22. See Bury, *Idea of Progress,* pp. 228-229; James Bonar, *Malthus and His Work* (New York, 1924), pp. 7-44; Joseph J. Spengler, "Population Theory in the Ante-Bellum South," *Journal of Southern History,* II (1936), 361-362.

population laws expounded by the conservative English curate.[23] Tucker was aware of Malthus' theories as early as 1813, when he rejected them as "gloomy" and inapplicable to America's destiny; and not until the 1830's did he become an avowed Malthusian. Although Tucker seemed to "out-Malthus Malthus" in some of his later economic writings, he so frequently contradicted himself and so thoroughly qualified Malthus' population theories when discussing America's future that one is forced to agree with the economist who believes that Tucker never anticipated population pressure in the United States.[24] Tucker may have reversed himself and espoused Malthus' inexorable population laws partly because, as he claimed, he found Malthus' reasoning valid; yet it seems clear that he did so more for reasons of expediency. As was pointed out earlier, Tucker discovered in Malthus a rationale for continuing and even expanding slavery. Secondly, just as so many Englishmen, disillusioned by the French Revolution and afraid of Godwin's radicalism, saw in Malthus a way to rescue their nation from the "precipice of perfectibility,"[25] so Tucker, who in the 1830's and 1840's feared that America's lower classes might follow the French and try to alter America's laissez-faire economic system, found in Malthus a healthy antidote for radical social theories. Thus, like the *Edinburgh Review's* Francis Jeffrey and Henry Brougham, Tucker could and did blend the theories of Scottish "conjectural history" and progress with the Malthusian apologia that the poor were as happy as they could ever be and, significantly, a good deal happier than the savage.[26]

LUXURY AND DUELING

In 1804 Tucker published an essay dealing with "luxury," one of the most controversial topics of the eighteenth century and one of paramount concern to Scottish advocates of gradual progress. For

23. For the influence of Adam Smith on Malthus' ethical theories, see William P. Albrecht, *William Hazlitt and the Malthusian Controversy,* University of New Mexico Publications in Language and Literature, No. IV (Albuquerque, 1950), pp. 13, 20-24; and Bonar, *Malthus,* pp. 367-370. Kenneth Smith, *The Malthusian Controversy* (London, 1957), pp. 258-259, notes that Malthus drew almost exclusively from William Robertson's *History of America* for his delineation of the American Indian.

24. Spengler, "Population Theory," pp. 362, 372-373. For other discussions of Tucker's attitude toward Malthus, see Spengler's "Population Doctrines in the United States," *Journal of Political Economy,* XLI (1933), 433-467, 639-672; George Johnson Cady, "The Early American Reaction to the Theory of Malthus," *Journal of Political Economy,* XXXIX (1931), 601-632; and Helderman, "Social Scientist," pp. 148-174.

25. Bury, *Idea of Progress,* pp. 230-231.

26. Albrecht, *William Hazlitt,* pp. 13, 25.

many, the industrial revolution made concrete the discussion of progress. Primitivists who believed in the theory of degeneration found support for their position in the popular conception, inherited from classical thought, that luxury or "refinement" in a nation led to corruption and decadence, and they praised the virtues of the savage's primitive, ascetic life. These opponents of luxury—supported by some of the Scottish moralists who otherwise were firm believers in progress—argued that luxury tended to foster avarice, to increase vice in government, and to enervate men and make them effeminate. On the other hand, statesmen and economists, men pleased with the growth of commerce and industry, were anxious to prove that luxury could often be beneficial. Wealth and its concomitant luxury received a classical defense in Bernard de Mandeville's *Fable of the Bees;* but Mandeville's position, as Lois Whitney points out, was too drastic for many people to accept, and a more popular, less libertine defense appeared in the political and economic essays of David Hume and in Adam Smith's *Wealth of Nations.* Mediating between the positions of "the men of severe morals," who condemned even moderate luxury as evil, and the Mandevillians, who saw the most excessive luxury as a social blessing, both Hume and Smith defended luxury in terms of utility and both stressed the advantages of civilized society over the savage state.[27]

Tucker's position in "On Luxury" is essentially that of Smith and Hume, both of whom he was reading at the time he wrote this essay.[28] Though Tucker some twenty years later was to cite Adam Smith as the one who proved beyond doubt that luxury was beneficial to society,[29] his early essay strikingly reflects the influence of Hume. As Eugene Rotwein observes, Hume's "conjectural" view of historical process allowed him to assume, like Smith, that the "refinement" of his age was necessarily superior to the "savagism" of the past, that progress in economic activity is always accompanied by cultural and

27. Whitney, *Primitivism and Progress,* pp. 44, 55 ff. See also Rotwein's introduction to *David Hume,* pp. xci-xcii, who says that Smith's and Hume's position was founded partly upon their recognition of "the social origins of a sense of morality," and he points out, for example, that Hume believed that as men "flock into cities" to demonstrate their wit, breeding, good taste, and manners, they naturally learn more and provide one another with "pleasure and entertainment" (pp. xcix-c).

28. In his essays "On Banks" in the Richmond, Va., *Enquirer* (July 28, Aug. 1, 8, 22, and 25, 1804), Tucker referred frequently to *The Wealth of Nations* and Hume's economic essays, usually disagreeing with Hume that banks tend to lessen trade by raising the price of commodities.

29. See Tucker's "Political Economy," *American Quarterly Review,* I (1827), 309-310.

intellectual refinement. As Hume said, *"industry, knowledge* and *humanity* are linked by an indissoluble chain, and are found . . . to be peculiar to the more luxurious ages." The era, said Hume, which produces great politicians also produces great poets and great carpenters; as men become more social they develop the qualities of virtue and honor and become polished in their tastes.[30]

In his essay, Tucker defined luxury only briefly as "the love of enjoyment" and argued that the desire for luxury keeps men industrious and productive, keeps them working beyond the time needed merely to subsist. His defense of commercial life is based upon an assumption of the desirable progress of society from "rudeness" to "refinement."[31] Tucker argued, first, that all the arts and sciences are interconnected and reach unparalleled development in a "refined age," thus establishing the virtues of a cultivated stage of society over the "bleak and barren poverty of savage life." Gray's odes and elegies, Tucker said, never could have been written if it were not for the fact that the age and nation which produced them "also produced the pottery of Wedgwood, the Duke of Bridgewater's Canal." Luxury, when not excessive, not only stimulates the development of arts and sciences but, by encouraging the accumulation of wealth, which affords the means and invites the "exercise of generosity," counteracts avarice, America's greatest vice. "On the whole," said Tucker, setting forth what he continued to believe for all his life:

. . . it appears . . . that the seeds of luxury are grafted on the first principles of our nature: that it is . . . productive of more good than evil, that the ancients' objections to luxury do not apply to this country or these times; and that when properly regulated, it is favorable to the happiness of the individual; and to the welfare and safety of the nation.[32]

30. Rotwein's introduction to *David Hume,* pp. xci-xciv. Hume's statements are in his essay "Of Refinement in the Arts."

31. "X," "On Luxury," Richmond, Va., *Enquirer,* Dec. 22, 1804. "O" [James Ogilvie] discussed the problem in a similar fashion in "On Luxury," Richmond, Va., *Enquirer,* Oct. 27, 1804. He defined luxury as "something procured or prepared by labours, ingenuity and art; or something, the enjoyment of which presupposes a sensibility awakened and refined by the excitement of culture incident to civilization." In a concluding essay, however, Ogilvie warned readers to beware of luxury which stemmed from pride and vanity and pleased only the senses ("On Luxury—Part 2d," Richmond, Va., *Enquirer,* April 19, 1805). For Ogilvie's authorship, see Jay B. Hubbell, "William Wirt and the Familiar Essay in Virginia," *WMQ,* 2nd ser., XXIII (1943), 142-143.

32. "On Luxury." In lectures on political economy given in 1842, Tucker attacked "sumptuary laws" as prohibiting luxury, which, when supported by the industry of the community, improves manners and arts ("Notebook of Robert Lewis Dabney," "Notes on Political Economy," Dabney Papers, University of Virginia Library).

Tucker's defense of modern society in this essay against one claim set forth by many primitivists is of particular interest for showing how he purposefully applied the Scottish doctrine of evolutionary progress to defend the custom of dueling. In order to illustrate the significance of this issue in Tucker's theory of civilization, it is necessary to begin with a statement from "On Luxury" and, departing from the chronological scheme generally followed in this chapter, to see how Tucker amplified his discussion in 1822, when he wrote an essay "On Duelling." In his 1804 essay Tucker took the position that, more than any other quality, "honour" proved the superiority of a "refined" over a "savage" age:

The sentiment of honour is . . . peculiar to luxurious and refined society. Whatever religion or reason may say to some of its dictates, it surely well supplies the place of savage courage. The dictates of opinion, the sensibility to shame, produce the same effect on the man of honour, as instinct and passion produce on the savage: thus we find that our modern Duellists are as ready to bid defiance of fear, and even to court death, as the most ferocious tribes of barbarism.[33]

33. "On Luxury," Richmond, Va., *Enquirer*, Dec. 22, 1804. Dueling was much discussed by members of the "Rainbow Society." The unsigned "Reflections on Duelling, Part 1st" (Richmond, Va., *Enquirer*, Jan. 18, 1805), argued that dueling could be eliminated once public opinion was directed against it and cited "Dr. Moore" and William Paley as supporting the contention that anti-dueling laws were sometimes effective. See Hubbell, "William Wirt and the Familiar Essay," pp. 142-143, who says that George Hay, the probable author, never published the announced second part of the essay. "G," the unknown author of "On Duelling" (Richmond, Va., *Enquirer*, Jan. 5, 1805), also opposed the institution and predicted its demise as a result of the "progress of society and science": "The history of human society, from primitive ignorance and barbarism, to the most refined and expanded civilization, is little else than a detail of the evils which have arisen from inveterate errors and the means which philosophy and reason has [*sic*] successfully employed for their gradual extirpation."

Tucker also seems to have entered the controversy. "Vindication of Duelling," signed "X," which appeared in the *Enquirer* on March 30, 1805, probably is his. As Hubbell notes ("William Wirt and the Familiar Essay," p. 144), Tucker's two acknowledged articles for the "Rainbow Society" are similarly signed "X," and "Vindication" defends dueling in generally the same fashion as did Tucker in his 1822 essay "On Duelling," discussed above in the text. Furthermore, sentences in "Vindication" are exact reproductions of those in yet a third essay which, though signed by a pseudonym, is surely Tucker's. "An Argument for Duelling," signed "Eugenius," appeared in the *Enquirer* on Aug. 11, 1804, as a replacement for No. IV of "Eugenius'" series of articles "On Banks." The author of these banking essays refers to "our essay which appeared in Mr. Davis' Virginia Gazette of July 4th, 1804. We may entitle it a first number of the 2nd series of Candidus" ("On Banks," No. V, Richmond, Va., *Enquirer*, Aug. 25, 1804). Malcolm Lester, who claims to have examined all the Virginia newspapers of this period, attributes to Tucker the first series of articles signed "Candidus," which appeared in the Virginia *Gazette and General Advertiser* on Feb. 11, 18, 25, and March 7, 10, 17 (see the bibliography to Lester's "George Tucker: His Early Life and Public Service, 1775-1825" [University

In 1822 Tucker defended the institution more completely than he did in 1804. Closely following the discussions of William Robertson and David Hume, both of whom he later praised—Hume as best explaining "the source of the sentiment of honour" and Robertson as being especially "full & satisfactory on the development of chivalry"[34] —Tucker traced the historical development of dueling. Stressing that it was not "founded in nature since it exists nowhere in the rude stages of society" and that it was not practiced even in the "most polished nations of antiquity," Tucker pointed out that, though its origin could be traced back to the judicial combats of the Middle Ages, dueling appeared only at that point in history when men began to value self-respect and honor—in that same age in which, because of society's progress and refinement, the horrors of war were diminished and men ceased to think of woman as "the plaything of the sensualist" and treated her with a "delicate and respectful attention." Once dueling had been introduced into private disputes by the challenge issued to Francis the First by Charles the Fifth, it became highly regarded as the symbol of refinement. At the present time, said Tucker, dueling is so "interwoven with the manners, sentiments, and education of the polished classes of society" that it would be useless to try to legislate it out of existence.[35]

Tucker's explanation of dueling as the natural accompaniment and manifestation of progress and civilization is less interesting or important, however, than the reasons he gave for preserving it. One of the most devastating claims of the primitivists was that modern commercial society tended to make men effeminate and cowardly. The charge, of course, had wide implications, since it not only praised the courage of the simple savage and condemned the enervated modern, but also buttressed the assertion that advanced civilizations necessarily nourish the seeds of their own corruption and destruction.

of Virginia M.A. thesis, 1946]). To these should be added the lone number of the second series which appeared on July 4, 1804, and was written by the same author. These various essays defending banks are probably those for which Tucker was rewarded with a directorship of the Richmond Bank in 1805 (see Pt. I, p. 14).

34. "Lectures on Rhetoric and Belles Lettres," Lecture XXV.

35. "On Duelling," *Essays on Various Subjects of Taste, Morals, and National Policy* (Georgetown, D.C., 1822), pp. 249, 251-254, 260, 267-268. Cf. William Robertson's account of how dueling was introduced into polite society as a natural effect of mankind's advancement from "barbarism to refinement" in *History of the Reign of the Emperor Charles V: With a View of the Progress of Society in Europe, from the Subdivision of the Roman Empire to the Beginning of the Sixteenth Century,* 2nd ed. (London, 1777), II, 13-14; III, 14-18. See also Hume's *The History of England from the Invasion of Julius Caesar to the Revolution in 1688* (London, 1773), IV, 84-85.

Tucker admitted the danger but argued that modern society had developed a remedy for it:

Nations, in their progress towards wealth and refinement, are in danger of becoming enervated, and of losing with their ferocity, that courage and energy of character which are essential to their defense. The sense of honour, however, is found to supply their place; and when aided by discipline, to make every modern civilized nation, however luxurious, an over match for any savage nation, however fierce and brave.[36]

Despite Tucker's later recognition of great social and economic problems as threatening the nation as the nineteenth century grew older, he always felt that if America's dissolution should occur, it would be the result of effeminacy and enervation. Tucker had greater admiration for the patrician planter class than for middle-class merchants, and he felt considerable disdain for many of the non-aristocratic social values prized by a democratic business society. Yet, envisaging and desiring a commercial and industrial future for America as the only path to wealth and national power, and accepting it as almost settled that America would always be democratic, he sought to perpetuate some of the values of the aristocratic class which, as he made clear in *The Valley,* was, with the progress of society, passing away. Thus, in 1822, he argued that dueling would preserve the qualities needed in the future to combat the "jealous and unsocial policy of the Chinese"— it nourishes "the flame of honour among us; and preserves, in undiminished force and purity, that courage, and courtesy, and generosity, and fidelity to engagements which our commercial habits, . . . political institutions," and, Tucker added for the benefit of Southern readers, slavery have a "tendency to weaken."[37]   Though he later found substitutes for dueling which were more suitable to the changing times, Tucker never ceased to believe that some means had to be employed to keep Americans from becoming listless. Some code of

36. "On Duelling," p. 269. Cf. Hume's defense of luxury in his essay "Of Refinement in the Arts," which in some editions he entitled "Luxury": "Nor need we fear, that men, by losing their ferocity, will lose their martial spirit, or become less undaunted and vigorous in defence of their country or their liberty. The arts have no such effect in enervating either the mind or body. . . . And if anger, which is said to be the whetstone of courage, loses some what of its asperity, by politeness and refinement; a sense of honour, which is a stronger, more constant, and more governable principle" more than takes its place, especially when accompanied by "discipline and martial skill, which are seldom found among a barbarous people" (*David Hume,* ed. Rotwein, p. 25). Hume saw "refinement in the arts" as a species of luxury or as "innocent luxury," and he frequently used "refinement" or "wealth" as equivalents for "luxury" (p. 19 n.).

37. "On Duelling," *Essays* (1822), pp. 269-270.

conduct had to be erected to replace that masculine courage which was, after all, one of the few virtues of the earlier stages of society.

POPULATION AND PROGRESS

Like many of his countrymen in the early decades of the nineteenth century, Tucker was an emotional nationalist, embarrassed by America's cultural backwardness and lack of refinement but confident at the same time of "the brilliant prospects of our future destiny."[38]   Assured by the Scottish moralists and historians that societies naturally evolve from a state of rudeness to one of opulence and refinement, and learning from the condescending essays of Jeffrey and Brougham in the *Edinburgh Review* that America would reach a position of eminence perhaps comparable to England's if and when her population density approached that of Europe,[39] Tucker looked forward to a teeming America. Then Adam Smith's principle of the diversification of labor would operate, canals and roads would be built to link together all the states, commerce and industry would thrive, wealth would be accumulated, and America would achieve world power and prestige. In this "advanced" society, Tucker believed, literature and the arts—"the offspring of luxurious opulence"—would flourish, and all but the lower classes, who must inevitably become poor and brutish in the process, would be happy.

Since Tucker so warmly looked forward to that day when America would rival and even surpass Europe as the cultural and power center of the world, he found it necessary to come to grips with the economic writings of Malthus, whose "cheerless . . . view of human society," Tucker said, seemed to offer nothing more than "an apology for bad government."[40]   In three papers in his volume *Essays on Various Subjects of Taste, Morals, and National Policy* (1822) which have been described as badly confused but pioneer Southern criticisms of Malthus,[41] Tucker made use of Scottish social and economic theory to celebrate America's inevitable progress, and, by extolling the benefits enjoyed by populous nations, attacked Malthus' theories.

38. *A Letter to a Member of the General Assembly of North Carolina on the Navigation of the Roanoke and Its Branches* (Richmond, Va., 1811), pp. 64-65. Cf. "On the Future Destiny of the United States," *Essays* (1822), p. 5.

39. Clive, *Scotch Reviewers*, pp. 167-169.

40. Tucker made the statement in "The Malthusian Theory. Discussed in a Correspondence Between Alex. H. Everett, and Prof. Geo. Tucker, of the University of Virginia," *United States Magazine and Democratic Review*, n.s. XVII (1846), 298, when he tried to explain why he had opposed Malthus early in his career.

41. Spengler, "Population Doctrines," pp. 435-436, says that Tucker seemed never to understand Malthus. Cf. Cady, "Early Reaction to Malthus," pp. 616-617.

In his first essay "On the Future Destiny of the United States," first published in the *Port Folio* in 1814, Tucker painted a glowing picture of the America of the future. With the "progress of civilization"—in a "century hence"—America, with a population of 120,000,000 persons, will be "the most opulent and powerful empire on earth," with her borders extending to Mexico and Canada. The essay also contains predictions that the mutual interests of the western and eastern states will keep both sections in the Union and that the nation will contain many large cities "embellished with the choicest productions of art," magnificent canals and roads, excellent colleges, a great navy, and a sizable, though not oppressive, revenue.[42] Once the nation becomes densely populated, her economy will be primarily industrial, for, Tucker explained, ninety-five percent of the population in order to survive will be forced to exchange their labor for the surplus produce of the landed gentry. In time, then, with the cheap price of labor, the West will become "the Flanders of the United States . . . covered with populous cities, and be the seat of wealth, of luxury, and of arts more or less liberal. . . ."[43]

With his nationalistic optimism thus concretely expressed in his vision of America's future industrialization, Tucker hoped to add theoretical support for his view. To this end and with obvious enjoyment, he utilized a cyclic concept of history, which many of the Scottish moralists used and which the haughty *Edinburgh Review,* America's patronizing critic, frequently found helpful in explaining Britain's world dominance. In comparing the Old and the New Worlds, Tucker made the popular eighteenth-century analogy between societies and individuals, but combined it with the theme of the westward course of culture in such a fashion as to predict the probable decline of Europe—specifically including Britain—and the historically certain eminence of America:

. . . once a powerful nation begins to decline in opulence and strength, who can set bounds to its downward course? or say, whether it will merely resume its former station, before its power had received a factitious increase —or by a decay in the emulation and spirit of its people, it may sink a degree lower—or finally, by the continued operation of the same moral languor, it may reach the lowest point of natural degradation? Perhaps it is unalterably decreed that communities like individuals, should have not only their periods of infancy and manhood, but also of old age and dissolution; and in the same way as those countries of the western part of

42. "On the Future Destiny," *Essays* (1822), pp. 4-5.
43. *Ibid.,* pp. 19-20.

Asia, which were once flourishing and populous, have now become the abode of poverty and sloth, so may the opulent and powerful nations of Europe experience a similar reverse, and looking towards this continent see, in the moral as the physical world, the setting sun of their prosperity, illuminating in meridian splendour, their rising progeny in the west.[44]

In a second, complementary essay, "On the Density of Population" (1815), Tucker continued his oblique refutation of Malthus. Assuming as axiomatic that dense populations are economically desirable, lead to the cultivation of the arts, and increase national safety, Tucker intended to prove that a people's "morals and happiness" as well are enhanced as the density of population increases. It was, seemingly, to refute the Jeffersonian agrarians, who thought that cities were "pestilential" to the happiness of the people, that Tucker, citing the "ingenious and profound Hume," directed much of his energy.[45] First of all, Tucker said that the poor of large cities prefer "the evils of a precarious existence, chequered as they are with some of the pleasures of a town life" over certain employment in sparsely settled, rural areas. But even if it were granted that in a crowded industrial and commercial community the great multitudes are wretched, "it does not . . . follow that there may not also be a greater sum of happiness. While a larger number may suffer for want . . . those who are exempt from this evil may be also more susceptible of enjoyment." And if in Europe "the fruits of progressive art, science, and civilization" are monopolized by a small portion of the community, this is a consequence only of unjust institutions. In America, where the government does not interfere with the people, there would, of course, "still be inequality," but "it would be no more than would be salutary or just," "according to the industry, prudence and good fortune of each individual." Furthermore, what would ordinarily be wasted by the luxurious rich in sparsely settled areas, in cities would be used to increase the comfort of the poor. To ascribe evils to cities and dense populations was, Tucker felt, absurd, fruitless, and pessimistic, for cities are manifestations of man's social instinct and the inevitable accompaniment of the progress of civilization and, therefore, must *enhance,* not retard, human happiness and comfort, especially for the man of "unvitiated feelings."[46]

44. *Ibid.,* p. 23.

45. Tucker did not refer to the agrarians in this essay, but in his *Life of Thomas Jefferson,* II, 71-75, he repeated many of the arguments of the *Port Folio* essay to criticize Jefferson's contention that cities were "pestilential to the morals, the health, and the liberty of mankind."

46. "On Density of Population," *Essays* (1822), pp. 70-72, 76-77, 81-84.

As society advances in refinement, the *moral sense,* as well as every other faculty, will become more susceptible of impressions; and though an increased sensibility may often lead to evil as well as to good, yet the good will be most promoted, if there be more of it than of evil in the world—a proposition which, however it may be disputed by the gloomy misanthrope or frivolous declaimer, every man's conduct and feelings acknowledge to be just. In short, if men are superior in happiness and virtue to brutes, then also is civilized society superior to that which is rude and uncultivated. It would . . . be against the universal economy of nature . . . if man who is perpetually urged to form societies and to advance in civilization, should, by so doing, be laboring for his misery instead of his happiness.[47]

"On the Theory of Malthus" (1822), Tucker's last assault on the theories of the English don, is chiefly interesting in revealing that, though Tucker was still temperamentally and intellectually at odds with Malthus' "gloomy" views of society and did not believe his principles pertinent to America's unique situation, he saw, like so many of his contemporaries, the great value of Malthus' denigrations of heretical social doctrines. Tucker repeated many of the points of his previous attacks on Malthus, insisting that civilization itself provides all necessary checks to over-population, that, in short, "human habits and institutions," not ungovernable "laws of nature," control man's destiny.[48] Again he made use of "theoretical" history to stress the benefits of the march of civilization, this time by contrasting the life of modern man to that of the American Indian, a favorite and much maligned victim of Scottish social historians. It could "scarcely be doubted," Tucker said, "that the savage hunter had a less comfortable, a more precarious, existence than a citizen of the poorest class among us."[49] And even if the comparison be unfair because America might be, as some argued, in "that middle state which is equally remote from the miseries of rude and of civilized society," then it should be made clear that even the lowest orders of citizens of Europe are also better off than the primitive Indian.[50]

On the other hand, for the first time Tucker commended Malthus

47. *Ibid.,* pp. 78-79.
48. "On the Theory of Malthus," *Essays* (1822), pp. 305-306.
49. *Ibid.,* p. 322.
50. *Ibid.,* pp. 322-323. This argument, based on "conjectural history," was used by Francis Jeffrey to defend the Industrial Revolution: when the "arts of civilized life have reached a certain point" the working classes must be content to work for a "pittance barely adequate." Yet the poorest paid laborer in Europe was better off than the savage (see Clive, *Scotch Reviewers,* p. 137).

for establishing the fact that poor laws in the long run only served to make the miserable more wretched, and, most importantly, for discrediting those "useless or pernicious remedies" put forth by Godwin and Condorcet to correct the evils of modern life. Tucker agreed with Malthus that it was indeed unwise to try to revolutionize society, but, Tucker suggested, Godwin's "visionary system" could best be answered with a theory "derived from the moral laws of our nature":

Godwin's theory pre-supposes principles which do not exist, and which would not be well fitted to advance individual happiness, though they did— he is mistaken in his principles, and were they even right, his reasoning would be false. Man is impelled to action by his feelings and passions, and by them alone. His reason is merely an instrument for their use. These passions and feelings are principally selfish, but in some degree sympathetic. These somewhat regulate or modify the former, which, however, chiefly direct his actions: and it is by obeying this regulated self love that man can, in the best possible mode, advance his own happiness: for this primary passion points to it as truly and invariably as the needle to the pole. Our sympathies may be deadened; our self love never can. Our sympathies may be mistaken in what will gratify another; our self love can never be deceived in what will please ourselves. And so long as sympathy for others is subordinate for one's self, the happiness of individuals will be greater, when every man bends his efforts to gratify his own feelings, selfish and sympathetic, than if they were directed to the general good, which he can neither so well understand, nor so much regard. In a word, our pursuit of happiness, the great business of life, like every other business, is managed with greater diligence, better judgment, and more success, when every man acts for himself, than if he merely acted as the member of an extensive partnership.[51]

Tucker's explanation of universal human nature, upon which he built for all his discussions of progress and society, is clearly a simplified account of that proposed by the Scottish moralists, who, as Gladys Bryson points out, arrived at a secularized ethics in which human happiness was the standard of value. Rejecting the claim that reason was the great motivator of man, but unwilling to embrace the idea of greedy self-interest advanced by Hobbes and Mandeville, the Scots, great compromisers, decided that it was enlightened "self-interest" which, in advancing the happiness of the individual, increased the happiness of society and made the world go.[52]

51. "On the Theory of Malthus," *Essays* (1822), pp. 331-332.
52. *Man and Society*, pp. 21, 27-28, 215-216.

SUMMATION OF PROGRESS

Thirteen years elapsed after the publication of his 1822 *Essays* before Tucker turned again to the discussion of progress. "A Discourse on the Progress of Philosophy and Its Influence on the Intellectual and Moral Character of Man" is Tucker's most general and optimistic publication dealing with the idea of society's advancement. Defining "philosophy" as "that power of perceiving truths which are not obvious" or as "a system of thought and action" which appeals to reason and common sense for its precepts, Tucker hoped to prove that philosophy had diffused itself over the world and

. . . that it now mingles in all human concerns, and gives to the present age its distinguishing characteristics,—that its progress must still continue, and more and more influence the character of man in civilized society, and that in no country is this influence likely to be more extensively or beneficently felt than in this.[53]

Civilized man's intellectual power, so superior to that of the savage who is capable of strong feelings but helpless when confronted with "profound and comprehensive thoughts," continues to grow at an accelerating rate, because the "elaborate deductions of one age become the obvious truths of that which succeeded it, and each succeeding generation is more capable of intricate processes of reasoning than its predecessor." Because of this, civilized man can feel nothing but "contemptuous ridicule" for those achievements which commanded the veneration of his ancestors.[54]

To emphasize his point, Tucker catalogued the accomplishments of modern society, juxtaposing the past and the present and sometimes indicating the course of the future. In the fields neglected in the past, in the physical sciences—chemistry, physics, geology, mineralogy, and medicine—Tucker found a comprehensive triumph of man over matter. The discovery that "ligneous substances" can be changed by chemistry to provide "wholesome aliment" and even the "wonders now wrought by steam" are but precursors of even more marvelous discoveries to be made in the future. Because man's admiration is reserved for those scientific achievements which help humanity, the seven wonders of the world have been replaced as objects of pleasure and astonishment by such projects as the New York Canal, the Manchester Railroad, and the Thames Tunnel.[55]

53. "A Discourse on the Progress of Philosophy and Its Influence on the Intellectual and Moral Character of Man," *Southern Literary Messenger*, I (1835), p. 405.

54. *Ibid.*, pp. 405-406, 411.

55. *Ibid.*, p. 409.

The writing of history and the study of philosophy also have partaken of the "spirit of the age." The historian, who once contented himself with reciting the actions of princes and giving accounts of battles, now deals with those subjects which are concerned with the dignity and happiness of man, with "the progress of society and the arts of civilization." In tracing the development of mental philosophy, Tucker admitted that progress was slow because of the difficulty of the subject, but he asserted that the moderns have progressed in analyzing compound states, in reducing many seemingly diverse operations to one simple principle, as witnessed by "the theory of associations, as it now is compared with the slight and vague notice of it by Locke." In the related field of morals, Tucker added, Locke, a pioneer, made other mistakes, since corrected: he erroneously claimed that there was no propensity for man to deem one action virtuous and another vicious, and he showed great credulity and ignorance in denying, on scattered and inadequate reports, the existence of innate propensities, especially that of parental love.[56]

In discussing Christianity, Tucker assumed that religion in "every stage of society" is "dependent on the laws of our emotions, which are as unchangeable as our forms"; but it, like all institutions, he said, was removed from the "mists of barbarity" by the "progress of society." The "reformation must have taken place had Martin Luther never existed, or had the Dominican friars never carried on the traffic in indulgences; though it might not have happened at the precise time, or in the precise manner in which it did occur." It was as natural, said Tucker, that the religion of the Middle Ages should have been barbaric "as that after the discovery of printing, the revival of letters, and the general progress of science and philosophy," the "foul exhalations" of superstition should disappear, and that the modern age, with its great numbers of "Churches, Bible Societies, Missionary Societies, Seminary Schools &c" should be not only the most philosophical but also the "most ardently devoted to Christianity."[57]

Political economy received much of Tucker's attention. Expounding the doctrines of classical economics, he asserted that "all enlightened men" thoroughly agree that national prosperity is best enhanced when "schemes of government" are not allowed to interfere with the "sagacity of individuals." Philosophy, he said, also discovered that "a community will have the most industry, skill and thrift where

56. *Ibid.*, pp. 408-409.
57. *Ibid.*, p. 407.

property is best protected—when every one can freely exercise his talents or his capital and securely enjoy the fruits they have yielded."[58]

By thus summarizing the triumph of man over nature and the inevitable increase in happiness, prosperity, and virtue, Tucker praised the march of progress. But he called attention to the existence of sectional strife between North and South and to the political and economic troubles caused by the growing power of the laboring classes, both of which issues he was to treat more fully in a later publication on progress. Insisting that he tried to avoid both "gloomy" views and perfectibilian "dreams," Tucker argued for an interpretation of the future which was justified by a realistic estimate of society and history.[59] Pointing out, for example, that it was "part of man's inevitable destiny" to wage war, Tucker said that it was idle folly to lament over war, since it was a result of incontrovertible human nature. It was important to remember that all was purposeful, that though war did cause some misery, it also called forth "some of the noblest traits of our character—courage, patriotism, generosity, disinterestedness and every form of virtuous self-denial." Obviously thinking of society's tendency to become enervated and, perhaps, also of America's desire to extend her boundaries, Tucker said that the Creator seems to have ordained that "war as well as peace" is necessary for the development and preservation of some of our highest qualities as well as for the fulfillment of "our destiny."[60]

DANGERS OF A DEMOCRACY

In the last twenty-five years of his life, Tucker watched with general satisfaction the growth of America's population, industry, and wealth. Despite his optimistic temperament and his assumption of society's constant progress, he was disturbed by certain contemporary political and economic trends. Of all the troubles which beset America in the decades between 1830 and 1860, none caused him more concern than the threats that the Union might be dissolved by the

58. *Ibid.*, p. 409.

59. *Ibid.*, p. 418. Tucker explicitly attacked "those visions of future excellence or perfection . . . such as the dreams, first of Condorcet, and afterwards of Godwin."

60. *Ibid.*, pp. 418-419. Cf. Kames's attack on those who repine at the dispensations of Providence and curse war. In a refined state of society, Kames said, wars "give exercise to the elevated virtues of courage, generosity, and disinterestedness." "Industry, manufactures, and wealth are the fruits of peace," he admitted, but when the "military spirit" is lost, both the men and the rich commercial states in which they live tend to become "effeminate and cowardly." See *Sketches of the History of Man* (Glasgow, 1802), II, 182-183, 184-186.

secession of Southern states and that America's laissez-faire economic system might be altered by the concerted action of the working classes.

Both issues concerned Tucker long before the 1830's, though not as intensely as they did later. In 1814, when he discussed the progress of America, he believed that it was the western states which were most likely to withdraw from the Union, but after 1820, when the issue of slavery was brought to the fore in the Missouri debate, he recognized that the great sectional division in the country was between North and South. The two areas, as he realized, became further separated as the North grew more industrialized and sought trade restrictions which the agrarian South opposed.

In considering the discontent and agitation of the working classes, Tucker made use of his economic interpretation of civilization's advancement, which, optimistic as it was, never allowed him to assume that all people could be equally happy or that all could be well fed. Like the Scottish moralists and economists, he believed that in a nation's progress from rudeness to refinement there would be created a class society made up of the privileged property owners, at one extreme, who would run the nation and enjoy the fruits of industrialization, and, at the other, of the brutalized laboring people, some of whom must necessarily suffer privation. Until the Jacksonian era, however, Tucker never thought seriously about class conflict. When then he pondered the upheavals of the 1830's and 1840's—and he apparently was alarmed by such manifestations of unrest and power as organized labor, strikes, the rise of the "Workingmen's Party" and Locofocos, and the New York food riots—he concluded, good Whig that he was, that Andrew Jackson, seizing upon popular discontent to further his own ambitions, had ushered in a new era in American politics. In his rule, thought Tucker, the "uncultivated," irresponsible masses found sanction and leadership for their attacks on the propertied. In Tucker's mind, the terrors of the French Revolution—an upheaval that he labeled as "a signal instance of the retrograde steps" which occasionally occur in the progress of society—might be enacted on American soil if unscrupulous demagogues like Jackson could work upon the emotions and hatreds of the poor. Less dramatically, he believed it possible that in a democracy, the many might appropriate the "property of the rich" by altering the tax structure or by limiting the "price of provisions," or they might, as he once said, "in some moment of madness or reckless injustice" pass a law redistributing private property.[61]

61. "Discourse on the Progress of Philosophy," pp. 412-413, 417.

In his last essay on the idea of progress, originally given as a speech before the National Institute for the Promotion of Science in 1845 and entitled "Dangers to be Guarded Against in the Future Progress of the United States," Tucker discussed these two problems in the light of his often-used thesis that nations must decline once they have reached maturity. Tucker's opening statement is indicative both of the tone and the content of his paper, in which he preached moderation and hope:

When we see so close an analogy between the natural body and the body politic, in their gradual advance from infancy to maturity, in their healthy and diseased action, and in their self-preserving power to remedy the evils they may chance to encounter, we are naturally led to extend it still further, and to suppose that, as the animal body has, by the laws of its structure, a certain term of existence which it cannot transcend, so must political communities have their old age and death, as well as their infancy and manhood. But this is carrying the parallel too far. Governments may be more correctly compared with the species than with individuals—while the latter flourish for a time and then pass away, the former have the power of perpetual renovation.[62]

The dissolution of the American government, then, was not a "necessary condition of its existence," and, contrary to the opinion of Tocqueville, whose interesting comments are weakened by a tendency to form a theory on "too small a number of facts," there is "nothing in our frame of government which is inconsistent with its perma-

[62] "Dangers to be Guarded Against in the Future Progress of the United States," *American Whig Review*, V (1847), 614. Cf. the opinion of Stewart, who disagreed with those writers of the past fifty years who, "resting their conclusions chiefly on the *past* history of the world, have taken for granted, that nations, as well as individuals, contain within themselves the seeds of their decay and dissolution;—that there are limits prescribed by nature to the attainments of mankind, which it is impossible for them to pass; and that the splendid exertions of the two preceding centuries in arts, in commerce, and in arms, portend an approaching night of barbarism and misery. The events which we ourselves have witnessed since the period of the American Revolution, have been frequently urged as proofs, that the reign of Science and of Civilisation is already drawing to a close.

"In opposition to this very prevalent belief, a few, and but a few, philosophers have ventured to suggest, that the experience of the past does not authorize any such gloomy forebodings;—that the condition of mankind at present differs, in many essential respects, from what it ever was in any former age; and that, abstracting entirely from the extravagant doctrine of some of our contemporaries about the indefinite *perfectibility* of the race, the thick cloud which at present hangs over the civilised world, affords no solid argument for despairing of its future destiny." *Dissertation: Exhibiting the Progress of Metaphysical, Ethical, and Political Philosophy, Since the Revival of Letters in Europe* in *Works*, I, 492.

nency."[63] But it was the duty of America's citizens to consider remote and present dangers which nevertheless might destroy the republic.

The first great danger—that of the break-up of the Union—Tucker dismissed as unrealistic. He sought to reassure his audience that the threats of both Northern abolitionists and Southern nullificationists were manifestations of mere temporary disagreements which would pass away and, at the same time, to advance the cause of industrial capitalism as the natural child of progress and civilization. He argued that the problem of the protective tariff, the only possible way of acquiring sufficient revenue at the present time, would eventually disappear as a source of sectional rancor. As the density of population increased, more and more states would become manufacturing centers, and the motives for seeking protection would diminish as the number of "consuming states" decreased; moreover, the depressed price of labor resulting from competition for jobs among the workers, along with the use of machinery and greater capital expenditure, would result in a "security for the home market which will defy all foreign competition."[64]

Likewise, Tucker, using Malthus' population theories, tried to show that slavery, when viewed in the proper perspective, was not a serious issue. Because all laborers must eventually work for a "bare subsistence," once the population has increased in density slavery will pass out of existence and the North and South will join hands as industrial partners. Indeed, the "most intelligent and respectable" citizens recognize that "time . . . is silently at work and will bring a remedy for this source of internal dissension" and agree that abolitionist propaganda is of interest only to those who follow the "craft and mystery of politics." While the "misapplied sympathy" of Northern agitators does "adulterate the purity of popular elections," it cannot disturb the tranquility of the Union.[65]

Though Tucker thus alleged that industrial capitalism offered built-in solutions for the tariff and slavery issues, he admitted, as accompanying the growth of cities and industry, the danger of class conflict. He pointed out that in all highly civilized communities there exists side by side with the intelligent and rich a much larger ignorant and needy group who, always hostile to "the peace and well-being of society," will follow the banner of any demagogue "who will give them bread, or promise it."

63. "Dangers to be Guarded Against," p. 618.
64. *Ibid.*, pp. 619-620.
65. *Ibid.*, p. 620.

Can these two classes live together in peace and harmony, when they possess an equal share of political power? or must our government change its character and have infused into it a new vigor and means of restraint, suited to the new order of things? And, lastly, suppose such a change requisite, will it be practicable?[66]

Some, said Tucker, advocate that America's form of government be altered so as to provide "adequate physical force" to deal summarily with unwanted commotions, and, by excluding the majority from the franchise, keep government in the hands of intelligent and independent men who will see to it that no laws are passed to tax unequally the rich or to help debtors defraud their creditors.[67]

Although Tucker in 1829-30 was in favor of limiting the franchise in Virginia,[68] in 1847 he felt that changing the federal Constitution would be unwise and unnecessary for the nation. First of all, it might give the president power which could be "brought to bear on the honest and loyal, as well as the vicious and lawless"; and it conceivably could "lead to the rearing of a monarchy on the ruins of republican government."[69] Although he thought signs of unrest in some of America's larger cities did give weight to arguments of those who would alter the form of government in order to ward off the changes "which strike at the root of society," he expressed confidence that in unique America the terrors of Europe would not be repeated. The working classes in the United States would never be as poor or proportionally as numerous as those in Europe, because, said Tucker, contradicting his statements on slavery, Americans, habituated to a high standard of living, would voluntarily adopt checks against over-population. Moreover, the tendency of the lower classes to obey the law in the hope that they themselves might some day have wealth could be strengthened by educating them. Lastly, said Tucker,

. . . it must also be recollected that if, in the progress of society, the influence of intelligence and property is, on some accounts, diminished by the increased numbers and votes of the ignorant and necessitous, that influence is, on other accounts, augmented by the increased dependence of the destitute class on the other's employment and subsistence. Every large land-owner or ship-owner, every great manufacturer or miner, has an

66. *Ibid.*, pp. 623-624.
67. *Ibid.*, pp. 624-625.
68. Tucker's wish to limit the franchise in Virginia was a result of his desires to protect slavery (see Pt. III, pp. 193-195) and to insure Jackson's defeat in the state (see Pt. I, pp. 36-37).
69. "Dangers to be Guarded Against," pp. 624-625.

influence over those he employs, far greater in dense, than in thin populations. . . .[70]

The strength and nature of Tucker's optimism is best seen in the
concluding portion of his address, in which he asserted that America's
political system was, paradoxically, more in danger of destruction from
its strength than from its apparent weaknesses. In the course of a few
generations, America would be so great and powerful that there might
exist nothing to keep alive her martial spirit. It seemed to be true,
said Tucker, that nations must either "engage in a career of conquest"
or fall into a "state of torpor," and the great question facing America
was whether, as a result of "democratic jealousy" or lack of opportunity
for expansion (Canada and Mexico, he assumed, would probably already have been absorbed), her citizens would "sink into a listlessness
similar to that of the Chinese." Even without great national rivals,
America would continue to "increase in numbers and advance in the
race of improvement" because there existed within the Union itself
the same source of emulation which made, in turn, the Greeks, the
Romans, the French, and the English take the lead in "letters, science,
arms, and the useful arts." Those very sectional discords and political
quarrels which superficial observers felt were destroying the Union
not only were indicative of a secret national harmony but also, in
Tucker's mind, by creating competition and providing the stimulation
which the mind craves, served as a kind of national dextrose which
would fully develop all the faculties and ultimately fulfill "the most
splendid visions of national glory."[71]

An incorrigible optimist, Tucker continued to preach this com-
placent doctrine until the eve of the Civil War. His interpretation of
civilization's advancement, which was based upon the assumption that
modern "civilized" society evolved from a barbarous age as a result
of a law of history and not because of the actions of zealots, who only
impeded progress, allowed him to promise improvement, not utopia,
and to argue that if the *status quo* were not disturbed, if property—
including slaves—were carefully protected from the encroachments
of the mob, the "total" sum of man's happiness would be increased.
By applying this interpretation of progress to the United States, by

70. *Ibid.*, pp. 625-626. Cf. Tucker's statement in "Discourse on the Progress of
Philosophy" (p. 418), in which he expressed confidence that, because of "received or
expected" favors, habit, laws, and the "restraints of morality, of indolence, and fear,"
"all that the indigent class can effect for their own advantage by combination, may not
prove a sufficient antagonist to the influence the rich will be able to exert over them."

71. "Dangers to be Guarded Against," p. 628.

seeing it as ordained that the nation should be the world's greatest industrial-commercial power and should perhaps encompass all of the North American continent, Tucker found philosophical support for the doctrine of manifest destiny and—as a safeguard against enervation —an ethic for the wars required for expansion. But this concept of history did not help him to cope with immediate realities, with the problems which were working against his idea of nationalism. When he finally recognized that secession was almost inevitable, he continued to elaborate the theme that "time is silently at work and will bring a remedy" for keeping the nation united. But as his words fell on deaf ears, he became almost incoherent, believing all the while that it was the rest of the nation which was unrealistic and crazed.

SUMMARY OF TUCKER'S THOUGHT

For over half a century in his various roles as lawyer, legislator, man of letters, and professor of moral philosophy, Tucker wrote and lectured upon subjects whose range was broad enough to relate him to many of the most important intellectual currents of his age. Unrestricted by formal boundaries of subject matter, he not only was a highly reputable theoretician in philosophy, aesthetics, economics, and literature, but also he was a frequent commentator upon such significant controversial issues of nineteenth-century America as the slavery problem, the dangers of Jacksonian democracy, and the need for the South to industrialize. Few men in the ante-bellum South deserve a higher place in America's intellectual history than does Tucker. He well merits the accolade "Southern thinker."

Tucker has, of course, long been accorded high status as a thinker, but the fact is that the nature of his thought has been largely misconstrued. He is usually depicted as one of the last of the "revolutionary liberals," a life-long supporter of Jefferson's political and social doctrines, and a firm opponent of slavery. A careful analysis of his writings, however, reveals a different Tucker. When he came to the United States from Bermuda in 1795, he was an ardent republican, impressed favorably with the possibilities of a democratic society, and, like many of the Virginians with whom he associated, he opposed slavery on social and economic grounds. But before many years passed, Tucker shifted his position, moving further and further from Jefferson's political and social theories, becoming more and more conservative, more and more inclined to view slavery as permanent and profitable—as the sole answer to the South's racial problems and as a useful institution in the South's economic growth. Marriages into rich and socially prominent families strengthened his alliance with the Tidewater aristocracy, whose economic status, by the 1820's, demanded the continuance of slavery and whose position of leadership in the Old Dominion depended in large part upon the maintenance of unequal economic and political rights. And combined with this motive of self-interest in forming Tucker's anti-democratic, pro-slavery policies was an instinctive distrust of the judgments of uneducated, propertyless men. But most important in the molding of Tucker's social and political thought was his interpretation of the idea of progress and civilization. His prediction of society's advancement caused him to attach an overwhelming importance to the perpetuation of the *status quo,* to feel that any theoretical values a democracy might have were outweighed by the threats which it posed to property and to the stability of the social order. Although he had an unbounded faith in progress, Tucker's vision of the "future destiny" of the United States was a dark one for the great masses of men. He envisioned the coming of a densely populated commercial-industrial society in which the gulf between rich and poor, ruling and ruled, would be widened by technology. The economic progress of the nation, he argued, depended upon the growth of manufactures and thus upon the existence of great cities, thronged with brutalized factory workers whose political powers had to be curtailed, lest they be exploited by irresponsible politicians of the stamp of Jackson.

Perhaps more significant than Tucker's attacks upon agrarianism or his disaffection from his early Jeffersonian persuasion is his intelligent treatment of purely speculative ideas. His high reputation in the history of Southern culture must rest in great part upon his orderly, disinterested examination of fundamental problems in aesthetics, philosophy, and social economics at a time when most Southern intellectuals were exclusively occupied with immediate, sectional problems. Yet the historian of Southern culture is as much interested in the origins of Tucker's ideas as in the ideas themselves. For an understanding of the aesthetic, social, and economic theories which molded Tucker's literary criticism and philosophy, and which influenced his social and economic policies as well, not only elucidates the scope and nature of his thought, but also helps us to understand his age and culture.

In almost all discussions of American thought, there appear frequent references to the influence of the Scottish "philosophy of common sense." Pioneering studies such as I. Woodbridge Riley's histories of American philosophy, William Charvat's *Origins of American Critical Thought,* and Leon Howard's *Connecticut Wits,* and such a more recent work as Robert D. Jacobs' unpublished "Poe's Heritage from Jefferson's Virginia" have suggested how pervasive this influence may have been. But there has been no detailed examination of the influence of the writers of the Scottish Enlightenment on significant American figures and institutions. Such a lack is especially apparent in scholarship dealing with the South, for cultural historians generally agree that the philosophy of common sense flourished there more than in the North, where, except at Princeton, its conservatism was challenged by new philosophic and social movements. Tucker closely followed the major tenets of Scottish common sense philosophy and literary criticism, and his interpretation of America's destiny was based upon Scottish social and economic thought. His absorption of Scottish culture, then, supports past generalizations about the great impact of Scottish philosophical and social theory in the South. It also suggests, however, that the philosophy became popular earlier than has usually been thought, and for reasons not heretofore emphasized, and, finally, that it appealed to the intellectual laity as well as to Presbyterian and Methodist clerics.

The full effect of Scottish thought upon the Southern mind has yet to be determined. The philosophical speculations of Dugald Stewart, Thomas Reid, and Thomas Brown served Tucker with the means to attack skepticism and materialism. But it is important to note that Tucker's interest in the "science of metaphysics" was first awakened by the aesthetic theories of such prominent Scottish thinkers as Hugh Blair, Lord Kames, Archibald Alison, Adam Smith, and Stewart. From the ideas of these men, Tucker formed an interesting interpretation of the cyclical development of the arts as well as a set of generally conservative literary tastes, which favored the rational world of the eighteenth century over the "romantic" one of the nineteenth century. Yet, at the same time, it is possible to trace the Scots' influence in Tucker's coherent theory of the nature and function of poetry, an aesthetic creed which may have helped form the background for the literary theory and practice of that arch romantic Edgar Allan Poe.

In estimating the impact of the Scottish gospel of social and economic progress, which was at once conservative and "progressive," causal relationships are yet more difficult to draw, but the thinking of Tucker raises the interesting possibility that, by means of the social doctrines of the Scottish writers, the seeds of the New South were implanted during the age of the Old, only to flourish in the late nineteenth century, after the slavery issue had been settled. What is rather vaguely called "the Southern way" of life and defined in part by the stress which the Southern aristocracy placed upon the "amenities of life" was not, perhaps, at all points inimical to industrial and commercial progress, as Neo-Agrarians have argued. Tucker was a member of the "landed class," from whom, it is said, derived the "traditional Southern characteristics," and he articulated in the best Southern manner the pleasures of quiet and refined living and the need to preserve and cherish the sense of honor. But, like many in the South today, he was at the same time convinced of the desirability and inevitability of the triumph of industrialization and "progress."

BIBLIOGRAPHY

BIBLIOGRAPHY

I. TUCKER'S WORKS

A. Manuscripts

1. TUCKER'S LETTERS

Cabell Deposit, University of Virginia Library.
Jefferson Papers, University of Virginia Library.
Johnston Collection, Historical Society of Pennsylvania.
Madison Papers, Library of Congress.
Miscellaneous Papers, Henry E. Huntington Library.
Miscellaneous Papers, New York Public Library.
Tucker-Coleman Collection, Colonial Williamsburg.
Tucker-Harrison-Smith Papers, University of Virginia Library.

2. OTHER PAPERS

"Autobiography" [1858], Tucker-Harrison-Smith Papers, University of Virginia Library.
"A Century Hence: Or a Romance of 1941" [1841], Tucker-Harrison-Smith Papers, University of Virginia Library.
"Lectures on Rhetoric and Belles Lettres . . . at the Seventh Session, 1830-31," Tucker-Harrison-Smith Papers, University of Virginia Library.
"Pleasures Left to Old Age," poem dated Aug. 20, 1860, Tucker-Harrison-Smith Papers, University of Virginia Library.
[Remains of] "Poems by George Tucker," Tucker-Harrison-Smith Papers, University of Virginia Library.
"Three Days Before Marriage," poem written for Miss M. J. Brown, n.d., Tucker-Harrison-Smith Papers, University of Virginia Library.

B. Contributions to Serial Publications

1. GENERAL PUBLICATIONS, LISTED CHRONOLOGICALLY

Anonymous, "In Memoriam," Bermuda *Gazette* [1797].
"Agrestis," "To a Young Lady on Her Birth Day," Richmond, Va., *Argus,* n.d.

"An Inquirer," "To the Editor of the *Virginia Argus,*" Richmond, Va., *Argus* [Sept., 1803].

"An Inquirer," "To the Editor of the *Virginia Argus,*" Richmond, Va., *Argus,* Oct. 19, 1803.

"Candidus," seven untitled articles on banking, Richmond, Va., *Virginia Gazette and General Advertiser,* Feb. 11, 18, 25, March 7, 10, 17, July 4, 1804.

"A.B.," "Written in a Garden," Richmond, Va., *Virginia Gazette and General Advertiser,* June 9, 1804.

Anonymous, "On Banks," Richmond, Va., *Enquirer,* No. I, July 28, 1804; No. II, Aug. 1, 1804; No. III, Aug. 8, 1804; No. V [IV], Aug. 22, 1804; No. V, Aug. 25, 1804.

"Eugenius," "An Argument for Duelling," Richmond, Va., *Enquirer,* Aug. 11, 1804.

"X," "On the Illusions of Fancy," Rainbow, 1st ser., Richmond, Va., *Enquirer,* Sept. 29, 1804.

"X," "On Luxury," Rainbow, 2nd ser., Richmond, Va., *Enquirer,* Dec. 22, 1804.

"X," "Vindication of Duelling," Rainbow, 2nd ser., Richmond, Va., *Enquirer,* March 30, 1805.

"X," "To Miss . . . on Her Birth Day, By One of the Members of the Rainbow Association," Richmond, Va., *Enquirer,* May 14, 1805.

"Hickory Cornhill," "A Letter from Hickory Cornhill, Esq., to His Friend in the Country," Richmond, Va., *Enquirer,* Jan. 9, 1806.

Anonymous, "A Card of Apology, to All Whom It May Concern," Richmond, Va., *Enquirer,* Jan. 16, 1806.

"Peter Schryphel," letter in "Old Bachelor" Essay XV, Richmond, Va., *Enquirer,* March 5, 1811.

"Richard Vamper," letter in "Old Bachelor" Essay XV, Richmond, Va., *Enquirer,* March 5, 1811.

"Thoughts of a Hermit," "On American Literature," *Port Folio,* 3rd ser., IV (1814), 44-59.

———, "On Style," *Port Folio,* 3rd ser., IV (1814), 192-198.

———, "On the Future Destiny of the United States," *Port Folio,* 3rd ser., IV (1814), 382-397.

———, "On Architecture," *Port Folio,* 3rd ser., IV (1814), 559-569.

———, "On Beauty," *Port Folio,* 3rd ser., V (1815), 148-162, 220-230.

———, "On Banks of Circulation," *Port Folio,* 3rd ser., V (1815), 417-428.

———, "On Simplicity in Ornament," *Port Folio,* 3rd ser., VI (1815), 82-91.

———, "On Density of Population," *Port Folio,* 3rd ser., VI (1815), 164-175.

———, "On Rhyme," *Port Folio,* 3rd ser., VI (1815), 371-376.

———, "On National Debts," *Port Folio,* 3rd ser., VI (1815), 574-590.

George Tucker, "Valedictory Address on the Retirement of President James Madison," *Acts of the General Assembly of Virginia* (1816-17), pp. 201-202.

——, "Missouri Question, Speech of Mr. Tucker (of Virginia), in the House of Representatives," *Niles' Weekly Register*, XVIII [VI, n.s.], (March to Sept., 1820), 453-458.

——, "To the Freeholders of the Counties of Campbell, Pittsylvania, and Halifax," Lynchburg, Va., *Virginian*, June 11, 1824.

——, "To the Freeholders of the Counties of Campbell, Pittsylvania, and Halifax," Lynchburg, Va., *Virginian*, April 21, 1825.

Anonymous, "Political Economy," *American Quarterly Review*, I (1827), 309-331.

——, "The Bank of the United States," *American Quarterly Review*, IX (1831), 246-282.

George Tucker, "Education in Virginia," *Quarterly Journal of Education*, IV (1832), 49-71.

"One of the Sovereign People," "The President's Late Act, No. I," Washington, D.C., *National Intelligencer*, Oct. 9, 1833.

——, "The President's Bank Manifesto, No. II," Washington, D.C., *National Intelligencer*, Oct. 12, 1833.

——, "The President's Late Manifesto, No. III," Washington, D.C., *National Intelligencer*, Oct. 16, 1833.

George Tucker, "Tucker to Governor Floyd," *Journals of the House of Delegates, 1833-34*, Richmond, Va., 1834, Document No. 1, p. 167.

Anonymous, "Apostrophe of the Aeolian Harp to the Wind," *Southern Literary Messenger*, I (1835), 396.

George Tucker, "A Discourse on the Progress of Philosophy and Its Influence on the Intellectual and Moral Character of Man," *Southern Literary Messenger*, I (1835), 405-421.

——, "Evil Effects of Great Cities," *Southern Literary Messenger*, III (1837), 462-463.

——, "Discourse on American Literature: Delivered Before the Charlottesville Lyceum, December 19, 1837," *Southern Literary Messenger*, IV (1838), 81-88.

Anonymous, "Pandemus Polyglott," *Southern Literary Messenger*, IV (1838), 203-207.

"H.C.," "Hickory Cornhill: A Letter from Hickory Cornhill, Esq. to His Friend in the Country," *Southern Literary Messenger*, IV (1838), 327-328.

George Tucker, "Historical Error Corrected," *Southern Literary Messenger*, IV (1838), 344.

——, extract from *Theory of Money and Banks Investigated*, *Niles' Weekly Register*, LVII (1839), 155-156.

———, untitled articles, *Hunt's Merchants' Magazine and Commercial Review,* II (1840), 89-100, 210-222, 441-450.

———, "The Currency," Washington *Independent,* Dec. 24, 1841.

———, "Psychological Observations on the Siamese Twins, Chang and Eng, Made in 1836," American Philosophical Society *Proceedings,* II (1841-42), 22-28.

———, selections from *Progress of the United States in Population . . . ,* *Hunt's Merchants' Magazine and Commercial Review,* VI (1842), 274-277; VII (1842), 31-42, 132-147, 241-245, 529-534; VIII (1843), 36-47, 157-164, 240-249, 330-335, 427-438, 503-512; IX (1843), 47-58, 136-144, 220-243, 509-516.

———, "The Currency," *Hunt's Merchants' Magazine and Commercial Review,* VI (1842), 433-439.

———, "Association of Ideas," *Virginia University Faculty Publication,* [1843].

———, "Washington's Levee," *Niles' Weekly Register,* LXV (1843), 226.

———, "On the Dangers Most to be Guarded Against in the Future Progress of the United States," National Institute for the Promotion of Science *Proceedings,* No. 3 (1845), 430.

———, "To the Legislature of Virginia," *Southern Literary Messenger,* XI (1845), 96.

———, "The Malthusian Theory. Discussed in a Correspondence between Alex. H. Everett, and Prof. Geo. Tucker, of the University of Virginia," *United States Magazine and Democratic Review,* n.s. XVII (1846), 298-302, 379-389, 438-441; XXII (1848), 11-18.

———, "A General Statistical Society for the United States," *Hunt's Merchants' Magazine and Commercial Review,* XVII (1847), 571-577.

———, "Dangers to be Guarded Against in the Future Progress of the United States," *American Whig Review,* V (1847), 614-629.

———, "Inhabitants of the United States," *American Quarterly Register and Magazine,* I (1848), 203-207.

———, summary of speech, American Association for the Advancement of Science *Proceedings,* I (1848), 134-135.

———, "Association of Ideas," *American Quarterly Register and Magazine,* III (1849), 466-477.

———, digest of paper, American Philosophical Society *Proceedings,* V (1850), 148-150.

———, "Statistics—Precious Metals," *American Quarterly Register and Magazine,* IV (1850), 266-269.

———, "Our Metallic Currency," *Hunt's Merchants' Magazine and Commercial Review,* XXVII (1852), 175-178.

Anonymous, Obituary Notice of Mrs. Robley Dunglison, Philadelphia *Pennsylvania Inquirer,* March 7, 1853.

George Tucker, "Banks or No Banks," *Hunt's Merchants' Magazine and Commercial Review*, XXXVIII (1858), 147-157.

——, "Description of Williamsburg in 1796," extract from *The Valley of Shenandoah, WMQ,* 2nd ser., XIX (1939), 192-196.

2. *Virginia Literary Museum,* LISTED CHRONOLOGICALLY

"Q," "Introduction," No. 1, June 17, 1829, 1-3.

"K," "Verbal Criticism," No. 1, June 17, 1829, 11-13.

"K," "The Policy of Encouraging Manufactures," No. 2, June 24, 1829, 17-20.

Anonymous, "The Policy of Encouraging Manufactures—No. 2," No. 3, July 1, 1829, 42-47.

"V," "Jefferson's Memoir and Correspondence," No. 4, July 8, 1829, 49-51.

"K," "Roads to Riches," No. 4, July 8, 1829, 55-59.

"K," "The Policy of Encouraging Manufactures—No. 3," No. 4, July 8, 1829, 59-61.

"V," "Jefferson's Memoir and Correspondence," No. 5, July 15, 1829, 68-70.

"K," "The Policy of Encouraging Manufactures—No. 4," No. 5, July 15, 1829, 77-80.

"V," "A Letter to a Member of the Approaching Convention in Richmond," No. 6, July 22, 1829, 81-84.

"V," "The Wilderness," No. 6, July 22, 1829, 85-86.

"K," "The Policy of Encouraging Manufactures—No. 5," No. 7, July 29, 1829, 103-107.

"V," "The Constitution of Virginia, Letter II," No. 8, Aug. 5, 1829, 121-124.

"V," "The Policy of Encouraging Manufactures—No. 6," No. 10, Aug. 19, 1829, 154-157.

"Q," "The Gold Seeker," No. 12, Sept. 2, 1829, 182-189.

"V," "The Constitution of Virginia, Letter III," No. 14, Sept. 16, 1829, 209-212.

"V," "The Constitution of Virginia, Letter IV," No. 15, Sept. 23, 1829, 234-236.

"V," "The Constitution of Virginia, Letter V," No. 16, Sept. 30, 1829, 241-247.

"C.C.," "Education of the People, No. 1," No. 16, Sept. 30, 1829, 249-253.

"Q," "The Confessions of a Pirate," No. 17, Oct. 7, 1829, 262-270.

"Q," "Political Economy: Ricardo's Theory of Profits," No. 18, Oct. 14, 1829, 273-276.

"C.C.," "Education of the People, No. 2," No. 19, Oct. 21, 1829, 298-303.

Anonymous, Note, No. 19, Oct. 21, 1829, 303.

"Q," "Universities," No. 20, Oct. 28, 1829, 305-308.

"Defensor," "Political Economy: Correction of Error," No. 20, Oct. 28, 1829, 316-319.

"Q," "The Convention," No. 22, Nov. 11, 1829, 337-339.

"K," "The Brothers," No. 22, Nov. 11, 1829, 339-344.

"C.C.," "Premises and Causes—Cause and Effect," No. 22, Nov. 11, 1829, 344-349.

"C.C.," "Education of the People, No. 3," No. 22, Nov. 11, 1829, 349-352.

"Q," "Universities," No. 24, Nov. 25, 1829, 369-372.

"C. Cruize," "Colonel Hazle," No. 24, Nov. 25, 1829, 372-374.

"C.C.," "Education of the People, Effects of Education on Practical Mechanics," No. 24, Nov. 25, 1829, 375-378.

"Cuspis," "Political Economy. The Free Trade Advocate," No. 25, Dec. 2, 1829, 394-398.

Anonymous, "The Convention," No. 25, Dec. 2, 1829, 398-400.

——, "The Convention," No. 26, Dec. 9, 1829, 414-416.

——, "The Convention," No. 27, Dec. 16, 1829, 429-432.

——, "The Convention," No. 28, Dec. 23, 1829, 443-447.

——, "The Convention," No. 29, Dec. 30, 1829, 460-464.

"C.C.," "Education of the People," No. 30, Jan. 6, 1830, 471-475.

Anonymous, "The Convention," No. 30, Jan. 6, 1830, 475-479.

"Q," "Census of the United States," No. 31, Jan. 13, 1830, 491-494.

"V," "Universities," No. 31, Jan. 13, 1830, 494-496.

Anonymous, "The Convention," No. 31, Jan. 13, 1830, 508-511.

——, "The Convention," No. 33, Jan. 27, 1830, 523-527.

"Q," "The Siamese Twins," No. 34, Feb. 3, 1830, 529-531.

Anonymous, "The Convention," No. 34, Feb. 3, 1830, 537-542.

"Q," "American Almanac," No. 35, Feb. 10, 1830, 556.

Anonymous, "The Convention," No. 35, Feb. 10, 1830, 556-559.

"Mercutio," "The Tariff," No. 35, Feb. 10, 1830, 559-560.

Anonymous, "The Convention," No. 36, Feb. 17, 1830, 571-575.

"Q," "Mr. Monroe's Claim," No. 36, Feb. 17, 1830, 575-576.

"Q," "The Convention," No. 37, Feb. 24, 1830, 585-590.

"C.C.," "Education of the People," No. 38, March 3, 1830, 593.

"C. Cruize," "Maiden's Adventure," No. 38, March 3, 1830, 594-600.

"Q," "Cotton Cordage," No. 38, March 3, 1830, 603.

"Q," "Relative Values of Gold and Silver," No. 38, March 3, 1830, 606-608.

"Q," "Banks," No. 39, March 10, 1830, 621-623.

"K," "The Country Belle," No. 40, March 17, 1830, 632-640.

"K," "Mr. Cambreling's Report," No. 41, March 24, 1830, 654-656.

"K," "Mr. Cambreling's Report," No. 42, March 31, 1830, 657-661.

"Q," "Fulton," No. 43, April 7, 1830, 684-686.

"K," "Mr. Cambreling's Report," No. 43, April 7, 1830, 686-688.

"K," "Julia Moncrief," No. 44, April 14, 1830, 689-696.

"K," "Julia Moncrief," No. 45, April 21, 1830, 706-714.

Anonymous, "Metaphysics," No. 46, April 28, 1830, 721-727.

——, "True Though Truant," No. 46, April 28, 1830, 732-736.

"Q," "Par of Exchange," No. 47, May 5, 1830, 737-739.

Anonymous, "True Though Truant," No. 47, May 5, 1830, 747-751.

"Q," "The Metaphysics of Language," No. 48, May 12, 1830, 753-757.

"K," "Etymology," No. 48, May 12, 1830, 759-761.

"K," "The Three Talismans," No. 48, May 12, 1830, 761-767.

"K," "Bank of the United States," No. 48, May 12, 1830, 768.

"K," "Natural Language," No. 49, May 19, 1830, 769-770.

"K," "The Principle of Imitation," No. 51, June 2, 1830, 803-806.

"Q," "To the Public," No. 52, June 9, 1830, 817-818.

"Q," "Fifth Census," No. 52, June 9, 1830, 823-824.

C. Contributions to Books, Listed in Order of Composition

"An Inquirer," "To the Editor of the Virginia *Argus*," in *The Letters of the British Spy*, 9th ed., Baltimore, 1831, pp. 72-87, 207-216.

"X," "On the Illusions of Fancy," in *The Rainbow; First Series*, Richmond, Va., 1804, pp. 49-54.

"Peter Schryphel" and "Richard Vamper," letters in Essay XV in *The Old Bachelor*, Richmond, Va., 1814, pp. 90-98.

George Tucker, "United States of North America," in George Long, George R. Porter, George Tucker, and Wilhelm Wittich, *The Geography of America and the West Indies*, London, 1841.

———, "United States of North America," in George Long, George R. Porter, George Tucker, and Wilhelm Wittich, *America and the West Indies, Geographically Described*, London, 1845, pp. 198-352.

D. Books and Pamphlets, Listed in Order of First Publication

Works starred with an asterisk are those publications which have been attributed to Tucker by Samuel Allibone and which seem likely to have been so published, but for which I cannot find substantiation.

"By a Citizen of Virginia," *Letter to a Member of the General Assembly of Virginia, on the Subject of the Late Conspiracy of the Slaves with a Proposal for Their Colonization*, Baltimore, 1801; 2nd ed., Richmond, Va., 1801.

"By a Citizen of Pittsylvania," *A Letter to a Member of the General Assembly of North Carolina on the Navigation of the Roanoke and Its Branches*, Richmond, Va., 1811.

Anonymous, *Letters from Virginia, Translated from the French*, Baltimore, 1816.

[George Tucker], *Recollections of the Life of Eleanor Rosalie Tucker. Addressed to Her Surviving Sister by Their Father*, Lynchburg, Va., 1818.

George Tucker, *Speech of Mr. Tucker, of Virginia, on the Penetration of Slavery in Missouri. Delivered in the House of Representatives of the United States February 25, 1820* [Washington, D.C., 1820].

"By a Citizen of Virginia," *Essays on Various Subjects of Taste, Morals, and National Policy,* Georgetown, D.C., 1822.

George Tucker, *To the Freeholders of the Counties of Campbell, Pittsylvania, and Halifax,* Lynchburg, Va., 1824.

"By a Citizen of Virginia," *The Valley of Shenandoah; or, Memoirs of the Graysons,* 2 vols., New York, 1824; 2nd ed., New York, 1828.

"Joseph Atterley," *A Voyage to the Moon: With Some Account of the Manners and Customs, Science and Philosophy, of the People of Morosofia and Other Lunarians,* New York, 1827.

George Tucker, *The Laws of Wages, Profits and Rent Investigated,* Philadelphia, 1837.

————, *The Life of Thomas Jefferson, Third President of the United States, with Parts of His Correspondence Never Before Published, and Notices of His Opinions on Questions of Civil Government, National Policy, and Constitutional Law,* 2 vols., Philadelphia, 1837; other ed. London, 1837, 1838.

*————, *Public Discourse on the Literature of the United States,* Charlottesville, Va., 1837.

"By a Virginian," *Defence of the Character of Thomas Jefferson Against a Writer in the New York Review and Quarterly Church Journal,* New York, 1838.

George Tucker, *Theory of Money and Banks Investigated,* Boston, 1839; *2nd ed., Boston, 1839.

*————, *Essay on Cause and Effect,* Philadelphia, 1842.

————, *Progress of the United States in Population and Wealth in Fifty Years, as Exhibited by the Decennial Census,* Boston, New York, Philadelphia, Washington, D.C., 1843.

*————, *Public Discourse on the Dangers Most Threatening to the United States,* Washington, D.C., 1843.

————, *Memoir of the Life and Character of John P. Emmet, M.D., Professor of Chemistry and Materia Medica in the University of Virginia,* Philadelphia, 1845.

————, *An Essay on Cause and Effect; Being an Examination of Hume's Doctrine, that We Can Perceive No Necessary Connexion Between Them,* Philadelphia, 1850.

————, *Progress of the United States in Population and Wealth in Fifty Years, as Exhibited by the Decennial Census, with an Appendix, Containing an Abstract of the Census of 1850,* New York, 1855.

————, *A History of the United States from Their Colonization to the End of the Twenty-Sixth Congress, in 1841,* 4 vols., Philadelphia, 1856-58.

————, *Political Economy for the People,* Philadelphia, 1859; 2nd ed., Philadelphia, 1860.

————, *Essays, Moral and Metaphysical,* Philadelphia, 1860.

II. GENERAL WORKS, LISTED ALPHABETICALLY

A. Manuscripts

1. Letters and Miscellaneous Papers

American Philosophical Society Committee Reports, American Philosophical Society.

Biddle Papers, Library of Congress.

Bryan Papers, University of Virginia Library.

Cabell Deposit, University of Virginia Library.

Dabney Papers, University of Virginia Library.

Gooch Family Papers, University of Virginia Library.

Jefferson Papers, University of Virginia Library.

Madison Papers, Library of Congress.

Monroe Papers, Library of Congress.

Tucker-Harrison-Smith Papers, University of Virginia Library.

2. Student Notebooks and University Records

"Minutes of the Board of Visitors of the University of Virginia," typed copy, University of Virginia Library.

"Minutes of the Faculty of the University of Virginia," University of Virginia Library.

"Notebook of Robert Lewis Dabney," Dabney Papers, University of Virginia Library.

"Notes on the Lectures of Moral Philosophy by George Tucker, Esq.," "Metaphysics," title page signed Merit M. Robinson, Cabell Deposit, University of Virginia Library.

"Notes on Mental Philosophy," signed William W. Harris, University of Virginia, October 7th, 1835, Tucker-Harrison-Smith Papers, University of Virginia Library.

3. Life Records

Dunglison, Robley, "Autobiographical Ana," 8 vols., Library of the College of Physicians of Philadelphia.

Tucker, Maria B., "Commonplace Book," typed copy, University of Virginia Library.

4. Unpublished Studies

Cauble, Frank P., "William Wirt and His Friends, a Study in Southern Culture, 1772-1834," University of North Carolina dissertation, 1934.

Dabney, William Minor, "Jefferson's Albemarle: History of Albemarle County, Virginia, 1728-1819," University of Virginia dissertation, 1951.

Jacobs, Robert D., "Poe's Heritage from Jefferson's Virginia," Johns Hopkins University dissertation, 1953.

Lester, Malcolm, "George Tucker: His Early Life and Public Service, 1775-1825," University of Virginia M.A. thesis, 1946.

Martin, Edwin T., "Thomas Jefferson and the Idea of Progress," University of Wisconsin dissertation, 1941.

Prince, William Stevens, "St. George Tucker As a Poet of the Early Republic," Yale University dissertation, 1954.

Turrentine, Percy Winfield, "Life and Letters of Nathaniel Beverley Tucker," Harvard University dissertation, 1952.

B. Magazines and Newspapers

Ahlstrom, Sydney E., "The Scottish Philosophy and American Theology," *Church History*, XXIV (1955), 257-272.

Anonymous, "An Answer to Hickory Cornhill, Esq. from His Friend in the Country," Richmond, Va., *Enquirer*, Jan. 16, 1806.

———, "Character of the Late Mrs. Maria B. Tucker," *Port Folio*, 5th ser., XV (1823), 350-352.

———, obituary notice of Tucker, Charlottesville, Va., *Jeffersonian*, April 11, 1861.

———, obituary notice of Tucker, Richmond, Va., *Enquirer*, April 13, 1861.

———, "Reflections on Duelling, Part 1st," Richmond, Va., *Enquirer*, Jan. 18, 1805.

———, review of *Essays on Various Subjects* . . . , *Port Folio*, 5th ser., V (1823), 252.

———, review of *History of the United States* . . . , *De Bow's Review*, XXIII (1857), 668.

———, review of *History of the United States* . . . , *Harper's New Monthly Magazine*, XIII (1856), 555.

———, review of *History of the United States* . . . , *London Athenaeum*, March 27, 1858, p. 398.

———, review of *History of the United States* . . . , *North American Review*, LXXXVIII (1859), 280.

———, review of *Laws of Wages* . . . , *Southern Literary Messenger*, IV (1838), 341-342.

———, review of *Life of Jefferson* . . . , *London Athenaeum*, May 6, 1837, p. 313.

———, review of *Life of Jefferson* . . . , *Southern Literary Messenger*, VI (1840), 642-650.

———, review of *Progress of the United States in Population* . . . , *Hunt's Merchants' Magazine and Commercial Review*, IX (1843), 487.

———, review of *A Voyage to the Moon*, *Western Monthly Review*, I (1828), 674-676.

"B.," "Literature of Virginia, To Professor Tucker of the University," *Southern Literary Messenger*, IV (1838), 684-689.

Bailey, J. O., "Sources for Poe's *Arthur Gordon Pym*, 'Hans Pfaal,' and Other Pieces," *PMLA*, LVII (1942), 513-535.

Bernard, Jessie, "George Tucker: Liberal Southern Social Scientist," *Social Forces*, XXV (1946-47), 131-145, 406-416.

[Brougham, Henry], review of *Life of Jefferson* . . . , *Edinburgh Review,* LXVI (1837), 156-186.

Cady, George Johnson, "The Early American Reaction to the Theory of Malthus," *Journal of Political Economy,* XXXIX (1931), 601-632.

Come, Donald Robert, "The Influence of Princeton on Higher Education in the South Before 1825," *WMQ,* 3rd ser., II (1945), 359-396.

Curti, Merle, "The Great Mr. Locke, America's Philosopher, 1783-1861," *Huntington Library Bulletin,* XI (1937), 107-151.

Dudley, Fred A., "Tintinnabulation: And a Source of Poe's 'The Bells,'" *AL,* IV (1933), 296-300.

Dunglison, Robley, "Obituary Notice of Professor Tucker," American Philosophical Society *Proceedings,* IX (1862-64), 64-70.

[Dunglison, Robley], review of *A Voyage to the Moon, American Quarterly Review,* III (1828), 61-88.

Everett, Edward, review of *Essays on Various Subjects* . . . , *North American Review,* XVI (1823), 45-58.

Forbes, Duncan, "The Rationalism of Sir Walter Scott," *Cambridge Journal,* VII (1953), 20-35.

———, "'Scientific' Whiggism: Adam Smith and John Millar," *Cambridge Journal,* VII (1954), 643-670.

"G," "On Duelling," Richmond, Va., *Enquirer,* Jan. 5, 1805.

Gross, S. D., "Memoir of Robley Dunglison, M.D., LL.D.," *Summary of the Transactions of the College of Physicians of Philadelphia,* n.s., IV (Feb., 1863-May, 1874), 294-313.

Helderman, Leonard C., "A Satirist in Old Virginia," *American Scholar,* VI (1937), 481-497.

———, "A Social Scientist of the Old South," *Journal of Southern History,* II (1936), 148-174.

Hooker, Edward Niles, "The Discussion of Taste, from 1750 to 1770, and the New Trends in Literary Criticism," *PMLA,* XLIX (1934), 577-598.

Hubbell, Jay B., "William Wirt and the Familiar Essay in Virginia," *WMQ,* 2nd ser., XXIII (1943), 136-152.

Jeffrey, Francis, review of Archibald Alison's *Essays on the Nature and Principles of Taste, Edinburgh Review,* XVIII (May, 1811), 1-46.

Johnson, Herman Patrick, "The First Chairman of Our Faculty as an Essayist," University of Virginia *Alumni Bulletin,* 3rd ser., IX (Oct., 1916), 520-524.

Jones, Howard Mumford, "The Influence of European Ideas in Nineteenth-Century America," *AL,* VII (1935), 241-273.

[Jones, Joseph Seawell], review of *Life of Jefferson* . . . , *New York Review and Quarterly Church Journal,* I (1837), 5-58.

Kelly, George, "Poe's Theory of Beauty," *AL,* XXVII (1956), 521-536.

Lovejoy, Arthur O., "The Parallel of Deism and Classicism," *MP*, XXIX (1932), 281-299.

Lubell, Albert J., "Poe and A. W. Schlegel," *JEGP*, LII (1953), 1-12.

Mabbott, Thomas O., "Poe's *Ulalume*," *Explicator*, I (Feb., 1943), Item 25.

"MRA," "Browsings," Lynchburg, Va., *News*, March 20, 1953.

"O" [James Ogilvie], "On Luxury," Richmond, Va., *Enquirer*, Oct. 27, 1804.

"O" [James Ogilvie], "On Luxury—Part 2d," Richmond, Va., *Enquirer*, April 19, 1805.

Pascal, Roy, "Herder and the Scottish Historical School," *English Goethe Society Publications*, n.s., XIV (1938-39), 23-42.

———, "Property and Society: The Scottish Historical School of the Eighteenth Century," *Modern Quarterly*, I (1938), 169-179.

Pearce, Roy Harvey, "The Eighteenth-Century Scottish Primitivists: Some Reconsiderations," *ELH*, XII (1945), 203-220.

Popkin, Richard H., "George Tucker, An Early American Critic of Hume," *JHI*, XIII (1952), 370-375.

Posey, Meredith Niel, "Notes on *Hans Pfaal*," *MLN*, XLV (1930), 501-507.

Scheffer, John D., "The Idea of the Decline in Literature and the Fine Arts in Eighteenth-Century England," *MP*, XXXIV (1936), 155-178.

Sherley, George Douglass, "Our University, II: George Tucker, Professor of Moral Philosophy in the University of Virginia, 1825-1845," *Virginia University Magazine*, XIX (June, 1880), 539-574.

Snavely, Tipton R., "George Tucker as Economist," University of Virginia *Alumni Bulletin*, 3rd ser., XVI (April, 1923), 109-130.

Spengler, Joseph J., "Population Doctrines in the United States," *Journal of Political Economy*, XLI (1933), 433-467, 639-672.

———, "Population Theory in the Ante-Bellum South," *Journal of Southern History*, II (1936), 360-389.

Stovall, Floyd, "Poe's Debt to Coleridge," *University of Texas Studies in English*, X (1930), 70-127.

Teggart, Frederick J., "A Problem in the History of Ideas," *JHI*, I (1940), 494-503.

Wayland, J. W., "The Virginia Literary Museum," *Publications of the Southern History Association*, VI (1902), 1-14.

Whitney, Lois, "English Primitivistic Theories of Epic Origins," *MP*, XXI (1924), 337-378.

C. Books

Adams, Herbert B., *Thomas Jefferson and the University of Virginia*, U.S. Bureau of Education Circular of Information No. 1, 1888, in *Contributions to American Educational History*, No. 2, Washington, D.C., 1888.

Albrecht, William P., *William Hazlitt and the Malthusian Controversy,* University of New Mexico Publications in Language and Literature, No. IV, Albuquerque, 1950.

Alison, Archibald, *Essays on the Nature and Principles of Taste,* Boston, 1812.

Allen, Hervey, *Israfel: The Life and Times of Edgar Allan Poe,* 2 vols., 2nd ed., New York, 1927.

Allibone, Samuel, *Critical Dictionary of English Literature and British and American Authors,* 3 vols., Philadelphia, 1876.

Alterton, Margaret, and Hardin Craig, eds., *Edgar Allan Poe,* New York, 1935.

Ambler, Charles Henry, *Sectionalism in Virginia from 1776 to 1861,* Chicago, 1910.

Aptheker, Herbert, *American Negro Slave Revolts,* New York, 1943.

Bate, Walter Jackson, *From Classic to Romantic: Premises of Taste in Eighteenth-Century England,* Cambridge, Mass., 1946.

Bateson, F. W., *English Poetry and the English Language: An Experiment in Literary History,* Oxford, 1934.

Beard, Charles A., "The Idea of Progress" in *A Century of Progress,* ed. Beard, New York, 1932.

Beard, Charles A., and Mary Beard, *The Rise of American Civilization in the United States,* Vol. IV in *The American Spirit: A Study of the Idea of Civilization in the United States,* New York, 1942.

Blau, Joseph, *Men and Movements in American Philosophy,* New York, 1953.

Bonar, James, *Malthus and His Work,* New York, 1924.

Brown, Thomas, *Lectures on the Philosophy of the Human Mind,* 2 vols., Boston, 1826.

Bruce, Philip Alexander, *History of the University of Virginia,* 5 vols., New York, 1920.

Bruce, William Cabell, *John Randolph of Roanoke,* 2 vols., New York, 1939.

Bryson, Gladys, *Man and Society: The Scottish Inquiry of the Eighteenth Century,* Princeton, 1945.

Bury, J. B., *The Idea of Progress: An Inquiry into Its Origins and Growth,* new ed., New York, 1932.

Cabell, Nathaniel Francis, *Early History of the University of Virginia, as Contained in the Letters of Thomas Jefferson and Joseph C. Cabell,* Richmond, Va., 1856.

Campbell, George, *The Philosophy of Rhetoric,* 2 vols., Edinburgh and London, 1808.

Campbell, Killis, *Poems of Edgar Allan Poe,* Boston, 1917.

A Catalogue of the Officers and Students of the University of Virginia, Charlottesville, Va., 1880.

Charvat, William, *The Origins of American Critical Thought, 1810-1835,* Philadelphia, 1936.

Clive, John, *Scotch Reviewers: The Edinburgh Review, 1802-1815,* Cambridge, Mass., 1957.

Coleman, Mary Haldane, *St. George Tucker, Citizen of No Mean City,* Richmond, Va., 1938.

Coulter, Ellis Merton, *College Life in the Old South,* rev. ed., Athens, Ga., 1951.

Crane, Ronald S., "Neo-Classical Criticism," in *Dictionary of World Literature,* ed. Joseph Shipley, rev. ed., New York, 1953, pp. 116-127.

Cruse, Peter H., biographical sketch of William Wirt in *The Letters of the British Spy,* 10th ed., New York, 1832.

Curti, Merle, *The Growth of American Thought,* 2nd ed., New York, 1951.

Davidson, Edward H., ed., *Selected Writings of Edgar Allan Poe,* Boston, 1956.

Dictionary of American Biography, ed. Allen Johnson and Dumas Malone, 21 vols., New York, 1928-1936.

Dorfman, Joseph, *The Economic Mind in American Civilization, 1606-1865,* 2 vols., New York, 1946.

Eaton, Clement, *Freedom of Thought in the Old South,* Durham, N.C., 1940.

——, *A History of the Old South,* New York, 1949.

Ekirch, Arthur A., Jr., *The Idea of Progress in America, 1815-1860,* New York, 1944.

Emmet, Thomas Addis, *An Account of the Tucker Family of Bermuda from a History of the Emmet Family,* New York, 1898.

Farnam, Henry W., *Chapters in the History of Social Legislation in the United States to 1860,* ed. Clive Day, Washington, D.C., 1938.

Foley, Patrick Kevin, *American Authors 1795-1895: A Bibliography of First and Notable Editions Chronologically Arranged with Notes,* Boston, 1897.

Forbes, Duncan, *The Liberal Anglican Idea of History,* Cambridge, 1952.

Gaines, Francis Pendleton, *The Southern Plantation: A Study in the Development and the Accuracy of a Tradition,* New York, 1924.

Gerard, Alexander, *An Essay on Taste,* London, 1759.

Harrison, Robert Lewis, "George Tucker" in *A Library of Southern Literature,* ed. Edwin Anderson Alderman *et al.,* Atlanta, Ga., 1907-1923, XII, 5515-5519.

Herold, Amos L., *James Kirk Paulding: Versatile American,* New York, 1926.

Hipple, Walter John, Jr., *The Beautiful, the Sublime, & the Picturesque in Eighteenth-Century British Aesthetic Theory,* Carbondale, Ill., 1957.

Hubbell, Jay B., *The South in American Literature, 1607-1900,* Durham, N.C., 1954.

——, *Virginia Life in Fiction,* Dallas, 1922.

Hume, David, *Essays Moral, Political and Literary,* ed. T. H. Green and T. H. Grose, 2 vols., new ed., London, 1889.

——, *The History of England from the Invasion of Julius Caesar to the Revolution in 1688,* 8 vols., London, 1773.

Jackson, David K., comp., *The Contributors and Contributions to the Southern Literary Messenger (1834-1864),* Charlottesville, Va., 1936.

Jefferson, Thomas, *The Works of Thomas Jefferson,* ed. Paul Leicester Ford, 10 vols., New York and London, 1904.

Jeffrey, Francis, *Contributions to the Edinburgh Review,* 2 vols., 2nd ed., London, 1846.

Jenkins, William Sumner, *Pro-Slavery Thought in the Old South,* Chapel Hill, N.C., 1935.

Jones, Richard Foster, *Ancients and Moderns: A Study of the Background of the Battle of the Books,* Washington University Studies in Language and Literature, n.s., No. 6, St. Louis, Mo., 1936.

Kames, Lord (Henry Home), *Elements of Criticism,* London, 1824.

——, *Sketches of the History of Man,* 4 vols., Glasgow, 1802.

Kennedy, John P., *Memoirs of the Life of William Wirt, Attorney General of the United States,* 2 vols., rev. ed., Philadelphia, 1850.

Kerr, Wilfred Brenton, *Bermuda and the American Revolution, 1760-1783,* Princeton, 1936.

Klingberg, Frank J., and Frank W. Klingberg, eds., *The Correspondence Between Henry Stephens Randall and Hugh Blair Grigsby 1856-1861,* University of California Publications in History, XLIII, Los Angeles and Berkeley, 1952.

Koch, Adrienne, *Jefferson and Madison: The Great Collaboration,* New York, 1950.

——, *The Philosophy of Thomas Jefferson,* New York, 1943.

La Rochefoucauld-Liancourt, Duc de, *Travels Through the United States of North America, the Country of the Iroquois, and Upper Canada, in the Years 1795, 1796, and 1797; With an Authentic Account of Lower Canada,* 2 vols., London, 1799.

Leary, Lewis, *The Literary Career of Nathaniel Tucker, 1750-1807,* Durham, N.C., 1951.

Literary History of the United States, ed. Robert E. Spiller *et al.,* rev. ed., New York, 1953.

Logan, James Venable, *The Poetry and Aesthetics of Erasmus Darwin,* Princeton, 1936.

Macaulay, Thomas Babington, *Essays, Critical and Miscellaneous,* rev. ed., New York, 1878.

MacCulloch, John Ramsay, *The Literature of Political Economy: A Classified Catalogue of Select Publications in the Different Departments of that Science, with Historical, Critical and Biographical Notices,* London, 1845.

Marburg, Clara, *Sir William Temple: A Seventeenth Century "Libertine,"* New Haven, 1932.

Martineau, Harriet, *Retrospect of Western Travel,* London, 1838.

Mathews, M. M., *The Beginnings of American English: Essays and Comments,* Chicago, 1931.

McCosh, James, *The Scottish Philosophy, Biographical, Expository, Critical, from Hutcheson to Hamilton,* New York, 1875.

McIlwaine, Shields, *The Southern Poor White from Lubberland to Tobacco Road,* Norman, Okla., 1939.

McKenzie, Gordon, *Critical Responsiveness: A Study of the Psychological Current in Later Eighteenth-Century Criticism,* University of California Publications in English, XX, Berkeley and Los Angeles, 1949.

Meek, Ronald L., "The Scottish Contribution to Marxist Sociology," in *Democracy and the Labour Movement,* ed. John Saville, London, 1954, pp. 84-102.

Meigs, William M., *Life of Josiah Meigs,* Philadelphia, 1887.

Poe, Edgar Allan, *The Complete Works of Edgar Allan Poe,* ed. James A. Harrison, 17 vols., New York, 1902.

Quinn, Arthur Hobson, *Edgar Allan Poe: A Critical Biography,* New York, 1941.

Randall, Helen Whitcomb, *The Critical Theory of Lord Kames,* Smith College Studies in Modern Languages, Nos. 1-4, XXII, 1940-41.

Randall, Henry S., *The Life of Thomas Jefferson,* 3 vols., New York, 1858.

Reid, Thomas, *The Works of Thomas Reid, D.D., with Notes and Supplementary Dissertations,* ed. Sir William Hamilton, Bart., 2 vols., 8th ed., Edinburgh, 1895.

Riley, I. Woodbridge, *American Philosophy, The Early Schools,* New York, 1907.

———, *American Thought from Puritanism to Pragmatism and Beyond,* New York, 1915.

Robertson, William, *History of the Reign of the Emperor Charles V: With a View of the Progress of Society in Europe, from the Subdivision of the Roman Empire to the Beginning of the Sixteenth Century,* 4 vols., 2nd ed., London, 1777.

Rotwein, Eugene, ed., *David Hume: Writings on Economics,* Madison, Wis., and London, 1955.

Schmidt, George P., *The Old Time College President,* New York, 1930.

Schmitz, Robert Morell, *Hugh Blair,* New York, 1948.

Schneider, Herbert W., *A History of American Philosophy,* New York, 1946.

Segerstedt, Torgny T., *The Problem of Knowledge in Scottish Philosophy* in Lunds Universtets Arsskrift, N.F. Avd. Bd. 31, Nt. 6, Lund, 1935.

Smith, Henry Nash, *Virgin Land: The American West as Symbol and Myth,* Cambridge, Mass., 1950.

Smith, Kenneth, *The Malthusian Controversy,* London, 1957.

Smith, Wilson, *Professors & Public Ethics: Studies of Northern Moral Philosophers Before the Civil War,* Ithaca, N.Y., 1956.

Spencer, Benjamin T., *The Quest for Nationality: An American Literary Campaign,* Syracuse, N.Y., 1957.

Stampp, Kenneth, *The Peculiar Institution: Slavery in the Ante-Bellum South,* New York, 1956.

Stewart, Dugald, *The Collected Works of Dugald Stewart, Esq., F.R.S.S.,* ed. Sir William Hamilton, Bart., 11 vols., Edinburgh, 1854.

Teggart, Frederick J., "The Idea of Progress" in *Theory of History,* New Haven, 1925.

Turner, John Roscoe, *The Ricardian Rent Theory in Early American Economics,* New York, 1921.

Tuveson, Ernest Lee, *Millennium and Utopia: A Study in the Background of the Idea of Progress,* Berkeley and Los Angeles, 1949.

Twelve Southerners, *I'll Take My Stand: The South in the Agrarian Tradition,* New York, 1930.

Tyler, John Gardiner, *The Old Colonial Capital,* Richmond, Va., 1907.

Van Becelaere, L., *La Philosophie en Amérique despuis les origines jusqu'à nos jours,* New York, 1904.

Webster, Daniel, *The Writings and Speeches of Daniel Webster,* ed. J. W. McIntyre, 18 vols., Boston, 1903.

Weld, Isaac, Jr., *Travels Through the States of North America and the Provinces of Upper and Lower Canada, During the Years 1795, 1796, and 1797,* 2 vols., London, 1799.

Wellek, René, *The Rise of English Literary History,* Chapel Hill, N.C., 1941.

White, Henry C., "The South's Contributions to Philosophy," *History of the Literary and Intellectual Life of the Southern States,* ed. John Bell Henneman, Vol. VII in *The South in the Building of the Nation,* Richmond, Va., 1909.

Whitney, Lois, *Primitivism and the Idea of Progress in English Popular Literature of the Eighteenth Century,* Baltimore, 1934.

Wilkinson, Henry C., *Bermuda in the Old Empire: A History of the Island from the Dissolution of the Somers Island Company Until the End of the American Revolutionary War: 1684-1784,* Oxford, 1950.

Younger, Edward, *John A. Kasson: Politics and Diplomacy from Lincoln to McKinley,* Iowa City, 1955.

INDEX

Abolitionist propaganda, effect in South, 195; Tucker on, 198-99, 226

Adams, John, 13

Addison, Joseph, 71, 131

Aesthetics, relation to philosophy, 155-57. *See also* Beauty; Honor; Sublimity

Agrarianism. *See* Anti-agrarianism

Alison, Archibald, associationism of, 121, 122; theory of beauty attacked by Tucker, 121, 122, 124, 156-57; *Essays on the Nature and Principles of Taste,* 121, 127, 156; on degeneration of literature, 127; influenced Poe, 139; mentioned, 117, 124, 131, 134, 231

Allan, John, 11

America and the West Indies (Long *et al.*), 35

American Association for the Advancement of Science, 43

American Philosophical Society, 42, 43, 163, 168, 169

American Quarterly Register and Magazine, 169

American Quarterly Review, 37, 98

Anstey, Christopher, *New Bath Guide,* 56

"Answer to Hickory Cornhill, An," 56

Anti-agrarianism, of Tucker, 45, 182, 218. *See also* Cities; Industrialization; Population; Progress, idea of

Anti-didacticism, in Tucker's literary theory, 134, 139; in Poe's literary theory, 139-40

Antigua, Tucker's plantation in, 9; Tucker visits, 10

Anti-Masonic Party, 36

Anti-slavery sentiment, in Bermuda, 177; economic causes for, 177; religious causes for, 177; social causes for, 177-78; in Virginia, 177-79; in *Letters from Virginia,* 182-83

Aristocracy, praised, 39, 62-63, 69; in *The Valley,* 81-82, 87, 88; criticism of, 86-87; in "A Century Hence," 105-6; in South, 200; Tucker on values of, 215

Associationism, Tucker satirizes Jeffrey's theory of, 93-94; principles of derived from human nature, 119; Tucker's theory of, 119, 121, 157, 169-71; Gerard on, 121; Kames on, 122; effect on beauty, 137; and imagination, 155-56; principles of, 155-56; in Britain, 156; physiological explanation of, 156; Stewart on, 156-57; Brown's theory of, 170; Reid on, 171

Avarice, counteracted by luxury, 212

Babbage, Charles, 38

Bacon, Francis, 98

Baltimore, 10, 29

Bank. *See* Second National Bank; Bank of Virginia

Bank of Virginia, Tucker defends as private institution, 14; regulation by Virginia legislature, 14; mentioned, 55

Barlow, Joel, 72

Bascomb, George, 4

Bauraud, Dr. Philip, 10

Beauty, as concept, 120-25; sources of in Tucker's aesthetic, 122-23; physiological explanation for, 123; defined by pleasure-pain, 124; compared with sublimity, 124-25; in poetry, 135, 136-38; as poetic effect, 137; sources of for poetry, 136-37; as poetic inspiration, 137; effect of associationism on, 137;